Agent for Change in International Development

Volume Two

AGENT FOR CHANGE IN INTERNATIONAL DEVELOPMENT

My Flight Path into the 21st Century

Volume Two

The Family Companion

LUDWIG "LU" RUDEL

ISBN: 1518762190
ISBN 13: 9781518762192
Library of Congress Control Number: 2015919617
CreateSpace Independent Publishing Platform
North Charleston, South Carolina

This is the companion volume to my book, titled *Memoirs of an Agent for Change in International Development: My Flight Path into the 21st Century,* published by Arlington Hall Press in 2014 as part of the "Memoirs and Occasional Papers" series of the Association for Diplomatic Studies and Training (see www.ADST.org). That volume describes my professional life.

This volume is not associated with the Association for Diplomatic Studies and Training (ADST) and is not part of their "Memoirs and Occasional Papers" series.

Names of persons in photos on cover; reading each photo from left to right:

Front cover; Upper left photo:	Ruthann Rudel, David Rudel, Joanna Rudel Devine.
Upper right photo:	Wolfgang Devine, Declan Devine, Emma Devine.
Lower photo:	Miranda Rudel, Caroline Rudel, Ezra Rudel, Ambrose Devine, Willa Rudel.
Back of cover:	The Eight Cousins - Miranda, Willa, Caroline, Ambrose, Emma, Ezra, Declan and Wolfgang.

CONTENTS

Photos that accompany this text may be accessed through a link at the website: www.rudel.net

PREFACE

IN THIS VOLUME, I discuss the more personal aspects of my life, as well as our family's life. I found these personal writings to be more challenging than the narration of my professional work. How does a man, having lived an active life for more than eighty years, look back to assess and relate accurately and objectively his fifty-three year long marriage and family life? Can he be counted on to faithfully reveal the drama surrounding the early years of his family, the rearing of his children, the intimacies of the spousal relationship, the management of his dual roles of breadwinner and husband/father – without inevitably resorting to rationalization and lies? The ups and downs caused by external pressures, each family member's hormonal mood swings, a traveling man's temptations, real or wrongly inferred disloyalties and infidelities, the emotional conflicts arising and subsiding as a family deals with the daily theater of an active household – each of these issues and events are bound to be perceived differently by each participant, particularly in retrospect.

Who would believe such a narrative of self-appraisal? Daily, we are exposed to examples of self-deception, easily recognizable in others, less so in ourselves. We understand the "Rashomon effect", how events are perceived and described one way by one party, another way by a second party, perhaps yet differently by additional participants to the same event. The search for truth is not easy, as Diogenes long ago proclaimed.

And yet, I want to make the effort for my family. Perhaps the most reliable way to present the family's last fifty-three years would be to limit my current narrative to the bare, hopefully indisputable facts. In chapter two,

I present past writings, some of which were written by me in verse, some authored by my children over the intervening years. I will draw from our Christmas letters to chronicle the more significant events, thoughts, and conversations dealing with personal family issues, written at a time much closer to the actual events. It is best to rely less on my recollections; rather let those earlier writings speak for themselves. As the Romans used to say, "Verba Volent, Scripta Tenent" – speech flies away, the written word remains.

This part of my memoirs also places emphasis on our global travels. It is an attempt to explain why we did what we did, rather than simply narrate what we did.

Why did we travel so much? Part of the explanation is that it was a requirement of my employment. But our quest to see and experience every nook and cranny of this planet went deeper than that. I have always had a fascination with the concept of "national character." When members of the human species identify themselves as part of a social, cultural or national grouping, how do these groupings differ in their collective behaviors? What is there about the German culture and values that can explain their behavior during the period leading up to World War II? Why cannot the Greeks get along with their neighbors, the Turks? How to explain the behavior of the various Arab societies toward each other? Or the French toward their tourists? Or the Poles toward the Jews?

During the early 1950s, while engaged in my undergraduate studies at City College of New York, one of the school's most distinguished professors, Hans Kohn, published his famous study, *The Idea of Nationalism* (1951). In it, he discusses the qualities, values and ideas that tie people together as a nation. I became keenly interested in his thesis, that "… in the eighteenth century, through the simultaneous emergence of nationalism, democracy, and industrialism, all three closely linked in origin and continuous interaction, an ever-quickening and ever-widening process of acculturation, economic exchange, and intensification of communications started ...."[1] He further elaborates that, "Nationalism is a state of mind, permeating the large majority of people...." I am persuaded that national character is an important factor to be taken into account when designing and negotiating economic assistance efforts.

In these pages, I have attempted to draw upon my observations in the course of these travels to describe and, perhaps shed some light on this subject, controversial though it may be, since it seems to play an important role in the process of international negotiation. To the extent I have come to understand what these observations signify, I report them to you for your own assessment. I summarize these findings and those on other matters in **chapter nine and in Annex 1B**.

---

1 *The Idea of Nationalism,* Hans Kohn, 1951, The MacMillan Company, New York, pages 3 and 16.

ACKNOWLEDGEMENTS

I DEDICATE THIS WORK TO my wife of 53 years, Joan Mae (Fogltanz) Rudel. She is, by any measure, the most significant of my "second thoughts". One of life's lessons for me has been the proclivity of the mind to be absolutely convinced, at one moment in time, of the right, the correct, the absolutely, unquestionably only valid action to be taken. And then, some time later, to begin a process of rethinking the same issue and coming to a totally different conclusion – a "second thought."

The decision that has had the greatest impact on my happiness, and also on my productivity and accomplishments, has been the decision to embrace this woman as my partner in life after my first effort at marriage revealed itself to have been a huge mistake. I fell deeply in love with her. Contrary to the advice and counsel of many wise persons, I chose her to help me find a meaningful life on this planet. It is my good fortune that she also decided to choose me.

All I have strived for is directly due to her inspiration. All that I have achieved, including the raising of our family of three children and eight grandchildren, as is described in this book and its companion work, is directly due to her wonderful and magnificent partnership.

I also acknowledge the contributions to my well-being that derive from my three children - Ruthann, David and Joanna. I could not have asked for a more supportive and compatible family. And then, the "eight cousins", Wolfgang, Emma, Declan, Ambrose, Caroline, Ezra, Willa and Miranda. These are the sum total of my blessings.

How Much Time?

Here's a short story. How much time have you got?

It's been 13 billion years since the "Big Bang".
The sky is full of stars, galaxies, black holes and what nots,
Each pursuing its mathematically predictable orbit.
And we ride on one small planet;
The only one known, in this vast, light speed measured universe,
That supports life.

First came water.
A billion years later, some life formed
In the massive seas,
Excreting oxygen to bubble up that, after eons,
Collectively became our atmosphere.

Eventually, some things crawled onto the land,
Evolved into species that breathe, adapt and procreate.
Complex processes essential to support life materialized
Over millennia to create a livable environment
On this small globe,
Making it unique among all known heavenly bodies.
It must have taken quite a bit of time.

Fourteen thousand years ago the latest ice age ended.
Even more recently, during this brief period

Of our planet's past we call "recorded history",
Toynbee tells us about 26 civilizations,
Each with a beginning, a middle and an end,
Some exploding; some imploding; some gobbling up another.

My universe began not that long ago - At conception? At birth?
You can look at it either way.
For me, that is when history began!
I found a fully formed planet containing many species of life,
With a social structure ready for my use.
Life came to me with mandates to study, learn, do good things.
A drive to "repair the world" seems hardwired into our genes.
From whence do these task orders derive?
Why do only some labor so, to create, to make things better?

Life on this planet, always an uncertain business,
Comes with no guarantees.
There is evidence of past catastrophic collisions from outer space
That almost ended life on earth.
But now, for the first time, it has entered the realm of possibility
For the human species itself,
To destabilize those miraculous processes
Essential to sustain earthly life,
Thereby bringing habitation of this planet
To an abrupt end.

Not to worry.
If all life on earth were catastrophically snuffed out,
The universe, its galaxies, stars and what nots,
Would unconcernedly proceed on their predictable course.
Pity, that our unique earth might take on the sterile status
Of every other known celestial.

Even without such "Armageddon events"
The duration of our individual lives is uncertain.
We are continuously subjected to hazards,
Some man-made; some resulting from curious twists of fate,
Each risky phase navigated through multi-perils to personal survival.
No guarantees.
Survival is determined, event after event,
More by random luck than skill.
Each person asks, "How much time have I got?"
Each draws a different answer.

We mourn our inevitable end,
Even when it comes as a capstone to a well worn life.
Why is that considered a tragedy?
Would that one had never been born? Had never appeared on this planet,
Avoiding the pains and heartaches that go with the wondrous gifts
Of reason and our five senses?
How fortunate for us that
We alone, in this light speed measured universe,
Are privileged to partake of our magnificent, brief moment.

So, here am I, pursuing my predictable orbit,
Living my personal civilization's beginning, middle,
And traveling at light speed toward its end.
Inevitably, the body's alarm clock will ring
To awake me from my dreams;
Reminding that my earth is about to disappear.

How much time have you got?
One needs to travel faster than light
To do all the things one dreams of doing,
In life's brief, allotted minute.

PART ONE

THE FAMILY

1

The Family: Its Early Years - 1960 to 1974

The Courtship -- 1960[2]

AFTER COMPLETING MY MILITARY service in January 1955, I spent a year in New York City with my first wife, Sandra. I pursued my MA in International Policies at New York University (NYU) while waiting for an appointment to the International Cooperation Administration (ICA) in Washington D.C. In the interim, I worked at the Inter-Oceanic Commodities Corporation at 17 Battery Place, which imported cocoa and coffee and exported grain. In January 1956, we moved to Washington D.C. where Sandra found work as a stockbroker.

There is no point in belaboring the problems of that marriage here. There are always at least two sides to the story. We had had a wonderful time in Japan during my military assignment. But once we settled in Washington, things got unstuck. In mid-1959, we separated and divorced the following year. There were no children to complicate things. My determination to end the marriage convinced my mother that she had been right all along in thinking her "number two son" was unstable.

2　Some of the material in this section has been excerpted and edited from Volume I of Memoirs of an Agent for Change in International Development.

One of my friends in my army reserve unit, a lawyer named Marv Perlis, helped me secure an "Alabama" divorce. In those days, it was difficult in many states to obtain a "no fault" divorce - except in Alabama. Since it was unseemly for a gentleman or a lady to appear in court in Alabama, the attorneys conducted all the proceedings. Neither party had to make a physical appearance; being in the state for twenty-four hours satisfied residency requirements. I flew down to Birmingham, took a taxi to the attorney's office, signed some papers, and handed the attorney our signed agreement. That was it. He did the rest.

Carter Ide, my boss and mentor while I served on the Iran Desk at ICA, was absolutely wonderful to me. Knowing I was going through a rough patch, both at home and at work, he covered for me and treated me gently.

I had been slated to take an overseas assignment. Once my divorce was final, I requested one with the ICA mission in Turkey. In late summer 1960, I transferred to the Foreign Service Reserve and was posted to Turkey. A new chapter in my life began.

—⚬⚬⚬—

My assignment in 1960 to the U.S. aid mission (reconstituted into USAID by President Kennedy in 1961) in Ankara, Turkey was a watershed in my life. I had learned the foreign aid business over the last five years and understood how Washington worked. I had developed a favorable reputation within the agency and was launched on an exciting career path. I was single again. I had completed all work for my MA in International Policies at NYU, including the thesis requirement and had graduated in 1959. I had sufficient income to feel a degree of financial independence for the first time in my life. The new assignment as assistant program officer in Ankara put me to work under some very experienced, smart and capable people. It promised to be challenging and interesting in a country that was very important to the U.S. And it was not too far from

Europe, which was appealing for travel purposes. It was, in every sense, a fresh start to my adult life.

In September 1960, I purchased a Peugeot 403 in Paris and set out on a drive through Holland, Germany, Italy, the former Yugoslavia, Bulgaria, and into Turkey. The aid mission got me a classy, two-bedroom, furnished apartment within walking distance from my office. First order of business was a visit to the military Post Exchange (PX) located in the center of Ankara to buy new supplies and adult toys (i.e. a neat hi-fi system) to complement the furnishings. Next was the recruitment of Gulsun, an elderly, slightly crippled, but sweet, devoted woman as my full-time housekeeper. Boy-oh-boy, at the tender age of thirty, I had arrived!

Two weeks after arrival, on a visit to the U.S. Embassy, I found myself walking up the steps behind a very shapely woman, also recently arrived, and working in the Economic Section. From my vantage point, I noted she had great legs. Her name was Joan Fogltanz. I say "was" because eventually the name would be changed to "Rudel."

How do I describe this woman? At five foot six inches and 116 pounds, with an open face, a sedate, yet self assured manner, and a warm smile, she was lovely to look at and easy to speak with. Her demeanor and sophistication belied the fact that she grew up on a small Wisconsin dairy farm. Her eight great-grandparents, true pioneers, had migrated from rural Bohemia (Czechoslovakia) during the 1850s to Wisconsin where they set to clearing land for dairy farming.

Joan received the first eight years of her education in a one room schoolhouse that required her to take a two mile hike from her farm on a country road, rain or shine, every day. After completing high school, at age seventeen, she left home to take a clerical job in Milwaukee where she attended evening classes at Marquette University. She desperately wanted a college education, something simply out of reach for a farm girl growing up in rural Wisconsin. When I got to know her, I learned that her younger sister, Marlene, had just completed high school and that Joan was trying to persuade her to enroll in a liberal arts college. She had actually set aside some money to help Marlene out--so strongly did she feel about the benefits of gaining an advanced education. If she had missed out, at least Marlene would obtain it, and Joan would receive vicarious enjoyment therefrom.

Being an adventurous soul, Joan had traveled to Europe in 1957 on her own, spending six weeks in Switzerland, France, Belgium, Holland, Germany, England and Italy. Later, she and a friend bought a car and traveled for a year around the U.S., finding temporary work to fund their touring through thirty-eight states. Her love of travel and of exploring distant lands had prompted her and her friend to join the Foreign Service. Turkey was their first assignment. She had arrived at post just two weeks before me. She evidenced a huge intellectual curiosity, a desire to learn about everything. Her mind was like a sponge, eager to soak up knowledge about the world around her. No subject was taboo for her.

Oh, and did I mention she was a practicing Roman Catholic?

During the next year, Joan and I gradually bonded. Much to the chagrin of senior embassy "poo-bah"s, Joan scandalously joined me for a three-week trip to England to pick up my new Jaguar and drive it back to Turkey. We slowly came to the realization that our love was too powerful to be forgotten when our tours ended. We finally understood and agreed that we must marry, in spite of our religious differences. What at first seemed impossible to both of us gradually became an improbability, then a possibility, a likelihood, and finally, an inevitability.

In May 1962, Joan and I boarded the Orient Express in Istanbul and traveled to Zurich where we married at the city hall. The room we rented was very modest indeed. Joan still remembers the plaid linoleum on the floor. But we were in love and did not care. Arranging to meet all of Switzerland's marriage rules and requirements was an ordeal but we had lots of friendly support from the U.S. consulate. I even managed to get the authorities in Vienna to promptly send a copy of my birth certificate to Zurich after learning it was needed. Finally, after three days of back and forth between the consulate and the Marriage Bureau, the bonds were posted at city hall for all to see. The appointment with the marriage officiator was set for the following Monday. We headed to a tavern, ordered fondue and several bottles of the local wine, got plastered and waited for Monday, when I would make an "honest woman" of Joan.

Irving and Sue Rosenthal, friends who were also posted at the aid mission in Ankara, had purchased a car in Dusseldorf. They coordinated their trip with ours and met us in Zurich, serving as witnesses as well as best man and maid of honor at our wedding. They then accompanied us on our honeymoon as we drove back to Ankara together in their new car. The Rosenthals would continue to cross paths with Joan and me, almost as though it were written in the stars. For the rest of our days, our lives would be intertwined. The four of us remain the best of friends to this day.

Our arrival as husband and wife was a great relief to the more conservative and senior members of the embassy and aid staff. They threw us a big wedding celebration, attended by the diplomatic community.

After several months I was sent to the U.S. for consultation. When I returned, I found Joan in the U.S. military hospital. She had suffered a miscarriage during my absence, as had Sue Rosenthal. When I had departed, I had no idea either woman was pregnant. Joan's miscarriage had an emotional impact on me. It also taught me something about the chemical changes in a woman's body during pregnancy and their effect on her emotional wellbeing in the event of loss of the fetus.

We were scheduled to depart Turkey in early December 1962, and so the farewell parties began. Joan and I were happy to move on. After Thanksgiving, we packed our things, got into our Jaguar and drove to Izmir. We watched the car get loaded onto a ship and then boarded it to sail for Venice, and drove to Le Havre. We checked into a first-class stateroom on the *SS America* and sailed for New York City.

It had been a wonderful two-year assignment with many opportunities to understand Turkey's amazingly complex culture. The work experience helped prepare me for positions of greater responsibility and enhanced my reputation within USAID. By the end of my tour, I had also improved my financial position. But the most significant development was my second try at matrimony. The satisfactions derived from my new marriage with Joan were to be greater than I had any right to expect. I had found my soul mate.

THE MARRIAGE -- 1962

Joan and I had wrestled with the question of marriage for more than a year while courting in Turkey. We concluded that the biggest problem to be faced in the future would be reconciling our different religious beliefs. She was a devout, church-going Catholic and I was a divorced agnostic with Jewish upbringing. We accepted the risks of this potential source of conflict and promised to bend over backwards to accommodate each other's practices. We were also concerned that our respective families would find it difficult to accept our marriage particularly once the children arrived. As it turned out, religious differences were the least of our problems. Both of us were somewhat estranged from our respective families, I more so than Joan, and decided we would seek their embrace but could do without it. In fact, both families quickly accepted us, and also our children as they came along. Unfortunately, my mother died before she could meet Joan.

Here is an extract from a letter to our friends sent in July 1962, two months after the wedding:

As you can see by the enclosed announcement, we were married in Zurich, Switzerland on May 22, 1962 by the "Standesbeamter" of the Zurich Canton. Since very few of you know anything about our courtship we thought something more than a formal announcement might be in order.

….Lu met Joan the first day he arrived in Ankara. He saw her leave the Director's office, took one look at her legs and made a mental note which, in all fairness, cannot be repeated here. They went out together from time to time. By early summer they were dating to the exclusion of others. Marriage was not in the sphere of consciousness of either mind since the differences in religious beliefs and outlook seemed insurmountable. Lu had been married once before. While divorce is permissible in his religion (he is Jewish) it is not so recognized in Joan's (she is Roman Catholic). But as time permitted each to compare their basic values of life - their ethics and aspirations, likes and dislikes – a significant similarity, or at least congruency became evident. And soon, in the words of a friend "what once seemed impossible, now seemed only very difficult" and soon thereafter seemed "difficult but inevitable."

In the spring of 1962, after much soul searching, each made peace with his/her own conscience and they decided to marry in a civil ceremony. Joan determined to remain as much a Catholic as the Church would let her be. Lu recognized the importance of Joan's association with her Church and agreed to help her maintain it as much as possible. Both recognized the differences in religious outlook and agreed to respectfully disagree, giving the children the best of both worlds and permitting free thought to reign in their household. And so … on May 15, Joan and Lu departed from Istanbul via the Orient Express bound for Zurich and were married a week later.

- Lu and Joan

On November 16, 1963, while we were posted in Washington D.C., Ruthann made her appearance. We selected her name to be representative of both the Torah as well as the New Testament, to symbolize our effort to bridge the religion gap. Ruthann was baptized and Joan's family came to Washington for the ceremony. However, when I proudly told a colleague, a graduate of the

Harvard University Divinity School, of our cleverness, he pointed out that the Biblical Ruth was not a Jew but a Moabite. But he added that, in the end, we did get it right because Ann, the mother of Mary, was Jewish!

In the spring of 1964, I was sent to study economics at the University of Michigan. By the time we moved from Washington to Ann Arbor, Joan was pregnant once again. David was born on the night of October 1, 1964, just ten and a half months after Ruthann's début. We were a growing family. Once again, Joan's parents flew to Michigan to help us and to participate in the baptism.

Our apartment in Ann Arbor was comfortable and I could see how Joan adapted so wonderfully to her new role as mother. I was less comfortable with the role of father. I had no role model since my father had died when I was seven years old. Jul was the only person who had been a father figure to me since I had never found anything in the behavior of Joe Rappaport, my stepfather, to be worth emulating. That poor guy had been a bachelor all his life until he married Pepi, my mother, at the age of fifty-five. Consequently, I threw myself into my work and left the household in Joan's capable hands.

I was also uncomfortable in my new role as a full-time student with no need to work. We had a handsome salary coming in regularly from my employer, Uncle Sam. My past experience in college was to squeeze as much time as possible out of my employment and do the minimum amount of studying necessary to pass the courses. Now I was a person with some leisure. I did not know how to handle that; my daily schedule seemed incomplete. And so, I took myself to the airport and learned to fly. I earned my pilot's license before leaving Ann Arbor in January 1965. Flying small aircraft in the world's "far-off-places" would become my favorite sport and, perhaps with the single exception of performing as an actor in live theater, my most enjoyable form of relaxation. It is described in greater detail in chapter eight, below. I also earned another masters degree to add to the one from NYU.

The academic year passed quickly and soon we found ourselves back in Washington D.C. for a short stay while preparations were being made for our new posting in New Delhi, India. Traveling with two children in diapers kept Joan and me hopping. But the burden fell almost entirely on her since I was asked to go to India in advance of the family, for six weeks to serve as a member of an evaluation team to review our aid program there.

ASSIGNMENT TO INDIA -- 1965 TO 1970

The family arrived in India in May 1965 after a long trip from New York on a Boeing 707. We settled into a fine house with a full staff of servants to lighten our burden. Ruthann was eighteen months old; David was seven months old. Joan and I were ready to take on the challenges of our new life on the subcontinent, and soon, Joan became aware that she was pregnant once again.

Here is the very first, albeit belated, Christmas letter our new family sent to our family and friends the following year:

Here it is the beginning of February 1966, and we have not yet sent out our Christmas/ New Year letter. It is living proof that things "just take a little longer" to get done on the subcontinent.

Well, what sort of year has it been? A year of change primarily. After celebrating a very white and cold Christmas 1964 with the Fogltanz family in Wisconsin, we bade farewell to the University of Michigan, packed our worldly belongings, pointed our two cars and two babies east and headed for Washington, D. C, to get oriented on Lu's new job with the USAID Mission in India. After the usual harried shopping, last minute briefing and farewells, (Lu took a short trip to New Delhi while the family got ready to migrate) the family flew to India, stopping in Rome and Tel Aviv. Because we visited the

Vatican as well as Israel, some unkind soul remarked that we were "praying both sides of the street."

The children are growing wonderfully. Ruthann has started school, is the youngest enrolled there (2 years, 3 months) and is developing into a remarkably lovely little girl. David is the clown of the family with blond hair and an ever present smile. He is just beginning to express himself. Both are being spoiled rotten by over-protective nursemaids and a staff of servants who seem to love the children every bit as much as their parents do. Progress is being made on the Rudel project for a four children (2 boys, 2 girls) family. By the time you get this letter the third installment will have arrived (no applause, please.) One more to go according to plan, but Lu keeps insisting that "a couple, plus three of a kind" is a "full house", We have not done as much traveling as we might have wished because of the pressure of workload at the office, Nevertheless, we spent some time at Himalayan mountain resorts during the summer (Kasauli and Naini Tal) and managed a week long trip by train and car from Delhi to Bombay. We also visited Agra (Taj Mahal), Jaipur and Udaipur on long weekends, becoming exposed to the Rajputs of Rajasthan. Lu just flew to Nepal last week and saw some of the more formidable mountains. In Nepal only those masses of terra firma rising above 17,500 feet are classified as mountains. Everything of lesser stature is considered a "hill".

Life in India is circumscribed by masses of people ever increasing in number, shortage of resources, and inequitable distribution of wealth. In between two colonies of attractive houses in which wealthy Indians and foreign diplomats reside, there will be a "village" of small huts or mud hovels in which construction workers, servants and beggars live. A typical hut will be the size of a camping tent and may house father, mother, four or five children, one or two grandparents and an aunt or sister-in-law. A common water well will be the social center of the community. Electricity is non-existent and cooking is done over an open stove. The men and women find work when they can, share their salaries and live a hand-to-mouth existence. When the price of rice goes up a small amount it poses a major crisis for the family as savings are virtually non-existent. The streets are filled with these emaciated people, wearing old tattered hand-me-down garments who, in summer heat, drift slowly from place to place, their eyes glazed, oblivious to the horn blaring chauffeur driven cars and scooter rickshaws around them. What seems to keep everyone going is a stoical belief that this life is but one phase of their eternal existence, and the more suffering they endure during this incarnation the higher the level and the better the existence in their next incarnation. A discussion of the dangers of socialized medicine becomes meaningless when one house call by a competent doctor costs the average common laborer about a month's wages. Either people are left to die in the streets or the state provides free medical services. The same rationale holds for many other governmental functions. Hordes of bullock carts, water buffalo, scrawny cows ambling down the road amidst masses of people on foot and on bicycles soon created a sense of total envelopment. There appears to be little reason to hurry. It will all be there tomorrow.

The war with Pakistan has, of course, been the pivotal event of the year on the subcontinent. It is almost unbelievable that these two poverty-stricken nations, with their undernourished, illiterate masses eking out the meagerest of livelihoods, with their foreign exchange virtually depleted and their development programs almost totally dependent upon external assistance, that these countries with such manifold common interests to remain at peace should be willing to undertake a military action at this time in their history, And yet the politicians on both sides cheer as their respective governments announce that troops have been sent to teach their adversaries a lesson. None of the traditional political theories explaining the causes of war seem to fit here. The economic determinists can't seem to find a basis in the two nations' competition for Kashmir's markets or raw materials. The geopoliticians seek solace in pointing out that Kashmir is the bridge between China and Pakistan. But the feud over Kashmir predates the current love affair between Pakistan and China; it goes back to the late 1940's. A more plausible explanation appears to be that this insignificant piece of territory has become an emotion packed cause celebré in a test of strength and power between two peoples who have a history of 400 years of mutual hatred. The sacrifices each appears to be prepared to make to wrest Kashmir from the other exceeds any rational measure of Kashmir's value.

Since each nation's news system reported that its respective military was winning, neither government found itself with sufficient flexibility to compromise its original position lest it be accused of losing at the conference table what its soldiers had won on the battlefield. It was in this context that the Tashkent talks were begun. That they succeeded at all is due in large part to the unbending policy of the U. S. not to resume aid (except for food and fertilizer) to either country until there was some evidence that peace was restored. The demise of Prime Minister Shastri just following the issuance of the Tashkent declaration also must be credited with staving off the critics and channeling the emotions of the crowd away from the issues (the inverse of the "scapegoat" effect; not unlike the sacrificial offering ceremonies of ancient times).

In spite of the seeming ageless and endless poverty and misery, things are changing rapidly in India. Just being an idle observer to these events would be exciting enough, but to be directly associated with these development efforts, even though our role is ever so insignificant, is almost more than one could wish for.

We are all learning a. great deal about Indian culture and are also bringing a bit of our own to New Delhi. Lu acted the part of Charlie Reader in an amateur production of "Tender Trap", became sufficiently interested in the theatre to revive the American Theatre Association of New Delhi and is currently its president. We will be putting on "Mary Mary" and "Hatful of Rain" during the first half of 1966.

Now that we are comfortably settled in our home, and Joan is back to her original shape, we (the five of us) are ready to travel and plan to see much of this part of the world during the next year. We hope somehow that you will find occasion to stop by to see us if you should be "in the neighborhood".

Fond wishes to you and yours.

- Joan and Lu Rudel

Our third child, Joanna, made her appearance on Valentine's Day, 1966. Born in New Delhi at the Holy Family Hospital, she was our "Indian miniature", a small wiry child with a solid bundle of nerves, full of dynamism and energy. Fortunately, we had ample household help and hired a second *ayah* to care for her.

BUSINESS AND FAMILY TRAVEL IN INDIA

Some travel was required by my work since AID projects were located throughout India. We were so heavily involved with India's development efforts that it was important to understand what was being done by the Indians themselves along with our own input. On some of these trips it was just Joan and me with the household staff attending to the children in Delhi. The U.S. had consulates in Madras, Calcutta and Bombay and the consuls wanted to stay informed about our activities in their areas of responsibility. I was working with people all over the subcontinent: in Ahmedabad and Baroda with the Indian Institute of Management; in Pune with the Institute for Economic Research; in Bombay with Tata Consulting; in Madras with the Central Leather Research Institute; in Calcutta with Dastur and the other Indian Institute of Management; and in Cochin with the Marine Products Export Promotion Council. I felt productive even though the winds were never at my back.

Our family also went on several holiday trips to southern India (Bangalore, Cochin, Madurai), to the Ganges Plain (Lucknow, Benares, Putna), as well as Pokhara in neighboring Nepal. We also needed to travel each summer to escape the debilitating heat of Delhi. During the winter months, Delhi's weather is ideal. But in March, the temperature begins to climb. It becomes intolerable in May and June until the monsoon begins to cool things down a bit in early July. During those sixty days in May and June, most Westerners find cooler places for their families to hibernate.

The foothills of the Himalayas are not too far from Delhi and allow a working member to join the family on most weekends. Kashmir was a most luxurious escape spot during our tour. The trout fishing there is world-renowned and we took advantage of places like Gulmarg and Pahalgam for extended stays. One summer, we camped at seven thousand feet, living in furnished tents large enough to house bunk beds. The household staff came with us and took care of all the camping drudgery. We even rented a houseboat, sometimes referred to as a little piece of England, on Dal Lake.

There were touristic trips to Rajasthan, including the cities of Udaipur and Jaipur as we traveled by rail, air or car. Transport and hotels were inexpensive; there were no cost constraints for travel in India. In 1968, Joan and I even rented the Maharajah of Siliserh's former palace in Rajasthan, about a hundred miles from Delhi, and invited thirty of our friends to celebrate New Year's day with us. The palace was located on the shores of a small lake. When the moon rose, the setting was spectacular and the party a hoot.

The two-week hiking trip to Nepal was even more spectacular. We traveled from Delhi by train to Lucknow, then north to Nautanwa right on the border, and walked into Nepal. It was late in the evening and the guards were gone so we were told to just go about our business and check in with the authorities the next day. We had a wonderful time trekking towards the Anapurna range, spending nights in our sleeping bags on the front stoop of a bungalow and eating canned beans. We carried our water in large Clorox bottles.

We also toured through south India and visited Goa, Cochin, Periyar Wildlife Sanctuary, Madurai, Madras, Ooty and the tea estates The people of south India seemed entirely different to us than those living in the Ganges Plains or in Rajasthan. Their economy was then dominated by fishing, cashews, coir and coconut products on the coast, particularly in Kerala, and tea estates in the center. Now, of course, Ootacamund, formerly the center of the tea estates, has become a center for outsourced computer services. I toured coir factories and cashew nut cleaning facilities and quickly understood why the people of Kerala vote for a communist government. The work in these facilities is almost inhuman drudgery. For example, cashew nuts in their shells were then imported from Africa, roasted and cleaned for export in India and then re-exported because the Africans would not do the final processing. The lacquer released during roasting of the cashew nut is used to make automobile brake lining. Imagine what that did to the hands of the workers. Labor at coir factories, using coconut shell fiber to make doormats, is just as brutal.

In late 1969, with our children approaching school age, I realized that my family needed to establish its roots in the United States. Our five years of life within the diplomatic community based in India had been a wonderfully fulfilling experience in many ways. It gave our children a unique perspective. But it also had denied them an acculturation in their own national society. It was time to return to the United States.

During our tour, we had learned of a support program for Tibetan refugees and met a young woman, perhaps twenty years old, who had walked across the Himalayan mountains into Nepal to escape from China. Her name was Yangchen Lhamo. We recruited her to help us care for the children. She had no education. When she began work for us in our New Delhi home, we gave her a tour of the kitchen. She had no idea how to open the door of the refrigerator.

There were the usual farewell parties--one included a fortuneteller--as we wrapped up our belongings and prepared to re-enter normal life in the U.S. The children and we said good-bye to our Indian friends, uncertain whether they and we would ever meet again. An important chapter in our lives was closing We departed India in 1970 together with Yangchen who continued to work and live with us in the U.S. for another four years. By the time she left our employment in 1974, she was on her way to becoming an American citizen and establishing her own family in Paterson, New Jersey.

Our family life in India is more fully described in chapter five of Volume I. Suffice it to say here that we enjoyed life as a growing family in a diplomatic setting and it was a very satisfying five years for us all

2

THE FAMILY MATURES: THE STORY IN VERSE AND LETTERS - 1974 TO 2015

HERE IS THE SITUATION in which our family found itself in 1974 as we returned to Washington D.C. after completing our two year assignment in Harrisburg with the Government of Pennsylvania. Our three children were eleven, ten, and eight years old respectively. We had purchased a home that was somewhat beyond our financial means in the best school district in the Maryland suburbs of the Washington area--Joan's iron clad criteria--so that our children could safely attend excellent public schools. Yangchen had moved on just as we were entering the busiest time of a family's growth.

Moreover, I was caught in AID's Reduction in Force (RIF) effort after having completed eighteen years of service, which, together with my military service, put me just five years short of retirement with an annuity from the Foreign Service. Preparing the appeal to have the RIF reversed was taking lots of time and was a source of great anxiety for Joan and me. Even when my RIF order was rescinded in 1975 and my employment with AID reinstated, it was clear that my government salary would be insufficient to finance the children's college education. Additionally, the Pennsylvania land development project was moving much slower than we had anticipated. Far from reaching its take off threshold, it was taking a lot of our spare time without yielding any revenue for us or for the shareholders. See part three of the previous volume for more about the land development in Appalachia.

And so, Joan had to return to the work force. She enrolled at the local community college for training in computer science, reasoning correctly that this was the next growth industry. She graduated with a 4.0 grade point average and was valedictorian of a graduating class of a thousand students. She entered the work force in 1978. At first, she had difficulty in convincing the recruiters that her age (she was forty-four years old) was not an impediment to the performance of her tasks. The use of computers was just beginning and very young folks dominated this fledgling industry. Eventually she was hired by a firm to work on the U.S. Army recruitment system. The system, similar to airline reservation systems, was intended to serve the recruiting stations by allowing them to match new recruits with the army's requirements and training slots. Ten years later, by the time Joan retired, she had been placed in charge of the company's task to service that entire system.

It was around the time we returned to Washington D.C. that I began to write poetry. Well actually, my work is best described as rhyme or verse, or doggerel even. It does not rise to the lofty heights of poetry. I found initial inspiration in a short untitled rhyme written by Mrs. Harold Wilson, wife of the then British prime minister. It read as follows:

> **If I can write before I die**
> **One line of purest poetry,**
> **Or crystallize for all to share**
> **A thought unique, a moment rare**
> **Within one sentence clear and plain,**
> **Then I shall not have lived in vain.**

When Ruthann, whom we sometimes called Principessa Divina after Puccini's *Turandot*, turned ten, I presented her with the following message to mark her birthday:

TEN

TEN is a much bigger number than NINE
  It is a new series.
  It has two digits.
TEN has such a mature sound to it.
TEN means you are in your TEENS – almost.
TEN is the smallest coin with silver in it.
  Silver is a precious metal.
  TEN is precious.
TEN sounds so TENder.
  It is a gentle number.
  So round and full and important.

TEN is the starting age for little ladies.
  It is the age of awareness.
  The age of sensitivity.
  The age of sensibility.
  The age of responsibility.
  These are all important words.
  And they have important meanings.
  You have to be at least TEN,
  Before you can really understand them.
  HAPPY BIRTHDAY PRINCIPESSA
  - November 16, 1973

Then one for David on his eleventh birthday:

Dear David Said ...

Dear David said that there is no point in washing a face
Before going to sleep because no one will look at it
'til morning anyway.
Dear David said that... Dear David.

Dear David said that he was going to finish his model
airplane, do his homework, his Horn practice, empty
the waste baskets and fold the clothes -- but first
he wants to watch television.
Dear dedicated, delightful, devastating David said
that -- he ready did.

Dear David said he was Jewish -- that was on Sunday when
Mother wanted him to get out of bed and go to church.

Dear David said He was Catholic -- that was when Dad asked
him to study Hebrew so he could be Bar Mitzvahed.
Dear, diligent, darling David said that -- He really did.

Dear David said he wanted to do some of the family chores
like trimming the grass that summer, but that
ought to be worth $100 to Mom and Pop.
Dear devoted dutiful David said that -- He really did.

Dear David
- is a good swimmer so we bought a swimming pool;
- is a good skier; so we built a ski slope;
- now if he became a good student, he would expect
us to buy him a school.

Dear David said he is very observant and should be a great
detective. He realized we were not going to the concert
at Wolf Trap when he sat down in his seat at the Kennedy
Center.

Dear David wants his older sister to stop getting stronger
so he can finally beat her at arm wrestle and swimming races.

Dear David wants his younger sister to get bigger and stronger
so he can punch her when she bothers him without feeling
guilty.

Dear David wants to be ... well we aren't quite sure.
But that was when Dear David was 10 years old --
Now he is 11 -- What will Dear David say now??

HAPPY BIRTHDAY to our downright, distinguished, debonair, dreamer!!
- October 1, 1975

And one for Joanna on her eighth:

Dearest Joanna

Today you are eight
You already can skate.
And there are signs of late
That you want to debate
And not leave it to fate.
But you should first gain some weight
At a very near date
Or we'll use you as bait!

Next year you'll be nine
If you walk a straight line
With a rhythm divine
As a partner of mine.
We can dance so sublime
And I'll make up a rhyme
To say, "we all love you"!!

- February 14, 1974

TEENAGE YEARS

Similar themes were the subject of birthday messages to the children as they made their way into their 'teens. Ruthann pressed us early on to allow her greater independence than we thought advisable. In 1979, at the tender age of sixteen, she set forth a plan to travel to Israel and spend her summer working on a Kibbutz. She had done all sorts of research, contacted the sponsors of the program, and developed a budget. She requested our approval just after she performed exceptionally well on the clarinet at a concert of the Montgomery Youth Orchestra. While we were still in a euphoric mood, enjoying the *naches* of having such a gifted child, she sprung the idea on us. Despite the butterflies in our stomach, we agreed to let her make the trip on her own.

A couple of years later, it was David's turn. After graduating high school, he decided to travel to India on his own and wandered the subcontinent for four months. He too, survived the experience without any mishap. He later reported to us an incident when he got lost in the Rajasthan desert with his camel driver. Still, he came back to us none-the-worse.

The family was caught up in its busiest period. The children were now seventeen, sixteen and fourteen respectively. The mood of the times is captured in our 1980 Christmas letter, which took the form of verse, to our friends and relatives:

An Apology From the Rudels

A working family are we.
Joan computes, 30 hours a week, does she
Clerking and baby-sitting do the children three
School, music and dance leave little time free
To go off for a skiing spree.
And as for me -
For an eternity,
Have I been shuttling to Pennsylvany
To sell another lot and tree.
Golly Gee!!
Can't you see
How weary
We must be?

So that's the reason for our fall.
We didn't write, we didn't call,
To send our greetings to you all,
For Hanukah, Yule, and your New Year's ball.

It's not that you were out of mind.
We loved your cards, they were so kind,
But time to write, we did not find.
This rat race has us in a bind.

Next year, for sure, we'll take more care
To play the year-end game fair and square.
We'll shoot the kids, and quit our jobs,
Default our mortgage and live like slobs.

But we will send a card to each of you ~
Personalized in thought, through and through,
To tell you which way the wind blew.
And then you'll see how much we grew!

– December 1980

That same year, I sent Ruthann the following message:

To Ruthann on her seventeenth birthday (with apologies to William Shakespeare)

To flee or not to flee; that is the question.
Whether 'tis nobler in Bethesda to suffer the gaffs and snubs of those with outrageous fortune,
Or to flee across town, and by so doing end the comfy life at home.

To sleep, ah yes, to sleep,
'Tis a consummation devoutly to be wished.
To sleep, perchance to dream, aye, there's the rub; for in that sleep what dreams may come-
There's the respect that is so hard to show - for one who would bear the whips and scorns of teachers, the oppressor parent's chore list, the proud sister's Japliness, the pangs of Driver's Ed, the brother's delay, the insolence of adults, and the spurns that patient merit of the unworthy takes.

Who would grocery packages and firewood bear, to grunt and sweat under a weary life, but that the dread of something after graduation puzzles the will, and makes us rather bear those ills we have, than fly to others we know not of.

Thus growing up does make rebels of us all,
Until the childhood fantasy of adult freedom, is sicklied o'er with the pale cast of thought,
And wild parties of great pitch and moment with disregard of curfew time, their currents turn awry and lose the name of action.
                    Love, Mom and Dad

   1980 was the year I retired from AID after completing twenty-five years of government service. Joan had begun her career in the fledgling computer business following her graduation. I could now devote my time to the Glendale project while continuing to perform short-term assignments with international development agencies.

   The family dynamics were rapidly changing. Joan was "in the rat race", tightly scheduled between her daily employment and the tasks of household management, while I was the one able to set my own schedule. The children were becoming more independent and mobile, as each earned his or her driver's license. Ruthann completed high school that year and we thought she needed a poem to enshrine the experience.

> For Seventeen summers has she grown,
> Now her form has got full blown.
> She passed grade school and went on high
> (In sophomore year she got real high).
>
> Her credentials show that she has led
> In music, grades and drivers ed.
> Of rock and roll she knows the beat
> And swims a lot to slim her seat.
>
> She's cool and calm at times of stress,
> But Lord, her room is still a mess.
> Colleagues say she's quite astute
> Her iron will is resolute.
>
> She goes off with the "Gang of Four",
> Life's deeper mysteries, to explore.
> And toils to earn a little bread,
> To spend on...well, enough said.
>
> This Princess who cares not for lace,
> Is right at home on Winterberry Place.
> But also travels far and wide,
> And moves with independent stride.
>
> When we, these contradictions hear,
> No way to label her is clear,

For she is one that's all her own.
She wants her roots, but room to roam.

So let us raise our cup of cheer,
Bid welcome to her eighteenth year.
For whether she be far or near,
She'll always be our "Princess dear".

———⊗⊗⊗———

A year later, on her eighteenth birthday, we wrote this letter to her:

A TESTIMONIAL FOR RUTHANN RUDEL
NOVEMBER 16, 1981

We have known her for some considerable time now, this child who has just reached the legal age of womanhood; - as much as modern parents can know their modern daughter in these times when the marvels of modern technology allow us to communicate instantly with the entire galaxy, but two people in the same room have perhaps more trouble sharing their thoughts than they must have had in ancient days.

She was born early in our marriage, the first of three to arrive in quick succession. And of course, this "Principessa Divina" had to bear the brunt of our experiments with parenthood. She spent her first year of life in Ann Arbor, just long enough to allow for the arrival of her brother. Then off to India, where she could be properly pampered by a staff of servants, living in an island of luxury amidst the most squalid poverty this modern world has come to know. She was barely 26 months old when her sister made an appearance on this worldly stage, an action she has to this day found difficult to forgive. Her long, thick mane of brown hair, so carefully groomed, was her hallmark as she attended, first the fashionable Playhouse School and then the British School.

At the age of seven she returned to America and had to learn to live in our normal environment, if one can use that word to describe life in the U.S. during the Seventies. The end of the Viet Nam War was followed by Watergate, a particularly ugly period in which to formulate one's mind and values. Who is friend? Who is foe? What is the meaning of loyalty? Who is responsible? These are complicated questions for a third grader.

The family moved to Harrisburg for two years, another wrenching of the roots and baptismal into a different culture. Living on the "Buckle of the Bible Belt" and looked upon by others as the only Jew in the school full of faith healers (though she herself might not even have thought herself Jewish), must have been a memorable experience. Still she made a few good friends and rolled with the punches, and through it all, got the "Headmaster's Award" at the Harrisburg Academy for the best student in her grade.

Back to Washington - this time to Bethesda, the bastion of the upper-middle-class-suburban-liberal-pseudo-intellectual professional. Another life style; a different set of values; new friends, classmates and neighbors. And the contrasts must have sparked the thoughts even before she could frame them into proper questions. Who am I? Where do I fit? What do I want? What don't I like? Why? Thoughts without sentences; substance without form. And here we found ourselves so powerless to help, except perhaps to set some limits to her explorations, lest she hurt herself beyond repair.

Growing up was never an easy task. Now especially! There are too many options available; seemingly too many choices, with image and reality confused by the media's marketing madness to pander to our weaknesses. It may be asking much of a young mind to sift through this flow of fluff and to ferret out fact from fantasy.

But discipline - yes, discipline - turned out to be her strong suit. Once she made up that well-constructed mind of hers, she stuck it out until she reached her goal. And so she molded her musical talent to become an excellent clarinetist. She pursued her interests in chemistry, math and other courses, to become a top-rated student and National Merit candidate. She knew she wanted the things money could buy and worked to earn it, taking pride in her discovery that work is the real road to independence. We watched her from a distance, suspecting that she wanted it that way and would look upon us as intruders if we tried to get too close.

She developed a strong sense of equity and justice and, except for a few well-known blind spots, demonstrates an objectivity and intellectual integrity beyond her years.

While she is prone to hide some of her emotions, there are times when they do burst forth. There was the time she vented her frustration with Glendale Yearound and its reluctance to be successfully completed, by crying out with a tear-choked voice, that "Capitalism sucks".

Her wanderlust (we can argue whether it is inherited - and if so, from whom) is realistically pursued, gives pleasure to her and those around her and adds visibly to her understanding of herself and the world in which she finds herself.

The forces of fate are fickle. Anyone can get into real difficulty. But it is the manner in which a person responds to adverse circumstances that is the mark of his/her character. While her tests in this regard fortunately have not been extreme, her response in those instances which caught her up is reassuring to those who care for her.

She has learned to deal well with people, and has gained the respect and friendship of those she chose to respect and befriend. It turned out she has the inner strengths to be flexible, and to change when it suited her. And she had the courage to avoid previously prescribed patterns and styles and to build one uniquely suited to her. Although we are not asked to pass judgment on it, we like what we have seen.

We find satisfaction in this person who has now reached the age and earned the rights of independence. While she still suffers from certain common childhood diseases - notably the ones that cause her to think she knows and understands more than she really does -- we have confidence in her and in her future. She has all the ingredients to create for herself a happy healthy productive and socially responsible life.

And we ask whatever powers there be, to let it be so.

Mom and Dad

There was a poem that year for Joanna, on her fifteenth birthday, as well:

TO A FIFTEEN YEAR OLD VALENTINE

It all began on the Ganges Plain,
Amidst a drought – there was no rain.
Mom's mirror showed her round with child,
She was surprised, to put it mild,
With two at home, to find that she
Would soon add one to make it three.
But then we knew it was too late,
To sulk and not accept our fate.
For Indian miniatures are fair,
And we knew that ours would be quite rare.

To make her debut she picks
Valentine's Day in Sixty-Six.
She looked around in shock to see
This hospital has no TV!!
So back inside she tried to crawl.
She really drove us up the wall.
It became clear for all to see
That she was not content to be
A normal, peaceful, average kid.
Her dramatic style could not be hid.
And lo, these last fifteen years
She set her rules. And we have fears
Her performances will do her in.
Her siblings view her with chagrin.

At fifteen years this lady knows
In dance and life, to strike a pose.
For she can charm the world at will.
And when she's mad, she's fit to kill.
So here's a wish for her from me –
Don't let your sparks burn down our (family) tree.

-February 14, 1981

David was going through a difficult time in high school. Without going into detail, here is the letter we wrote to him upon his graduation:

Dear David,

I had intended for this to be a poem. But somehow, the fondness I feel toward you; the impact of your graduation on your mother and me; the reminiscences of your past experiences as you grew, and the hopes and wishes we have for your future, are too complex to he placed in iambic pentameter - at least I can't do it.

You are a gentle, lovable guy! I guess that is the base layer of our feelings about you. We take great pride in the human values you chose for yourself - those with which you seem most comfortable. Your pride in workmanship - and your attitude towards the arts and artisan skills gives us great satisfaction. The classless mentality with which you perceive your colleagues is a sign of maturity beyond your years. While it may still take a while before you get past your enthrallment with the symbols of stature and distinguish between them and substance, the underlying set of values that governs your relationship with others I find highly attractive, rare in high school graduates, and makes me very proud to be your father.

This last year must have been very painful for you - and I regret the portion of pain I inflicted on you. If a valid excuse exists - and I am no longer certain it does - it was done out of a sense that I owed you one last effort to press you into fully exploiting the enormous potential in you. But that talent and skill that lies within you can only he tapped by you. Perhaps I should have known that all along.

I often find myself gazing at your pictures on the family room wall. They conjure up wonderful memories; some amusing, some prideful, some frustrating, but none angry. If it were possible for a father to design and structure his son exactly the way he might want him, I might have added one or two things to what you created for yourself, but I would not have changed the basic you. But then, you might have designed your father differently too, if you had the option.

I guess I'm trying to say that I feet much love for you, and am proud and glad that you are my son.

This really is the beginning of your adulthood. Whichever life-style you chose for yourself, you know I wish you well and that I want to give you whatever assistance I can. But most of all, I hope we can now become good friends.

- June 8, 1982

The family scene in 1982 is described in our Christmas letter:

1982 was a good year for the Rudels.

Ruthann: After a four-month solo backpacking trip through Greece,
she is now a freshman at Oberlin, studying chemistry and clarinet.

David: Graduated high school and now working as an apprentice cabinet maker and taking evening courses. He's off to India in February for four months.

Joanna: Has become stage struck. She's a junior at Whitman High, works two jobs and is very big on musical theater.

Joan: Continues to be the Whiz Mom of computers and holds the home together.
She joined Ruthann in Greece in the spring and Lu in India in the fall. Except for a week of camping in New England this summer, she hardly traveled at all this year.

Lu: Is getting the hang of selling computer language translation systems. Also did some consulting for USAID/ India and our dear friend, James Watt, the Interior Man.

Glendale: Survived this recession year in spite of the worst sales season ever.
But the bank has become more sympathetic and, as Leo Durocher used to say, "Wait 'til next year."

We hope 1983 will be a good year for you and yours, and for us and ours. Also, maybe for one or two others.
Happy Holidays from the Rudels

———<del></del>———

For Joanna, at age seventeen:

For Puppsie:

The Seventeenth Passage

One wonders what may lie in store,
Down this mysterious corridor.
The past is lit, the future dark;
My eyes search for some defining mark,
So I may know, not just surmise,
If goals and wants I'll realize.

Great aspirations have pressed me far,
I know I'm shooting for a star.
All sorts of barriers I have stormed;
And dancers legs I now have formed.

So much to do, so much to fear,
In these next weeks that make a year,
To learn to act, and sing as well,
And build self-discipline (Oh what hell!)

We're almost grown and on our own.
Who's gonna pay my telephone?

Will audiences value me?
Will producers pay my salary?

The seventeenth year will set me free.
How much I've longed for liberty!
And yet it's comforting to think,
That family will help me clear the brink.
One thing is sure. When I am done,
They'll know I've tried - It'll have been fun.

Happy birthday, Mom and Dad

———⚬⚬⚬———

And at eighteen:

Valentine's Day 1984

At last, she's gonna make eighteen,
Potential star of stage and screen.
Emoting each hour of the day,
She presses on to get her way.

This charmer has uncommon looks,
A canny sense not gleaned from books.
Her body's trained to jump and spin.
When she contests - she moves to win!

Oh! She can warm to those she likes,
And worm her way into their psyches.
But bearing, and cold, piercing eye
Says, "Dare to contradict and die!"

We had large doubts some years ago,
She'd survive teenage imbroglio.
But her close scrapes with injury,
Caused only parents the infirmary.

She may soon leave our homey nest,
The last to go. - Then we can rest -
If rest we want. But probably
we'll recall her tricks nostalgically.

We'll laugh to hear of her new stunts,
As Puppsie shrieks and moans and grunts,
Towards her ambitions and her goal.
From Broadway she'll exact her toll.

HAPPY BIRTHDAY!!   from Mom and Dad

COLLEGE DAYS
In 1985 we sent this to Ruthann on her twenty-second birthday:

Princess,

So far away ....
I'd like us to be close this Day.
As you pass through another door
That may distance you from us some more.

This distance issue's been with us
Since long ago. I do not fuss.

But how I long to bridge
The gulf betwixt us.

Did I imagine it to be?
I thought us close when you were three.
No judgments made when diapers wet.
Jumna did tend to it, just yet.

But later, while I did not look,
(Were you inspired by a book?)
Your mind began to soar,
And left me in the nevermore.

I doubt that I can catch up now.
You're on your way. And I do bow
To your ability to see,
Which lifestyle will set your soul free.

The inner satisfaction's there.
I watch your moves as you go where
I hoped you might.
I'll reach for you from time to time.
If you reach back ... oh how sublime.

Love, Mom and Dad
- November 16, 1985

Here is one we sent to David that same year on his twenty-first birthday:

The young man has reached twenty-one.
His race through life has just begun.
All compass points entice him so.
On which tack will he choose to go?

He's shown some signs of interest.
No question; he has wanderlust,
To see what is to see and feel;
Distinguish fantasy from real.

He jumps and twists from bars on high;
Teaches young ones how to fly,
And tumble, run, do flips and swim.
Gymnastics can't be whim for him.

His care for wood and craftsmanship,
Belie his awful penmanship.
And somehow he has learned to cook,
Exotic meals, not by the book.

Somewhere, lurking in his head
There is this talent. Someone said,
"He's got good music in his heart,
But no 'sitzfleisch' in his other part."

But most of all he reasons well.
And, 'though it's still too soon to tell,
He seems to be a humanist.
He's gentle; not the first to raise his fist.

He sees good things in other folks,
And knows that some need different strokes.
Not bad! Independence is yours, now.
Pursue your dream! And do not bow.

ILLIGETIMIS NON-CARBURUNDUM

- October 1, 1985)

Our 1985 Christmas letter was short and to the point:

These last few years, we never quite got ourselves organized to send out Holiday greetings. You may be pleased to know, however, that each year we would go through our card list and think of each person on it. So if our ESP was working, you should have received our message.

The Rudel nest is quite empty now. Three in college. Ruthann completing her senior year at Oberlin – honors in bio-chem; David a junior at Maryland – big in gymnastics; Joanna at SUNY Purchase vigorously pursuing the dance.

And a little bit of role reversal at home. Joan is in the rat race – head of Quality Assurance for a computer company. Lu doing some consulting and tending to Glendale (our Pennsylvania project). Some travel is thrown in. Nairobi and Bangkok for the two of us; Central America for Lu. Also, a great vacation, camping in the Outer Banks. There are not too many of us campers who carry our tents and sleeping bags in our own airplane.

Have a healthy and happy 1986; with our sincere wish to see you soon.

Lu and Joan

———⊛⊛⊛———

To Ruthann, at graduation from Oberlin College, May 1986

To Our Princess:

Many thoughts rush through our mind
On this, your graduation.
You really do not need to hear
Another high oration.
And yet we want to let you know
You have our admiration,
With love, affection, strong and long
And a touch of exasperation.

We hope all your accomplishments
That led to celebration,
Will serve you well and help you see
With some imagination,
That life's a process, not a thing
By which to seek qualification,
Of causes, conflicts, choices, paths
In search of improved relation.
The Art of living is to bring
Well being to your generation.

———⊛⊛⊛———

For Joanna at twenty:

TWENTY

Well, my pet, I guess you made it.
Out of your teens and still not jaded.
No boredom shows through your repose.
In school and dance, you're on your toes.

Excitement flashes in your eyes,
And dreams of greatness, I surmise
Still lurk within your heart and head.
Success could shine on you, it's said.

And yet your faithful following,
Concerned that you invectives fling,
Would like to urge you to go slow,
When anger's Gods make your bile flow.

With talent such as you possess,
There's no need to make a mess,
And every hostile thought express.
To all about you, cause duress.

As you pursue your life-long run,
Take care. Don't be a smoking gun.
Life could be a lot of fun
If you survive 'til twenty-one.

With lots of love and Happy Birthday Wishes,
Mom and Dad - February 14, 1986

—⊛—

The year 1988 was a very important and eventful one for the family. David graduated from the University of Maryland. Joanna graduated from the State University of New York (SUNY) at Purchase and got married. Glendale became viable, thereby slowly lifting the family's financial burden as the risk began to pay off.

Here is a poem written for David on his graduation:

This fellow has acquired some flair.
His manner is quite debonair,
And 'though He's always low on cash
Carries himself with great panache.

He likes to work with steel and wood.
Manipulates a mouse, and prints quite good.
Repairs his car (quite frequently),
He thinks four wheels do set him free.

He's good on the gymnastics court,
Brings balance, grace and strength to sport.
Channels the energies of the troupe,
Towards healthy lifestyles for the group.

To avoid life's conflicts and its strife
Is keynote in this fellows life,
And music soothes his savage breast.
His skill with song is of the best.

High school may not have gone too well -
In fact, it was a bit of hell!
Unlikely that he came prepared
for higher education. Yet, well he fared.

His early work was tenuous,
First dabbled with the obvious.
The grades were barely passable
And Dad got more irascible.

Then something clicked, fell into place.
He found his niche: that gave him grace.
He climbed onto the learning tree
And growing, reached for his apogee.

The fruits of this fine search for good,
Is a degree in bachelorhood.
No well trod road to a career.
His own self-search has brought him here.

He's now degreed and certified.
All doubts have since been cast aside.
He's set to run on life's long course,
Our love has he, right at the source.

Mom and Dad

- May 1988

This one was for Joanna on her twenty-second birthday:

For Joanna:

**So many valentines have passed
Since we've begotten you.
This one has great significance
But the catch is twenty-two.**

**At twenty-two, born to be bad
You'd break a heart or two.
You might have chosen to pursue
Fresh valentines anew.**

**A "femme fatale", you'd stir things up,
And keep us in a stew.
You could now play the numbers game
Instead of being true.**

**Before this year will come to end
You want to tie the knot.
Henceforth the valentine in singular,
Is bound to be your lot.**

**But parents have a special right,
And 'though your heart be Jack's,
You'll be our secret valentine.
Alas, no saving on our tax!**

**Happy birthday, Mom and Dad
- February 14, 1988**

And another for her graduation from SUNY Purchase:

Well! It now appears you did survive
Four years of training. Still alive,
You made the grade, got a degree,
Valid 'til immortality.

Such exultation, so intense!
Your victory is just immense,
The suffering artist, ankles taped,
Captive no more, is now escaped.

The world of dance is a strange locus.
The audience views things in one focus.
But those inside the mirrored hall,
Embrace narcissus most of all.

Apprentice nymphet's, embodiments of grace,
Orthopedist's nightmare, bones out of place.
Jump and skip, fly like a bird,
Pregnancy is perverse; "mature" a dirty word.

Still, when all is said and done,
You have achieved, and you have won
Our admiration for having tried,
'Though fate dealt cards against your side.

And through it all you honed your skills,
Mastered the arts, performed with thrills.
Made us see you in bright light
So that we came to know you right.

You did us proud, we came to view;
Now life goes on, you start anew,
Acknowledged, lettered in fine arts,
With love for you etched in our hearts.

Mom and Dad
- May 1988

There are always jokes about the "in-laws"! In my case, however, I was very lucky. My father-in-law, Roman (Romy) Fogltanz, a life-long dairy farmer from Wisconsin, and his wife, Emma, turned out to be warm, accepting, deeply sincere and kind humans. We became friends, as my eulogy to him, included below, will attest.

I also became good friends with Joan's younger sister, Marlene. She married Richard Herbst and continued to live in Wisconsin, (the Milwaukee area) to raise two wonderful boys, Stephen and Andrew. Around the turn of the century they retired and moved to Tucson, Arizona but, after about twelve years, returned to Wisconsin to be near their children and grandchildren.

Our growing family always made efforts to celebrate Christmas together. There were many wintery trips from Washington DC to Denmark, Wisconsin along the east-west turnpike network, speeding along in second-hand cars, some of the trips actually, a twenty-four hour non-stop ordeal with small children sleeping in the car. But it was highly rewarding. The children learned much from Emma and Romy, having to do with simplicity in style of living, manual skills, individual productivity and honorable behavior.

Here is a short poem I wrote for Romy's eightieth birthday:

> **The way he glides across the floor,**
> **With Emmy in his arms.**
> **You'd never guess his age, 'Four Score',**
> **And still so many charms.**
>
> **His smile, his warmth, his kindnesses,**
> **That twinkle in his eye,**
> **His gentle words that lessen stress.**
> **It's "Gramps". He's one swell guy.**
>
> **With our love, Joan, Lu and the children**
> **October 10, 1988**

EARLY ADULTHOOD

Joanna's wedding to Jack Devine in 1988 marked the beginning of the Empty-Nest Syndrome. Being the youngest child, it was inevitable, I suppose, that she should marry first.

> **Joanna:**
>
> **One journey ends, you start anew.**
> **How brief it was, in hindsight view.**
> **Our girl has come of age.**
>
> **Conceived in ancient eastern lands, this girl**
> **Now has her own flag to unfurl.**
> **We sing a song of passage.**

It all began in Mogul lands,
Such big brown eyes, such tiny hands,
    And an imperious visage.

She knew her pedigree to be
Mumtaz Mahal, and one could see,
    She'll draw from men, their homage.

It's time to launch her into flight.
These golden bangles are her right,
    To mark celestial bondage.

And as we smile, and watch you go,
Our love will follow, you must know,
    "Forever", is the adage.

Mom and Dad, 1988

For Joanna:

A SCORE AND FOUR

Childhood gone, adulthood beckoned.
Marriage transforms all, she reckoned.
Freedom from Dad's rules and stricture
Life is like a movie picture!

Who'd have guessed that playing house
With a live person, albeit a spouse,
May hold surprises in the murky fog,
Unlike Ken and Barbie's dialogue.

This gal of dreams and great ambition,
Whose emotions show in Vistavision,
Who responds with spontaneity,
From sad laments to acute gayety;

Who wants to make each passing day,
A perfect day in every way,
Is forced to reconcile her goals,
As life's reality unfolds.

Yet compromise is not her suit.
She's headstrong, very resolute.
Unwilling to give her dreams the lie,
Until she's made a solid try.

Last year the growing pains did show.
At times it seemed to lay her low.
Thank God the spirit's still alive,
To struggle on - to a score and five.

Happy Birthday Joanna,

Mom and Dad

P.S. "God, give us grace to accept with serenity the things that cannot be changed, courage to change the things which should be changed, and the wisdom to distinguish the one from the other."
Reinhold Niebuhr, The Serenity Prayer 1943

- February 1990

For Ruthann's twenty-sixth birthday, this was our message:

TWENTY-SIX

How shall we celebrate the path
   On which we tread?
Here's a hill there s a bend,
   Now and then we glimpse ahead,
'Though the trees block out the forest,
   And changing light disturbs our view.
Is it easier to see what was,
If our mind's eye makes excuses,
   Can't be trusted to be true?

So many branches this path offers.
   To which cut-off shall we yield?
The possibilities excite us,
   'Though some suspect our fate is sealed.
Are measurements required,
   To mark one's progress on the way?
They say birthdays are essential,
   Lest we lose count and go astray.

Comparisons can be irksome,
   Tend to misdirect our goal.
Chronological imperative
   Overrules enhancement of our soul.
The quality of life is what
   Makes our spirit soar.
If longevity is all that's sought,
   Life would be such a bore.

And yet, we grasp at signs that tell us,
    Progress has been made.
Counting years is so much fun,
    While low numbers still are played.
Our wish to you at twenty six,
    Is that fate ease your heavy load,
And that this day will serve you well,
    A marker on an endless road.

Mom and Dad
- November 16, 1992

CHILDREN START THEIR FAMILIES

Thus ended the period of our family's growth to maturity. Our children were beginning their own families now. Joanna gave birth to Wolfgang, our first grandchild, on January 10, 1992. Oddly enough, at this point in time, the family became closer and sought out opportunities to come together, often in far-off places. Our 1994 Christmas letter reads:

Ruthann in Boston with Elaine, has shifted from environmental risk assessment consulting to the "Silent Spring Institute", researching the links between women's health problems and the environment.

David and Sandra relocated to St. Lewis; he developing computer networks for a health insurance carrier; she enrolled in the M.S. program at Washington University in occupational therapy.

Joanna and Jack happily enjoying their new house in the woods, raising Wolfgang and Emma.

Joan and Lu preserving the empty nest for return visits, trying to keep healthy and traveling. Last winter we spent seven weeks in Australia and New Zealand. For domestic travel, Lu's airplane (only family member not shown on photo) keeps purring along.

—⊶⊷⊶—

Here is our birthday greeting for David:

Dear David:

Happy Birthday! You must be pleased to have your birthday the same day as the U.S. Treasury. October 1 is the beginning of the fiscal year. Maybe you should carry a flag (or a dollar sign) on your birthday?

So, what's happening? Are you being properly compensated yet? Is there any news about your pending move to the west coast? Does Sandra like her new internship?

Here things are just fine although I have nothing new about the sale of Glendale. The airplane is in Trenton getting a new interior. I have a nifty hand-held GPS unit which allows me to locate my position from satellites to within 91 feet. And I'm enrolled in some classes (Opera and theater play reading). I'm reading the dual autobiographies of Will and Ariel Durant; written in the mid 1970s just before they died. It is truly remarkable what they accomplished. And what a list of names they drop. From Charlie Chaplin to Bertrand Russell. Every thoughtful or talented person of the Twentieth Century was an associate of theirs. The fascinating thing about the book is their conclusions about life in general and philosophies applicable to our current problems which

derived from their research. It could make for interesting discussion, perhaps at Thanksgiving or next Passover.

So have a ball...enjoy your celebration of life. And remember that we are indeed among the fortunate few.

With love, Dad

- October 1, 1996

———∞∞∞———

Then, Declan Devine was born in August of 1996:

Dear Declan Joseph Rudel Devine:

Your arrival into this world on August 23, 1996, has been a cause for much celebration for your entire family. Your father was present when you made the grand entrance at the hospital. Of course, your mother was also there, giving you the first push of your life.

Don't worry; she will give you many more, as you grow older. Wolf, Emma and Opa were the next to gaze upon you. Oma soon followed. And what a thrill is was for each of us. You definitely got star billing and it was well deserved.

So, welcome to this planet. We hope you have a pleasant and constructive visit, I'm reading a book by a very learned man. In it he wrote, "If a man is fortunate he will, before he dies, gather up as much as he can of his civilized heritage and transmit it to his children. And to his final breath he will be grateful for this inexhaustible legacy, knowing that it is our nourishing mother and our lasting life."

Oma and I are certain that your parents will carry out this task. To make it easier, the enclosed check will begin a fund to pay for your education. Part of that education will help train you to earn a living. But education is more than that. It will allow you to understand the results of the hard work of previous generations and give you the building blocks to develop your own philosophy suited to your life.

Love, Opa and Oma

- October 19, 1996

By the time 1997 came along, the length of our Christmas letter would indicate that a more leisurely pace had set into our household, even though the text of the letter spoke of hectic activities:

Dear Friends and Relatives:

It is the end of 1997 and we admit that we have been remiss in maintaining our communication channels. Sorry about that. Somehow, things have been hectic for us - nothing really bad, you understand; Lady Luck continues to smile on our family - but our lives have been full of minor (but not trivial) activities, quite fulfilling and enjoyable but leaving little time for correspondence. So this letter is intended to let you know we think of you from time to time (Wonder what "what's-their-name" are up to?) and may help catch you up on our family's growth, activities and interests.

We had hoped to shed ourselves of Glendale this year and actually, came close last summer but it was not to be. The buyer could not raise the money to buy us out. So Lu is still running the company. We will try again in 1998. Joan divides her time between watching the contractor build a new porch onto our house, taking Bible History courses, working out at the health club and acting like a grandmother. She also continues to feed her "Wanderlust". Last year she and Lu traveled (four trips) to England, Brazil, Paris and the Swiss/Italian Alps. Lu separately spent three weeks in China with a side trip to Dakar. The work mostly involved evaluations of relatively small development projects, nothing that would grab newspaper headlines like weapons inspections in Iraq, Chinese human rights violations in Tibet, or currency crises in South Asia. But we did get to hear the bitterness of the Swiss on the subject of Senator D'Amato's attacks on their people for keeping the Holocaust victims' gold for 50 years after they should have settled up.

Our children are doing well. Ruthann (the family social conscience) thrives in Boston, bought a small house and works on environmental factors impacting women's health at Silent Spring Institute. She is getting quite a bit of her material published. David (our family hedonist) and Sandra moved to San Francisco (where hedonists belong); David with Ernst and Young performing consulting services on computer networks; Sandra practicing occupational therapy in Oakland. And Joanna and Jack ply their arts and keep fixing up their house in Seneca, as their family continues to grow. Wolfgang is now almost six, is in kindergarten and plays soccer. Emma is four, a real piece of work who will gladly mimic just about anybody. Declan is 15 months old and, well, what can I say, he is a beautiful baby.

This last year we spent an unusual amount of time in New York with Lu's brother and his family. The Washington Rudels and the New York Rudels seem to be drawing closer.

All of these are minor activities of ordinary people. None of us has won a Nobel prize, been nominated for an Oscar; not even a decent win in the lottery. But life continues to treat us well. We hope you and yours also are doing well and wish you our Season's Greetings and best wishes for 1998. Let's hope our paths will cross during the coming year.

Lu and Joan Rudel
- December 1997

Talking about drawing closer to the "New York Rudels", here is a letter we addressed to my nephew, Tony Rudel, on the occasion of his fortieth birthday:

Dear Tony:
As Joan and I prepare to travel to New York to participate in the celebration of your fortieth birthday, lots of thoughts pass across my consciousness. You were only five years old when Joan and I married. That may not have been as much of a shock to our family as my getting a divorce in 1959, but it came close. When I decided to divorce Sandra, your mother and father came to Washington on a special trip because they were told that I was deranged and felt that they had to check it out themselves.

When Joan and I married in Switzerland, they just took it in stride. Another crazy trick by the family black sheep. Your Grandmother then got sick and that upstaged everything else.

By the time my family returned from India in 1970, you were on the move to Bar-Mitzvohdom, and we all dutifully followed the lead of Uncle Herman to unify the family around that occasion. It worked. We all really got to like you and, from that time on, we became closer to you than we did to any other "New York Rudel". We used you as slave labor in installing drainage ditches near the swimming pool, got you out to Pennsylvania from time to time and generally embraced your presence as and when the occasion arose. You have no idea how important it was to all of us that you participated in Joanna and Jack's wedding ceremony. I sensed that you also felt a kinship with us.

It has been almost my primary purpose as a father to assure a friendship among my offspring for each other, a respect for the other with an appreciation and admiration for their respective differences. I'm sure you have noticed that Ruthann, David and Joanna have very different personalities, values and interests but they all like each other and will support each other, notwithstanding these differences. Joan and I relish these signs of camaraderie and we at least fool ourselves into thinking that it is a mark of our success. We are equally pleased that you and Kristy and your children have become a part of our wider family circle, and that you too, can accept those who have wide ranging differences from you.

So, all of this is to say that Joan and I are very happy to be a part of your celebration this year, wish you a very happy year or so, and hope that we can continue to share important moments in our respective lives.

Joan, Lud, Ruthann, David and Joanna

- July 17, 1997

The big surprise of 1997 was a message we received from Ruthann, the child who normally did not display her feelings about her ties to the family.

MY PLACE AT THE TABLE

It's the morning after Thanksgiving and I find myself thinking about friends who have returned to their parents' home for the holiday. I can picture them -- grown children sitting at the breakfast tables of their youth. Perhaps they are eating the same cereal out of the same bowls, but now they drink coffee instead of milk. I think about my place at the table in my parents' house. I think about how very mine it is, and how nothing can make it not be mine, and then I realize that it now probably belongs to Wolf, or Emma, or someone who visits more regularly than I do. But in the still glass case of my memory, the spot is mine and I can feel what it is like to sit there.

I am lucky to know my place at the table is still there, and in less than a month I will sit and have my cereal and coffee, and it will all seem so – familiar. How do I know that this spot exists, that it is still mine? How do I know what it will feel like to sit there tomorrow or the next day? Is this feeling a function of the physical space? the cast of characters? my experience of the moment? How does this feeling evolve as these things change? What can take this spot from me? This day-after-Thanksgiving, I am thankful for having that place at the table to call up in my mind when I am not there; for knowing it exists; for pleasantly anticipating my upcoming visit to it.

The feelings I associate with my place at the table have evolved as the composite of thousands of meals and moments. The table and the family members have been a constant through the years as so many things have changed. They have seen tortured teenaged tears, excited nest-leaving, warmth upon return, and the growing knowing of me as the early asymmetry of parent and child gave way to the more symmetrical relation of adults, though still parent and child. Individually, most moments can't be recalled - -they are insubstantial as a small thin piece of translucent paper. But piled up, one upon the next, they have generated something with shape, color, texture, and substance -- a sense of belonging that I only recently realized I was lucky to have.

The spot that is mine is at one long side of the oval pine table in the room two steps down from the kitchen. There is a south-facing window to my left from which I see flagstone, pool, fence, trees, and sky. David and Joanna sit opposite me; Mom to my left and Dad to my right. I can see the grains and knots of the table, feel the shape of the chair against my body, the hard floor against my feet giving way recently to short-napped gray carpet. I can recall the smell, the feel of the air in that room. This physical space is what came to me this morning, thinking about adult children at their childhood breakfast tables. Of course I have felt the sense of belonging with this family at other tables. The feeling doesn't disappear in a different space. And I have learned between meals at this table, that a physical space can't hold onto feelings not held in the heart. But that aside, my spot, the one I am thinking of, is at that table in that room in that house.

The other people I see at this table are Mom and Dad, David and Joanna. They are the main characters - the beings whose energies I sense more than I see; the individuals I know more subconsciously than consciously; the family that welcomes me home. There are many things, basic things, that I do not know about them. Much of our shared experience is way in the past. Much of our experience isn't shared at all. Sitting at the table now we visit each other on the site of our time together. We have each evolved and come to the table transported across both space and time. We bring along our new families. As our evolved selves we share (infrequent) meals and talk about what a surprise it is to find ourselves enjoying each other so much. These new meals join the long line of old ones and we add a few new pieces of tissue paper to the existing pile.

Our recent gatherings are infused by our growing awareness of how lucky we are to have this table to return to. I sense in all of us a mixture of disbelief and fear - fear of change, of loss, of the inevitable future. Disbelief that these bizarrely unique and different individuals might have somehow succeeded in being some kind of happy functional unit. Perhaps underlying our marveling over our good fortune is a profound appreciation for the combination of luck and skill it has taken to create and maintain this space. With that in mind, I give thanks to whoever has been watching out for us and to my whole family. And I especially give thanks to my parents for their commitment, stability, and love.

- December 1997

From Joanna in 1997:

THE JOY OF COOKING, THE JOY OF SEX, AND THE JOY OF LIVING

The Joy of Cooking has been a constant resource for my mother, Joan. She has taught me my love for the culinary arts. Mom always made a variety of foods and on a slim budget. In fact, Jack says he has never eaten the same food twice at my parent's home. Now, I have permanently borrowed Mom's dog-eared plastic covered copy of the Joy of Cooking. I use it for pancakes, biscuits, stuffed cabbage and Sachertorte. We have moved beyond The Joy of Cooking to Gourmet Magazine and now Cooking Light. My mother is a constant cooking companion.

The Joy of Sex was first found under Mom and Dad's bed by David and Ruthann. I discovered my brother and sister sitting on my parent's bed deeply engrossed in a book. I knew they were avid readers. It was quite interesting and answered a lot of unexplained questions. I believe a few years later the book was moved to Dad's underwear drawer. (not very imaginative, guys).

The Joy of Life was written by my parents, Joan and Lu Rudel. It has been an inspiration on how to live my life and how my children can experience their childhoods. Mom and Dad's interests in religion, art, music, theatre, nature, travel, under-developed countries, developing better lives for people both abroad and stateside, and cuisine have certainly broadened by life and my views on the world. I certainly could not have selected more interesting, loving and generous parents if I had hand-picked them myself. (And we all know how picky I can be.) God Bless the both of you for loving each other through the good times and bad, through sickness and health, through rich times and poor, through Glendale, children, SAC, Montgomery College, State Department, ballet lessons, music lessons, India, Camp Hill, Romy and Emma, Uncle Julius and Rita, drugs, boyfriends, girlfriends, Oberlin, Univ. of Maryland, SUNY Purchase, live-in children, Jack, Sandra, Elaine, weddings, weddings, weddings, Wolfie, Emma, and Declan. I love you.

Joanna

- August 1997

A 1998 birthday message for David:

DAVID - THE HAPPY HOMEOWNER AT 34

Looks like our son is doing well,
From FAXes sent we're sure to tell.
Pays debts to us on time; no laxes.
And he's now complaining about high taxes.

A Republican in Oakland? Please!
Do they allow such anomalies?
Mayor Jerry Brown was selected to rule
Over the "Preppy Set". How cool!

He subscribed to daily paper as a tool
To track the housing market. He's no fool.
But now that residence is acquired,
Let's hope subscription won't be expired.

Two cars, a house with mortgage set,
A sailboat whose keel doesn't get wet.
A pair of DINKs with job satisfaction,
Seems they've mastered sound interaction.

So here he stands at thirty-four.
Productive, active; life's no bore.
A man of means, panache and flair,
Faces the millennium well aware.

His training in philosophy is reflected in how he thinks.
His values show a thoughtfulness; he treasures family links.
The rights and wrongs of life to him are not perceived as whimsy.
Basing one's behavior solely on self interest is patently too flimsy.

Some years ago as a "teenager",
I might have made a proper wager,
David would not do so well. He gave us fright,
That he wouldn't sustain himself in life's light.

Well, we of little faith are chastened.
Now all good things seem to have hastened
To his end. David, you have done us proud.
We can sing your praises very loud.

We wish you well as you mature.
Enjoy your life in its grandeur.
With Sandra standing at your side,
You'll "…let your conscience be your guide."

With love, Mom and Dad

- October 1, 1998

EULOGY FOR ROMY FOGLTANZ March 1999
I come here to pay my respects to Romy.

I hope that, somehow, Romy can observe what is happening today, here in this church at his memorial service. Many things have been said here about his importance to family members and others with whom he came in contact. Often we don't get around to saying these things to people until it's too late. I hope he knows how we feel about him.

I met Romy thirty-seven years ago when Joan and I returned from Turkey, after having married in Switzerland. Joan presented me to him as his new son-in-law. I'm sure when Romy was thinking about the kind of person he would like to have marry his daughter, he definitely did not have someone like me in mind. And yet, when he met me, he accepted me. He accepted me just as I was. He never put any pressure on me to change. He always made me welcome in his home. He respected my views and my beliefs and he never tried to impose his beliefs on me.

He led a full life and we should really celebrate his life rather than be sad about him, even though we will miss him terribly. He was a teacher to my children and he taught them and me by the example he set. His values, show-ing respect for the world around him, the environment, the tools he used, the ideas of others; these values will pass on and remain alive in all of us.

So now, Romy, I hope you heard all the things our children said, about how important you were to them.

And, if you should see my mother up there, please talk to her. Because, right now she must be wondering what I'm doing here, standing on the dais of this church, and talking. Just tell her ... I'm saying "good-bye" to a friend.

——— ∞ ———

THE CHILDREN AS PARENTS

Along the course of the past twenty or so years, our relationships with our children have turned much more egalitarian, relationships befitting mature adults, as illustrated best by our correspondence below. Here is an exchange with Ruthann:

RUTHANN AT 36

Regrets Only

I wish I had not done that!
Yelled, when she needed a pat.
That time, when she was outrageous,
Treated her like she was contagious.

The oldest, no matter how young and frail,
Is called upon to forge the trail.
In feudal times there was reward,
Through primogeniture from the Lord.

Most regrets, I must now admit,
Are about things I did NOT commit.
I should'da done that, I should'da done this.
I should have made time. Oh, the things we did miss.

But, said a wise man from afar, now gone,
The "moving finger, having writ" moves on,
No piety nor wit can bring back
Opportunities missed. No way to re-track!
Not now, anyway. With my eighth decade quickly approaching,
Even massive amounts of your mother's loud coaching,

Can't structure scenarios suitably ranging
To compensate. During all this time, our roles have been changing.
It seems you successfully weathered the storm,
At thirty-six you've exceeded the norm.
A fine home, productive career and wed.
No regrets here. We get "naches" instead.

Not all past contacts 'twixt us were harmful.
Truth is, you were really an armful.
Now, our family ties bind us strongly together,
As this past year has shown in good measure.

We're pleased you seek fairness and justice for all.
Your social conscience is always on call.
Your life's work is "Tikun Oulom", make the planet survive;
Nay, repair it from what was, when you first did arrive.

If value be drawn from our mixed permutation,
The task now falls to your generation.
To her offspring, Joanna will not raise her voice.
In place of a shout, she's made a wise choice.

You too, may wish to improve on the past.
You're the first born; and you learn so fast.
As for all those "regrets", there'll be no amends.
Still, I hope we shall always, in all ways be friends.

Happy Birthday - with all my love. Dad
- November 16, 1999

Here are two more Christmas letters in verse form, the first to welcome the millennium, the second written two years later:

CHRISTMAS 199999999

Hello, out there. You, whom we number as our friends.
Too long ignored by us; we'd like to make amends.
Life has been good for us but hectic was the pace.
Sad; no time we spent with you, dealing face to face.

Joan and Lu are doing fine, their children are grown up,
The grandkids now take their drinks from the old sippy cup.
The children lead productive lives, much too far away,
But they provide for us parents, some neat places to stay.

Ruthann, with partner Elaine; in Boston still reside.
Committed to each other, and for their community they provide.
David, and Sandra, make Oakland, California their nest.
Orange trees and roses in their back yard - all facing west.

Joanna and Jack with their young brood, nearby dwell.
So we see them a lot, and we think that's just swell..
Their newest, (the fourth) is due any moment, we are told.
They bought a big old house and barn - a farm - how bold!

What a great time it was to be alive! This Century did range,
From laconic to supersonic. Yearly, increasing its velocity of change.
Can this rate of change perpetuate another hundred years?
It boggles this old mind, and raises some fears.

Y2K you ask? Well, we respond, why not?
The Rudels are all well; we're a happy lot.
Another Christmas together - some will sleep on a cot.
And we welcome the new century. What choice have we got?

All our best wishes to you and yours for the Holidays and a Happy New Century. And we hope our paths will cross with yours in the not too distant future.

    The Rudels

HAPPY HOLIDAYS TO YOU AND WELCOME TO 2002

This past year has been one of fundamental contradictions;
Our private life benefited from reduced emotional frictions.
Lu finally sold Glendale, most of it anyway,
Retained the expanded farmhouse - what a great place to stay!

Galapagos and Machu Picchu for a winter holiday.
The West Coast and Tucson, (a bit hot in May).
A week at Rehoboth. Sand, surf, six grandkids with their parents frolick-
    ing at ease,
Perfect weather, much camaraderie, no shark attacks reported as yet;
    we did as we please.

Until 9/11; when aviation was turned on its head.
Civilian technological achievements became weapons instead.
Lu's airport was closed, restrictions imposed on freedom to fly where
    his spirit led.

Undaunted, we traveled to Central Europe again; Hungary, Vienna and
Prague,
And nary a drop of rain. (Not in Spain! That's a different refrain.)
Surrounded by ghosts of past generations, feeling their pleasure and
unspeakable pain.

In this age of miniaturization, bigger bangs are achieved
With ever smaller containers. How easy to be deceived!
The rate of technological change accelerates, approaching infinity;
No end in sight! Our near term future cannot be conceived.

We'll gather our clan again at our home. Christmas/Chanukah make a
wonderful system.
They have candles in common, and noble thoughts. such as Dona Nobis
Pacem
From "Great Grandma Emma" down the line to our latest "Gem'a",
Wolf, Emma, Declan, Ambrose, Caroline, Ezra,
We'll count all our blessings. That will be no dilemma

So, we say "hello" to the New Year 2002! Should we welcome or be in
dread of you?
Perhaps some of each; a bit of a stew. Tune in same time next year for a
formal review.

Our best wishes to you and your loved ones in these uncertain times,
Lu and Joan Rudel - November 2001

David and Sam had their first child in 2000:

HAPPY ARRIVAL, CAROLINE HOPE

Welcome to the world, my dear.
And to our family. We all draw near,
That we may sense and see and feel
Your persona; and to know you're real.

Small and dainty were you, on arrival.
But no questions as to your survival.
Yet, those pictures really gave us fits.
To see little you held in your dad's big mitts.

I think you'll like your mom and dad.
They'll teach you lots; tell good from bad.
Both practice open friendliness.
Your mom's the "Queen of Cleanliness".

Your dad likes tools; builds things with grace.
He earns your bread in cyberspace.
But, when a tool, his hands embrace,
It seems a light shines from his face.

You're in good hands, young Caroline.
We hope your life will be just fine.
You've loads of uncles, aunts and cousin.
They'll visit you; you'll do your fussin'.

Oma and Opa will love you, day to day.
Can't wait to hear what you have to say.
We think of you; our hearts do "kvell".
We hope the world will treat you well.
To Life - L'chayim

With love, Oma and Opa
- June 2000

———⊶⊙⊷———

Two more messages, prepared for Thanksgiving 2000 and Christmas 2001, describe my perception of our family and how we navigated through the events that befell us.

THANKSGIVING 2000

Welcome to our Turkey Pull,
Thanksgiving in year "two-triple-null";
Four generations at the table.
To recount our blessings while we're able.

With new arrival, Caroline
We link hands; each makes their sign.
We thank whatever Gods there be,
That we are well, and we are free.

Fortune smiles upon us now.
Nary a wrinkle on our brow.
Through luck and pluck our 'bed is made"
We now can sleep in the cool shade.

And yet, these "seven years of plenty",
May not persist 'til Twenty-Twenty.
We'll do our share for those now in need.
"All of life is temporary". We must take heed.

Please forgive. I do not wish to be a scold.
So now, if I may be so bold,
Notwithstanding my tendency for "expostulation".
Let us give thanks for procreation.

Word has come from our Boston segment,
Ruthann, the Princess, now is pregnant.
Next year, in April, there's due to be
Another miracle. I'm filled with glee!

Make room for fast growth to our family tree.
Elaine and Ruthann are set to be
A set of parents, just like you and me.
Let us give thanks. And may our love flow free.

— ∞∞ —

A FAMILY CHRISTMAS

There are at least two weeks of preparation.
Each dawn brings ever rising expectation,
We move and prepare, as in a trance, with growing anticipation.
"The children are gathering"; once more, another family celebration.

Is it Christmas? Someone's Birthday? A Beach Party? Passovers?
The subject hardly matters. A warm spirit descends on "7600" and
    hovers.

We fall into the grip of nostalgia! But memories can play tricks.
Painful events are repressed; we relish those that gave fun and kicks.

I ask myself, "You, who never considered raising a family an important
    objective,
Focused your energies to 'change the world' and 'get rich', (later found
    those goals deceptive),
Now get such pleasure from the results of efforts which you only mar-
    ginally pursued.
Do these emotions betray a change away from goals you now find crude?
Is this caused by failure of the "false Gods" you long ago did not have
    the strength to defy?
Or is it the new evidence of accomplishments by those whose existence
    began as a simple gleam in your eye?"

First there were only two of us. And that was enough!
We were in our "Twenties", engaged in worldly-most-important "stuff".
The history of our planet we had learned in 25 years.
It wouldn't take long to change its direction, if we work hard with our
    peers.

First Ruthann made her appearance, then David and Joanna.
Within 26 months! (Should we have worked harder at being a planner?)
So then there were five of us. During those initial formative years
We had lots of help. Diapers got changed as we gave little cheers.

The 'teen ages arrived; we lived in a safe neighborhood.
The focus was school, learning to understand and to be understood.
And "five 'round the table" was the normal slate.
Though there were times when tension levels did not fully abate.
How did these children perceive their world? A clear message they did give;

"To live to toil" takes away from the moment; it is not as rewarding as
    "to toil to live."

Still, I think we must have done a few things correctfully,
Though there may have been times when things were not said respectfully.
One by one, the three offspring sprung off, their own flags unfurled,
College at first, then to explore the world.

Again we were two at the table. Chairs reserved for those far from
home.
Lots of travel and phoning, to keep track of them while they roam.
Then came the choosing of partners. Now that was a blast!
The youngest was first and the oldest was last!

That was just the beginning! Each child did beget; our family's expanding.
And each child, to their children, was gentle of speech; not overly
    reprimanding.
As new issues arrive our family gatherings' decibel count rises.
But I'm growing more deaf, so am content to draw surmises
Of things that are said. But I know for a fact, long after I'm gone,
These family gatherings, with their camaraderie, will forever go on.

- December 2001

Here is an exchange with Joanna and her husband, Jack:

Happy Birthday, Jack (February 1) and Joanna (February 14)

ORDINARY THINGS

Morning - The four children sleep soundly as a rule.
Time to wake them, prep for school,
Dress, eat breakfast, make their lunch,
Pack their homework, transport that bunch
To their school busses. Off they go.
That routine followed, come sun or snow.
These are ordinary happenings, ordinary things.

She, at thirty-six, he at forty-two,
Have learned to pace their family through
The routine of their daily lives.
They enjoy the way each member strives
In their own way, as each one's personality may dictate
To face the day, the challenges, the quirks of fate.
These relationships, varied and complex from event to event,
Represent ordinary conduct, ordinary things.

One can sense much pleasure derived from these interactions.
As we see how these parents gain their satisfactions
By giving of themselves to their young
Daily making things work, and making life fun.
How very ordinary these things seem,

And yet, it seems a miracle is occurring before our very eyes,
We older folk who think we are so all knowing and wise.
How did this little girl whom we worried through her- 'teens,
And this young fellow who courted her with hardly any means,
How did they gain such worldliness that they could embrace
A family of their own, and maintain that hectic pace?

We are proud of you both, as we observe
Your efforts and your achievements. You serve
to remind us of the innate abilities of a child who has grown
Into a fully matured adult with skills of their own.
No ordinary thing at all. An extraordinary couple we know you
    to be,
Happy birthday to you both. In all matters of note, may you
    always agree.

With Love and Admiration,
Oma and Opa
- February 2002

Joanna and Jack were the first to experience their children's teenage years.

Dear Wolf:

I congratulate you on this very important occasion -- receiving the Sacrament of Confirmation and your passage into adulthood. I hope your preparations for this occasion are going well for you.

I think you know that I am very proud of your talents and intellect. And I enjoy your questioning mind. You do not assume that everything said by higher authority is factual and truthful, and reserve for yourself the right to question; to gather information with a view to form your own conclusions. This is a gift that should be used with discretion so that you don't question for the sake of argumentation.

If I am pressed to remind you of anything it is this: Our family, the family you were born into, is deserving of special treatment from its members; all have a special priority claim on each other's allegiance and are deserving of the benefit of special consideration even when they, at one moment or another in their long relationship with each other, may act to give some of us a sense of discomfort. This is particularly relevant for you as you deal with your younger siblings. And when one of them (or us) faces special challenges in his/her life, it becomes all the more important to "give a little extra" for the general well being of our family.

This is particularly true because it is a part of the human condition that we tend to remember the things we do for others, while we tend to forget those things others do for us. As a result, it is easy to think (wrongly) that others are taking advantage. Opa and Oma always keep this human failing in mind and try to bend over backwards to do more than we feel is our share. We have found that this is one of life's little secrets that, if kept constantly in mind, will bring about many rewards in terms of one's own peace of mind.

With love and admiration,

Oma and Opa
- October 2005

FOR EMMA

Emma (you who sing and dance) Devine,
Will you be my Valentine?????
I think you are so very pretty.
I also think you're somewhat witty!

You have great talents that can beguile.
At concerts you don't act infantile.
You play the piano with a smile,
And sketch pictures with a handsome style.

So take this flower. It comes straight from my heart.
And smile at me, so I'll know from the start
That you love me as I do you,
And that will see me the whole day through.

Happy St. Valentine's Day. 2005
Opa

—————

A message from David to me:

FOR DAD ON HIS EIGHTIETH BIRTHDAY

Eighty to One

Eighty years to look back upon
   Up ahead? Who knows, we must just plow on.

Three hundred and twenty seasons
   Did warm your skin or your bearded cheeks was freezin.

Four thousand one hundred and sixty weeks
   A seeming unequal balance but the paycheck speaks.

Twenty-nine thousand two hundred nights dreams of passion, dreams of
   yearning, sleepless nights tossing and turning.

Seven hundred thousand eight hundred hours
   The lunch hour, the happy hour, time to stop and buy Mom a flower.

Forty two million forty eight thousand of Kipling's unforgiving minutes
   Each filled with sixty seconds worth of distance run.

   Only

One son who loves you for ever and ever.
David
- July 5, 2010

DAVID AT FIFTY-ONE

I can't believe, our little son,
Has reached the age of fifty-one.
He just ran off to school last week,
Forgot his cap. He looked so meek.
I recall well, how young he seemed.
When he played the horn, his mom just beamed!

Intervening years passed; visits became few.
Meters became miles. Many distances grew.
He'd been so clever with his tools,
Fixed and upgraded our woodwork, stools,
Cabinets, showers. We should not grouse.
We admire his marks throughout the house.

But now, there's wear and tear to see,
On woodwork that had come to be

A staple of our reverie, for times when he
Resided here. Before he chose to be
Adult and free.

His quality of work cannot be matched.
Still we must try. Mustn't let it look patched.
So here's a sample of our restoration.
I'd like to be a fly on the wall at his station,
To listen in on the conversation,
As he critiques his "old man's" tribulation.

With great admiration - and much love, Dad
- October 1, 2015

⸙

From Joanna on the golden jubilee of Joan and my wedding:

Dear Mom and Dad,
On this day of your 50" Wedding Anniversary, I think about all the gifts you have given to me. I wouldn't call them "simple gifts", as I find them the most complicated and intricate gifts of all.

First of all you gave me the gift of life. Even though I know God had a large part in helping you with this gift, the love you two share for each other was the catalyst for this most special gift.

You gave me the gift of love. The love you two share for each other, your family and especially the world around you has shown me the intricacies of love and the importance to share, communicate, compromise and to love unconditionally.

You have given me the gift to love God in whatever way I choose. Being brought up both Catholic and Jewish I have an understanding that there is no "one" way to love God and to worship Him. You have taught me the importance of faith in my life and the importance of family history and tradition.

You gave me the gift of service to others. Dad, in your work with the State Department, Glendale and all your projects, you have always worked for service to others and to make the world a better place. Mom, your volunteer work with our schools, SOME and your community have shown me that my hands, heart and head can do more for others than for myself.

You gave me the gift to love Music, Dance and Theatre. Music was always playing in our house and you gave me the opportunity to learn to play the piano, violin and finally how to explore the dancer inside of me. Your love avid support of the Arts has been an inspiration for me, and a source of great pleasure.

You have given me the ability to appreciate the joys of life, such as fine cuisine, being a gracious host, gardening both for food and aesthetic, and the curiosity to always keep learning about the world around me.

But most of all you have given me the gift to be confident enough to be anything I want to be. Your support of me through out my life, in loving Jack, and raising Wolfgang, Emma, Declan and Ambrose, has fostered in me strength to persevere and to pass on. your gifts to my children and to share them with Jack.

For all these gifts and to you, Mom and Dad, I am ever grateful.
Happy 50th Anniversary! Joanna
- May 2012

JOAN AND I

Most illustrative of our household's emotional environment are perhaps the communications between Joan and myself. The following are four poems I wrote for my beloved wife:

> Dearest shrink, won't you explain?
> Forgot her birthday! What a strain!
> No gift. No card. No birthday wish.
> Out of my thoughts. I'm a dead fish.
>
> What meaning does this lapse convey?
> Did my unconscious go astray?
> Do you suppose I can't abide
> Her getting older by my side?
>
> Dearest shrink I do declare,
> There was romance. We once had flair.
> I thought of her incessantly,
> And sought to please her constantly.
>
> Do you suppose that in my head,
> Now, near three decades since we wed,
> She's seen to have eternal youth.
> To count her years might seem uncouth.

Yes, yes. That's it! I see it clear.
I missed her birthday out of fear
That I'd offend my "Heaven sent".
It was the highest compliment.

Happy Birthday, Joan
From your loving husband,
Lu (Alzheimer) Rudel

- August 12, 1990

DEAR JOAN:

I know large numbers frighten you,
When we discuss our budget.
Your never ending search for truth,
Just doesn't let you fudge it.

Well, now the time has come to tell
Your total years by number.
And 'though you're looking mighty swell,
'Specially when you slumber,

Still there's no way to dodge the fact,
In God's computer of this year,
(We want to say this with great tact),
For you, the digits six and zero now appear.
'Though time, unlike a bank account,
Tolerates no withdrawals.

We don't care what your balance amount.
We're chronological amorals!

You swim and dance with great agilities.
You still laugh at my jokes.
The glint in your eye conveys possibilities,
That in me, possibilities evokes.

So, I celebrate your binary,
Let sixty be "... a lot of news."
I bet you still fit into finery,
Sized at the square of the hypotenuse.

With continued love and admiration.
　　Lu - August 11, 1994

DEAR JOAN:

With love's endearments, past passions still smoldering,
Thus obscuring boring realities while our lives
　　continue unfoldering,
I write to tell you, head held high,
('Though you won't join me when I fly,)
That I adore you. 'Tis no lie!
And, likely will, until I die.

I know you've heard these words before.
(I better stop before I bore!)
And yet, I need to say once more,

Your presence in my life opened a door
To a New World, unparalleled, at the core
With anything I had experienced before.

How these passions work is a deep mystery
That might be explained through "chemistry".
And when, through forty years, they still do reign,
While feelings of warmth, tenderness and love sustain
Their clutches on my heart as I glance at you,
It's a miracle of sorts; I see you yet anew.

I hope you view your life to have been as rewarding
    as you have made mine.
And that you think it worth the effort
    to continue "for auld lang syne."
We could pursue our satisfactions for another forty years,
I'll vow to cherish you as always. You'll let me know
    should I fall in arrears.

Happy Anniversary, Lu
- May 22, 2002

TO JOAN: A TRIBUTE

Half a century. What a grand life lived,
Thanks to you, my Treasured Gift.
Those thirty years - before you came,
Hardly prepared me for our game.
Yet, I sensed – there - at Ataturk's tomb,
My children should be conceived in your womb.

Anyone who knows us well,
If asked, is guaranteed to tell,
That inequality twixt us is real,
'Cause I got the better of the deal.

How wise I was - you, to ensnare.
You've enriched my life beyond compare.
A comfy home peopled by a great crowd.
Three children of which we can be proud.
We merged our income for every quarter.
Our mortgage never went under water.

When I peer into the future, it seems elementary.
Eight grandchildren on track to penetrate the 22nd century,
The values you espoused with great perseverance
Should serve these kids well if they gain adherence.

Each day I say I'm glad we have each other.
If not for you, I'd hardly bother.
There may be more in store for us.
If good health prevails in our calculus.

And yet, of all my desires, I sense there's one,
Not yet fulfilled, despite our long run.
You'd be so shocked if I told all.
But there's no risk; 'cause I no longer recall!

With Love, and Thanks - Shalom,
    Lu
- May 22, 2012

For me, the most rewarding aspect, the ultimate result of our parenting, is that our three children like, support, and care for each other. When one of them finds him or herself in need, the others rally around and rise to the occasion. There is no score keeping among them. And now I perceive that the same feeling of mutual care flows among the eight cousins.

OUR FRIENDS

Joan and I formed a large circle of friends during the extraordinary five years we spent in India. The caliber of the staff, at both the embassy and the aid mission, was well above the norm for such postings. Many of the officers at the embassy went on to receive ambassadorial appointments, among them Tony Quainton, Roger Kirk, Nick Veliotis, and Bill Brown. Dick Celeste became governor of Ohio. Doug Bennett later headed Radio Free Europe. Ernie Stern became executive vice president of the World Bank. Many, such as Ed Lindblohm, Alan Mann, and John Lewis, returned as faculty to their Ivy League universities. Despite the variety of paths each of our lives took us down, our work and experience bonded some of us and we remained friends for the rest of our lives.

The Glendale project had eight shareholders, almost all of who had served in India with us. We would have the annual shareholders' meeting at our farmhouse each autumn. That meeting would turn into a party. Over time, as the project matured and became viable, these annual fall meetings turned into the Fall Foliage Festival. These annual festivals ranged over perhaps twenty-five years and other non-shareholder friends who had connections to our service in India were invited to join. [3]

Several of the exchanges below provide insight into our most cherished friendships. Perhaps the most important long-term relationship our family had was with W. Carter Ide, a man who I looked up to as my

---

3 These festivals are recorded in a photo album with text of some of the very humorous activities that were included into the weekend programs. See photos at www.rudel.net.

mentor during my government career. He also held a stake in the Glendale project. In 2000, I wrote this for his eightieth birthday:

March 11, 2000

Dear Carter:
　Happy Birthday!

　I have had the privilege of working and socializing with you for 43 years.

　As an immigrant to these shores, I often think back of the opportunities that have been offered to me in this country during my life. One of the most important such events was my interview and acceptance to work as your assistant at ICA's "Iran Desk" in the autumn of 1956. That opportunity to work with you at the tasks jointly before us has always been regarded by me as a most enjoyable and productive way of earning a living. It was not the beginning of my adult education but it allowed for the evolution in me of a new perspective, a broader vision of the world, much of it garnered from your vision.

　Not all of our encounters were sweetness and light. You let me know when my zeal and intolerance for those colleagues less clear minded or energetic got the best of me, sometimes in very direct language. But you also were very understanding when my own work slacked off as I tried to straighten out my marriage and my life. Most important, you showed me that one's first cut of analysis may not always reveal the entire truth and that one has to listen and consider, more seriously than I tended do, other's views as well.

Then there was also our business relationship. I suppose it can be said that neither of us were astute investors. But it was a tribute to your faith in me that you agreed to become a shareholder in my enterprise. That venture did not go as we anticipated, any more than aid produced the anticipated results in the former colonies of the imperialist powers. But it provided wonderful opportunities to wrestle with new and different problems and, in the end, it yielded some tangible benefits for each of us as well.

One thing I have always admired was your excellent judgment in selecting a spouse. I did not do too well the first time, but, perhaps in the course of observing you, my skills improved and, by 1962, I figured out how it is done. You and Helen have created a fine family. Each of your children is most fortunate to have had such wonderful parents.

You bring many qualities "to the table" to share with your friends. Your love of trekking, your interest in observing, and your ability to understand varied cultures, your remarkable gifts in producing watercolors of pastoral landscapes, are all qualities I find admirable. They make me envious from time to time.

Since our respective retirement from AID, we have continued our friendship and it has given me great satisfaction. I look forward to the next decade and wish you all the best in all you do.
Lu Rudel

———✦———

Ronald Ridker, an economist who was stationed in India with us, later served at the World Bank. Here is a poem I wrote to the tune of "Danny Boy" for his birthday:

Oh, Ronnie Boy, I hear protesters calling you.
The world's a mess; your theories are all wet.
Your World Bank friends imposed their will on innocents
The world owes you a monumental debt.

These Luddites thank you theorists very earnestly,
You've given them a cause that they can fight,
They found their enemy and it is all of us,
Globalization surely cannot be all right.

Oh Ronnie Boy, your politics, once radical,
Now seem so tame. You've no credibility.
The poor are fruitful and they sure have multiplied,
Let's hear a cheer for productivity.

You went to school, and blamed the old colonialists,
For exploitation of the distant poor.
Today, that exploitation's done by local folks.
A big improvement, you'll agree, I'm very sure.
     - December 1981

Donn Block joined the US foreign aid program a couple of years before me. A mid-westerner from Davenport, Iowa, he and I inexplicably became friends as well as colleagues. I replaced him on the Iran desk in 1957 when he was offered an assignment to Lahore, Pakistan. Later we served in India together. He had earned a Ph.D. in economics from Harvard, was a bachelor who earned his bread in government but his fundamental life interest lay with the performing and other arts. Over the years, we spent many happy days with him at his Rehoboth, Delaware beach house. Here is a rhyme I sent him for his fifty-fourth birthday:

FIFTY-FOUR (40) OR FIGHT
(WILL YOU SETTLE FOR FORTY-NINE?)

This, dear Donn, you might surmise,
Is "junk mail" notice of a prize
That you have won, and now can claim,
If you'll just tour our vast domain.

Instead, the gift that now is due,
Comes from the turning of the screw,
As time, its endless course does trace,
And seniority has you in honored place.

We envy you for what you've got.
Your appreciation of "the arts" is hot!
Of economics you know a lot,
Although you think it's mostly rot.

A man of many parts, you've wrung
From life, the best that's writ and sung.
Your body's fit, from heart to lung,
But none's a match for your barbed tongue.

Your wit and wisdom and that face,
Has seen you through to win – or place.
Your breads and cakes, your cookies too,
Are sought by all. (You part with few!)

Some envy you for what you lack.
No female albatross perched on your back.

You wend your way, completely free,
To mix with Art's celebrity.

Now that you'll strive for fifty-five,
You'll know it's great to be alive.
But as you move on up to speed,
Ignore the law. You must exceed!

You've always had one claim to fame,
Right in the spelling of your name.
Distinction came with stroke of pen.
I wish my name had a double "N"

With love and best wishes for your birthday,
Joann and Ludwinng - July 16, 1982

Two decades later, Donn encountered some serious heart problems:

DONN'S VALVE JOB

We've always known that you were smart,
But not so sure you had a heart.
So, it was news - in some ways - sorta,
A new valve's been placed in your aorta.

How fortunate that they could find,
A bovine with a turn of mind,
That could be used to fix and mend
Your vital organ; thereby the murmur end.

Will your demeanor be the same?
Will your politics still be insane?
Maybe that udder will endow
Your observations to be greeted with "Holy cow".

Give those medics a cigar!
They saved the Chief of ILR.
If other parts need replaced this Yule.
We urge you, next, to find a mule.

With love, and other good wishes.
Lu and Joan   January 2001

Donn got some mileage out of the surgery but then deteriorated, ending up in an assisted living facility. He had never married, thus had no family. But he enjoyed the good fortune of having many loyal friends. One such friend, Federico Roman, devoted himself to Donn's final care. Donn died in 2015. At the memorial gathering, I read the following:

Donn's Friends, Roman, Countrymen, Lend me your ears.

I come to reminisce about Donn, and to praise him.
The evil that men do lives after them. The good is oft interred with their bones.
So let it NOT be with Donn.

A noble friend has said Donn was overly frugal.
If it were so, it was a grievous fault.
And grievously has Donn answered for it.

And yet I gaze at the four woodblocks hanging there, and recall that occasion, many years ago, when Donn ripped them off my wall because they were mounted on acid paper, and reframed them as a gift, probably more for Joan than for me.

Then, there is the matter of that VIOLIN, given for no apparent reason, except from the heart.

He also contributed mightily to just causes and to the performing arts.

Frugality should be made of sterner stuff.

But we, all honorable men, did notice a reticence by Donn to part - even temporarily - with some of his fine belongings, notably his resistance to lend to us any of his vast CD collection.

He was my friend, faithful and just to me.

He had brought many of his captives, me included, to his Rehoboth beach house.

And would have charged a King's ransom for that privilege unless we invited him along to join us there.

You did see that on his 75th birthday Joan and Jackie presented him with cookies and cake - every bit of which he did accept, and much of it he took home with him. How many of us, noble friends of Donn, had noticed his quick acceptance of morsels that catered to his exquisite taste buds.

These foibles gave us, many times, cause for mirth to laugh with - or perhaps even - at him.

He did not suffer fools, gladly! Nor Republicans! His quick wit and barbed tongue for many years, gave us great amusement even when we ourselves were the butt of them.

Let us put out of our minds how these talents and gifts deteriorated in recent months.

You all did love him once, not without cause.
What cause withholds you then, to mourn him now as well as to celebrate his fascinating life?

Bear with me. My heart is still with Donn, and I must pause till it comes back to me.

John Cool was a colleague of Pat Moynihan (they went to the London School of Economics together) and served with the Ford Foundation in India:

JOHN COOL AT SEVENTY

He is the very pattern of a modern intellectual,
His knowledge base has storage place for fact and fancy textual.
He knows of obscure origins for things anthropological,
With very little prompting he'll quote lessons quite historical.

He ponders issues from all sides, be they personal or political,
Can debate with equal skill, both the vapid and the critical.
Abhors a value judgment and accepts with equanimity,
Behavior that is strange to us, from outrageous to just finicky.

He treats his fellow humans with kindness and gentility,
Enjoys a pun and can have fun with random acts of levity,
When speaking to an audience he never stoops to brevity,

So now, let us all celebrate our dear friend's long longevity.
The Rudels
- November 7, 1996

—⧉—

Elinor Berg, wife of Alan Berg--the World Bank's malnutrition maven--decided to establish a small vineyard to grow grapes from which she would make her own wine.

Dear Elinor:

I'm searching for a rhyme
That works with "wine".
How about "divine"
Or a new twist in your life's "paradigm"?

If I knew more about the ins and outs of vintage
Perhaps I could credit you with creating a "new mintage".
And that picture of you is worth a thousand words,
As you spray your grapes to keep away the birds.

It seems a new high in self-effacement
To be making wine in one's own basement.
Did your shrink figure out the psycho roots of this compulsion?
Maybe a return to the basics for some Galitzianer ancestor's expulsion?

Whatever the driving force may be,
For your output of liquid creativity,
The product was really delicious!
(Ask Alan if you can label it "nutritious".)

I would put in my order for next year,
If my pedestrian taste didn't run to beer.
Thanks for letting us partake of this elixir
It makes for one helluva social mixer.

With love, Joan and Lu
- July 2002

⎯⎯⎯⎯∞⎯⎯⎯⎯

One of our close friends living in Washington D.C., Elyse Smith, was a gifted pianist although she earned her keep as director of the Overseas Education Fund of the League of Women Voters. We encouraged her to have her Steinway piano rebuilt, irrespective of the cost. She finally did it.

To: Lee Smith – On Rebuilding her Piano

NEW HARMONIES AT CHEZ ELISE

Does Lee seem like a risk taker?
A gambler, plunger, a fortune staker?
Hardly. And yet on close examination,
That twinkle in her eye leaves room for contemplation.

Her piano, full of high potential,
Sat in repose, while Lee, the quintessential
procrastinator, waited… and waited.
Counting her pennies; resources understated.

One day while she was counting birthdays,
Concluded that pennies have limited worthdays.
She broke open her piggy bank,
And into the piano, her savings sank.

Did you ever see a smile so warm?
Eyes shining like beacons in a storm.
Her fingers float on polished keys,
Sounds produced that way do please.

How rash! Such big time cost incur.
But music did her passions stir.
For once, she did just as she'd please,
Now sounds invoke her ecstasies.

We offer libation. A toast to banish thrift,
As we drink from a "diminished fifth".
Let's dance and sing with this pianissimo whiz,
At Chez Elise where the new action is.

The Rudels - March 1997

Eric Griffel, one of our friends, and an investor in the Pennsylvania project, is eleven days younger than me. Our friendship ran back to 1957, when we both were interns at the Agency for International Development. Here is a birthday wish we sent to him.

To Eric Griffel

It pains me to say it, as I put it to you.
Your rhymes are quite clever for an old Polish Jew.
Offering homage to me, 'cause I'm now seventy-two
In the manner prescribed for juniors like you.

But, look out below! There's no respite for you.
The moving finger moves on. Soon you'll be seventy-two too.

Then the score will be even for some three hundred odd days.
We'll just be two weird old men, each set in his ways.

You'll be that hairless old man offering insightful advice,
Who critiques the world's foibles in manner concise.
While I, with the help of my guru, George Will,
Shall root for Republicans to go in for the kill.
We'll each, in our way, enjoy this land of the free,
And hope to make it to seventy-three.

Happy birthday, Lu
- July 2002

Eric fell while walking in the woods on our farm, while attending at our annual fall festival in Pennsylvania. A few days later Joan fell while pruning flowers in our back yard and injured herself the same way. Eric also had a habit of giving sunflowers to his friends. It gave rise to this message:

THE SUNFLOWER BOUTONNIERRE

My dear friend with pate so bald
Who walks in woods, eyes glazed, so enthralled
He fails to raise his foot enough
Then falls to ground with sonic "huff".
His mighty chest and rib cage ache
As if they'd tied him to a stake.

This sage, this wizened man of letters
Now suffers daily pain from his internal fetters.
But soon events conspired to lift his mood.

He heard that Lu did now brood,
'Cause Joan had followed his example!
Slammed her ribcage on flagstones ample.
Tripped in her yard and fell to ground.
And soon she too was X-ray bound.

Misery loves company! Hoidy boidy!
Here's some room for Schadenfreudy!

But no! My dear friend with pate so bald
With kindness would respond when called.
He'd say that he would use his power
To uplift Joan from her spirits dour.
And likely give her his calling card; a sunflower.

This is truly a man with flair
Even though he has no hair.
So, ... to one who is so aware
Of other people's feelings, we do declare
Him worthy of this (sunflower) boutonniere.

Lu - November 30, 2010

And, of course, there would be some untimely deaths. Lou Stamberg, my AID colleague from India whose wife is Susan Stamberg of National Public Radio fame, died in 2007.

Susan:

Here is what I would have said at the Memorial Service, had there been time.

I'm Lu Rudel, the "task-master" at the Program office of the former USAID Mission in India, to whom Jim Levinson referred earlier. It was my privilege to work with Lou Stamberg and Jim Levinson in New Delhi in 1965 and 1966. It was a glorious time in all of our careers because of the unique collection of extraordinarily talented professionals that Chet Bowles and John Lewis were able to amass there at that time to work at the Embassy and the AID Mission. We have since referred to ourselves as the "India Mafia". Many of us have remained in close contact for the past forty years.

I add my voice to this chorus to sing praises for Lou Stamberg for a life well lived!

He was my friend and colleague. When Joan and I talk about him, the words "decent, gentle, kind" come to mind (with the possible exception of his views of the current occupant of the White House). He was never pompous or pretentious.

He graduated from Harvard Law School and decided not to practice law. That action alone deserves high praise.

He seemed to have unlimited curiosity - an inquiring mind, humorous and quick witted. He was one of the very few people who actually asked me how my Sewage Treatment Plant works. He never believed that the use of the question mark at the end of a sentence was an admission of ignorance.

He touched so many people, as is evident when one looks around this hall. Throughout his life, his prime motivation was to share the gains and benefits he enjoyed, with those who were

less fortunate – to make some contribution that would incremen-
tally improve the lives of the poor. He took seriously the mandate
"Tikkun Oulom" - repair the world.

Joan and I shall miss him deeply.

Lee Rosner and Kay Chernush, close friends for many years, celebrated
their tenth wedding anniversary in 2009. She is a photographer and he is a
scientist, reflecting the adage "opposites attract". Here is a poem for them:

THE SYMBIOSIS OF KAY AND LEE

Robert Service let his imagination run free,
When he wrote "The Cremation of Sam McGee".
So, I ask those here assembled to forgive me,
Especially the host,
If I offer a toast,
To "The Symbiosis of Kay and Lee".

Kay is a fine woman – it is clear,
She has class, plays the flute, with a smile to endear.
L.A. was her home,
But she needed to roam,
As a child of the sixties she showed no fear.
And her tastes run to champagne, rather than beer.

She longed for travel to places exotic.
(Unlike Lee, who delved into the table periodic!)
Immersed herself in Indian Spirituality,
Then opted for Parisian cordiality.

The emotions run high in Kay,
Injustices cause her nerves to fray.
She perceives gestalt concepts in a large panorama,
Then, with her camera she records global melodrama.

Lee comes from Brooklyn, knows Talmud and baseball.
An east-coaster, he chose the sciences to be his call.
His left-brain is immense, he's oh, so very logical,
Somehow he also learned about things gynecological!

Why fortune smiled upon these two opposites it's hard to tell.
But they did meet, and left-brain/right-brain linked ... and turned to gel.
He analyses everything, she intuits the way to go.
Sometimes she zigs while he zags as they go to and fro.

But in the larger sense they complement one another,
As a ship and a lighthouse tend to serve each other.
Ten years ago they pledged that nothing shall pull these two apart.
We glory to witness this cohesion of science and art.

"Symbiosis – the living together of two species of organisms; a term usually restricted to cases in which the union of the two animals or plants is not disadvantageous to either, or is advantageous or necessary to both, as the case of the fungus and algae which together make up the lichen." (The American College Dictionary 1963)

SO ... WHAT'S NOT TO LIKEN????

love, Joan and Lu

- October 2009

The Brothers, "Julo und Lutz"

On March 6, 2011, my brother Julius celebrated his ninetieth birthday. An album of sixty-three photos was prepared by the "Washington Rudels" to commemorate that event. "Julo" and "Lutz" were our respective nicknames while we were growing up. Here is the text that went with those photos. (see www.Rudel.net to view the corresponding photos)

1. IN THE BEGINNING ... the world in which our relationship began ... in Vienna! You were 9 years and three months old when I was born. Up to then, you had it all to yourself! Don't we look angelic?

2, 3. An upwardly mobile family, living a good life. 1932 and 1934 respectively.

4. After arrival in the U.S.A. You took me out of the orphanage to Central Park in 1939.

5, 6. By 1942 you were engaged to Rita but still living at home with Mom, her new husband, Joe Rappaport and me. In these photos we celebrated Grandpa's birthday in 1942.

7, 8, 9. Your wedding in 1942 to Rita. That was the big parting. You moved out. Subsequently you and Rita visited us weekly where you tried to help me grow up while I tolerated an unpleasant household situation.

10, 11, 12, 13. Your career in music takes off! You worked at what you loved to do. I was so envious!

4, 15, 16, 17, 18. Your family expands and grows (three children) and you establish a comfortable life style in NYC as you become a prominent, internationally recognized conductor.

19, 20, 21. My career also begins in the U.S. Foreign Service in 1956. Riding on the Consul General's boat on the Shat-al-Arab River between Iraq and Iran. The Bosporus, The Golden Dome Mosque

22. The Diplomatic Scene in Iran.

23. After a first "failed marriage", tying the knot a second time with Joan in Zurich in 1962.

24. My wedding reception in Ankara.
25, 26, 27, 28. Babies followed quickly. New assignments in India as the children grow.

29, 30, 31. The New Your Rudels and the Washington Rudels meet from time to time, mostly at weddings, bar mitzvahs and funerals.

32. Madeleine's wedding in 1974.

33, 34. Tony's wedding in 1984.

35, 36. We meet in far away places, Michigan in 1988 and Cairo in 1989 (But no photo of you there).

37, 38, 39. With our children on their own, we both dote on the grandchildren.

40. The ritual of attending each other's decennial birthday parties begins. My 60th in 1990)

41. You ask me to come to your 70th birthday party (nine months hence; in 1991) and I offer to do so IF you promise to attend my 70th birthday party. You give your standard answer: "I will try!"

42, 43. The New Your Rudels and the Washington Rudels find occasions to celebrate together. A joint SEDER with both families at Tony's house in 1999. This is odd since neither Jul nor Lu are REALLY Jewish!

44, 45. My 70th birthday in Pennsylvania (2000). Your 80th birthday in NY (2001) Again I ask you to make the same commitment to attend my 80th. Again you answer, "I will try!"

46. Pittsburgh in 2001
47. Charleston S.C.
48. Vienna in 2002.

49 – 54. New York City in the mid 2000s

55, 56, 57. The NEA Honors in Washington D.C. in 2009

58 – 61. My 80th birthday celebration in Washington and your request that I attend your 90th in NYC. Again I extract the same commitment from you to attend my 90th. It seems to have worked so far. Might as well keep going.

62, 63. After long journeys taken by you and me in our respective separate directions, they have yielded a fine crop of offspring.

THE CYCLE REPEATS

I began this chapter with a poem written to Ruthann when she was ten years old. Let me end it with a poem to my oldest grandson, Wolfgang Devine, when he reached the age of ten.

Wolf at TEN

I wonder, as I sit in my den, fingering my pen,
What must it be like to be the first child in the family to turn TEN?
"Adults are taller, they make all the rules and then,
They enforce them. I cannot tell THEM what to do,
But they tell ME what to do, and also when!

"My siblings are smaller, but not by much.
They get into my things and mess up everything their little fingers touch.
They watch when I get in trouble, and figure out how
To get around the problem that got me in trouble, ... or such.
It's just not fair!!!"

But, my dear grandson, I would gladly change places with you.
You're at a wonderful moment in life. Think of all the things you CAN do.
Your mind is so nimble, you can argue endlessly and put the adults in a stew.
Your body can flex, your form is complex; each passing day you learn to do
Something new.

You probably want to get older ...and bigger ... very fast.
If, tomorrow, (or, latest, next Thursday) you could become 20 ... at last!
You could drive a car, fly a plane (and really drive your folks insane),
Sail down the Amazon; Go to College, Make a big football gain.
You think that's going to be all fun and no pain?
Think again.

Decisions; decisions; decisions!
Responsibilities; responsibilities; responsibilities!
Competition, competition; competition!
People will want to know from you: "What and where will you study?

What will you work at when you are through?
How and when will you begin to earn your living?
Who will you marry? How many children will you have?
They'll say, "Time is getting short, boy! Make up your mind, boy!"

So, now that you are halfway to twenty,
Be glad there's time aplenty,
To think about all the choices to you available;
Like, you might choose from the seas that are sailable.

Try-out new things and experiment; see what you enjoy most.
Learn everything from pillar to post.
Then help your siblings deal with their needs,
You'll later reap big gains from those small seeds.

Happy Birthday Wolfie! From Opa,

- January 2002

3

My Jewish Identity and the Melding of Faiths

This year (2015), following the lunar calendar, Passover fell on Good Friday. As has been the case for many years, I found myself sitting at the large dining room table surrounded by our children and grandchildren. I was swaddled in my tallis, made in Israel and given to me by a close friend who traveled there to view the Wailing Wall. The participants at the table had their *Haggadas* balanced on their laps. I was the only full blooded Jew at this table.

And I lead the group in conducting the Passover Seder.

In the first volume of this autobiography, I describe how my escape from Europe in 1938 and my exposure to anti-semitism in the U.S. made me question my Jewish identity. "Why do I have to be Jewish?" was the question I kept asking myself, deluded that leaving Europe could have been avoided had I not been born Jewish. While I had great respect for the teachings of the Torah and the Talmud, I could not convince myself that the cost of being Jewish was worth it. The ease with which one could assimilate into American society made adherence to a Jewish identity all the more difficult. *E Pluribus Unum* was the mantra. Even my mother had begun to eat ham. After my first marriage to a Jewish woman collapsed and when I chose a Catholic as my second wife, I believed I could ignore or abandon the links to my Jewish past and leave religious matters in our family to Joan. Our children were raised Catholic and I have aided and abetted each of their independent choices for spiritual identification.

Yet each Passover, I find myself leading the family in conducting the Passover Seder. How can I explain this anomalous annual scene?

The explanation lies with my wife.

Early in our marriage, Joan enrolled in an adult course on the Old Testament at her church. She learned that Catholicism flowed directly out of Judaism. Her teacher, Brother Malachi, would remind his class that Jesus was born a Jew and died a Jew (just as Luther was born a Catholic and died a Catholic). James Carroll, author of Constantine's Sword, argues that Catholicism derives from Judaism and its followers perceive themselves as the successors to Jews as God's "chosen people".

All of this gave impetus to Joan's insatiable quest for knowledge and understanding. She pressed me to expose the children and her to the few insights I had about Judaism and to search for more to add to my limited knowledge. Soon we began to celebrate a yearly Passover Seder with friends. Then it was Chanukah at Christmas time. Her curiosity about these things, as well as the children's interest and receptivity to an ecumenical household, brought me back to the Jewish cultural richness that I had earlier abandoned.

Joan has helped me appreciate Jewish values such as the quest for learning the truth and the importance of debate while respecting others' points of view. Through her, I have come to recognize the importance of passing these values on to our children and grandchildren. Our children do not consider themselves Jewish; yet they enjoy celebrating the richness of our Jewish heritage. Occasionally, they show signs of a longing for more knowledge via Talmudic study and debate. I find that I myself am still an agnostic, but am more comfortable with my Jewish origins now than I have ever been.

Indeed I realize that it is some of Judaism's fundamental values that have directed so many Jews to work in the spirit of *Tikkun Oulom*, to try and repair the world. Their work has often been recognized by various prestigious awards, including the Nobel Prize, far more frequently than can be explained by their proportion of the population at large. These values also extol equality among humans; they are the antithesis of values that allow slavery and oppression. Rabbi Hillel is reported to have said in the first century BCE that, "that which is hateful to you, do not do to your fellow. That is the whole Torah; the rest is the explanation."

The Exodus, Book Two of the Bible, tells of the uprooting of an enslaved people who were resolved to improve their condition at the peril of their very lives. It is mandated by custom that this story be retold each year to succeeding generations because it contains important lessons concerning the willingness of humans to make personal sacrifices to achieve such freedom. I ponder on this biblical story, which always ends with the wish, "Next Year in Jerusalem", and consider its relevance to today's situation on the ground. Today, all it would take to hold our next Seder in Jerusalem is the purchase of an airplane ticket.

As a descendant of the tribe of Israel, I cherish and empathize with the culture, the wit, the morality, and the traditions of Judaism, but not its religious beliefs. I take pride in the fact that my tribe, through custody of the Torah, has contributed significantly through the ages to Western ideas of equity, justice, and morality. In short, I am a "Cardiac Jew." In my heart, I'm Jewish. I know, from personal experience, that there was a huge price to be paid for being a Jew in twentieth century Europe. In the 1880s, about ten million Jews lived in Europe. By 1950, the Jewish population in Europe was reduced to less than two million. During the intervening seventy years, many migrated to the U.S., Canada and Argentina. Others became Zionists and moved to Palestine. Most of those who did not migrate, either to the West or to the East, were murdered.

Events on the scale of the Holocaust have happened before, not just in the last century. Every couple of hundred years or so, it happens. Jews then pick up and move from one hostile environment to take root in a neighboring country or society that is more hospitable. There the Jewish people thrive for about a hundred and fifty years, as we are doing now in the U.S.. Then, something turns and many thousands or millions are killed. The Wandering Jews then move yet again to another country and the cycle repeats. Jews in Spain lived peacefully alongside their Muslim neighbors until 1492 when Queen Isabella expelled both groups, and the Catholic Church launched the Inquisition. Jews in Lithuania and Poland thrived until the partition of Poland in 1792, when the Pale of Settlement was imposed by the Russians. My ancestors' trail of flight can be traced from Poland, to Czernowitz in the Austria-Hungarian Empire (now Cernivtsi in Ukraine), to Vienna and now to the United States. A friend of mine, also a Holocaust survivor in the U.S., once expressed his feelings toward Europeans, "They murdered my father in 1940...." How much more powerful that accusation feels than the impersonal statement: "They murdered six million Jews." Yet, that crime is the mathematical equivalent to the murder of my friend's father, multiplied six million times.

I believe it will happen again.

Throughout most of recorded history, Jews were "stateless persons" and did not enjoy full citizenship in the lands of their birth. During the two thousand years since the destruction of the Temple in Jerusalem, how many societies, how many countries, have offered full citizenship and social acceptance to my Jewish ancestors? Even today, this mindset of Jewish statelessness prevails in many nations. If I were living in Argentina, most Argentines would view me as "a Jew who makes his home in Argentina." Here in the United States, I am accepted as a full and equal American citizen who has a Jewish heritage. My exploration of history has taught me that this acceptance has few precedents. Only a handful of nations would have accorded me this full national identity.

Even so, I have no desire to embrace the Zionist wish for a country of our own in the world, and thus "return to the Promised Land." I do not subscribe to the idea that God gave this land to the Jews. I believe those

Jews who chose to migrate west, and their descendants, did a whole lot better than those who went east. Yet, I identify with, and support those who choose to embrace Zionism and who attempt to govern themselves as a Jewish nation in a hostile neighborhood. Many Jews consider supporting the State of Israel to be their duty.

I ask myself what the early Zionists, those that moved to Palestine at the turn of the twentieth century, thought when they looked at the landscape dotted with poverty-stricken Arabs? My guess is their thoughts were quite similar to those of the colonists who came to the "New World" in the 1700s and saw the Native Americans. "We will buy (or trade) their lands. We will give them an opportunity to join our effort and thereby lift themselves out of their primitive existence by working for us. We only want a small sliver of land. The Middle East is so big. Those that do not want to join us will move." At least the Jews, unlike many European colonists, had no intention to convert the native population and save souls.

Some Jews tend to support the creation of the State of Israel, irrespective of the knowledge that Jews have not made Palestine their home for almost two thousand years, that Arab armies swept through and conquered that region in the seventh century, that a sophisticated Arab civilization thrived there between the tenth and fifteenth centuries and beat back the "dark-ages Christians" at every turn until Queen Isabella screwed things up, and that the Ottoman Empire ruled the entire region from the fifteenth century until 1914. While most of us recognize the weakness of the arguments surrounding the "promise" made by the British in 1917 to the Jewish Diaspora through the Balfour Declaration, we tend to accept the legitimacy of the 1948 United Nations' action to establish the State of Israel in the land of Palestine. And we would like to think that Israelis and Palestinians can find a way to live peacefully as neighbors.

I cannot prove this, but it is likely that the existence of Israel has contributed to the well being of Jews like me, living in the Diaspora. But I am not a Zionist or a religious believer. And I have serious doubts that

Israel can survive, as a nation with Jewish identity, in the neighborhood in which it is located. For the Palestinians, represented by Hamas and other groups, Zionism equals colonialism and imperialism, rather than the legitimate struggle of a long persecuted Jewish people for return to their homeland.

Then what is to be learned from the Story of the Exodus, as well as my own story of departure and relocation, with respect to my relation-ship to Israel and my responsibility to my family? Surely I am sympathetic to the early settlers, and their offspring, who lived there before World War II. And I have particular sympathy for the Holocaust survivors who migrated from Europe to settle there in the first decade of Israel's cre-ation. I take enormous pride in the accomplishments of these people who built a modern, productive, and significantly democratic society. I contrast these accomplishments to the autocratic rule and conditions of poverty in most other societies in that region. I deplore the constant warfare and terrorism that Israel's neighbors have inflicted, while refusing to relocate the displaced Arab populations living in their refugee camps, for what is now three generations, in order to use them for political pur-poses. Sixty-seven years after the creation of the State of Israel, the larger Arab world has not instituted any serious accommodation to allow these refugees and their children to live fulfilling lives. The Jordanians do not want to accept them in Jordan. The Egyptians will not annex Gaza. There seems little interest among other Arab nations in offering these displaced Palestinians another place to live. That is a factor in the push for "right of return" to Palestine.

However, I also have the sense that the Israelis have not yet recon-ciled themselves to life in the neighborhood they have chosen for them-selves. One thoughtful observer, a prominent Egyptian writer, suggested that the Israelis are standing on their Mediterranean shore-line, looking wistfully towards West Europe, seeking aid and comfort from that direc-tion as though they were an outpost for the West in the Middle East. He suggested that Israelis should turn a hundred and eighty degrees and focus their attention on their neighboring countries. If the Israelis perceive themselves to be a permanent society located on these lands, they must build long-term friendships with their neighbors, because these neighbors also will be there permanently.

Global events will dictate how the creation of Israel in 1948 will play out. However, with regard to my own family, I consider the words of the Torah with respect to proper conduct in social relationships, and compare them with the preaching of Jesus. I find very few substantive differences between these two, once one removes the stories of the supernatural, of the miracles and of the respective ritual practices. I do not ask my family to adhere to any organized church or synagogue because these institutions tend to develop a track record of rigidity and intolerance towards non-conformists. But the philosophy contained in religious teachings is a useful guide for life and addressing its challenges.

And so, I make the choice to allow, perhaps encourage, a distancing of my children and grandchildren from their Jewish religious identity while cherishing the moral and cultural values of the Torah. I have assimilated into the "American" culture. When I am asked by my wife to observe the requirement of the Torah to pass on to our children the values, cultural richness and ethical precepts of Judaism, I do so with a sense of jubilation because I take great pride in the contributions made by my Jewish forebears to our civilization.

At each Passover Seder, our daughter, Ruthann, asks that we add this story about the Baal Shem Tov. It goes like this:

> The Baal Shem Tov used to go to a certain place in the woods and light a fire and pray when he was faced with an especially difficult task, and it was done.
>
> His successor followed his example and went to the same place, but said: "The fire we can no longer light, but we can still say the prayer." And what he asked was done too.

Another generation passed and Rabbi Moshe Leib went to the woods and said: "The fire we can no longer light, the prayer we no longer know; all we know is the place in the woods, and that will have to be enough." And it was enough.

In the fourth generation, Rabbi Israel stayed at home and said: "The fire we can no longer light, the prayer we no longer know, nor do we know the place in the woods. All we can do is tell the story." And that too, proved sufficient.

I also, hope it will prove sufficient.

Paul Johnson, in the epilogue *to A History of the Jews*, describes Jewish contributions to social order in this way[4]:

Certainly, the world without Jews would have been a radically different place. ... All the great conceptual discoveries of the intellect seem obvious and inescapable once they have been revealed, but it requires a special genius to formulate them for the first time. The Jews had this gift. To them we owe the idea of equality before the law, both divine and human; of the sanctity of life and the dignity of the human person; of the individual conscience and so of personal redemption; of the collective conscience and so of social responsibility; of peace as an abstract ideal and love as the foundation of justice; and many other items which constitute the basic moral furniture of the human mind.

If the next generation of our family now abandons its ancient Jewish identity because of perceived future high risks, it should nonetheless continue to adhere to those strictures of the Torah that embody the values of equality and freedom as interpreted by Rabbi Hillel so long ago. Indeed,

---

4 Footnote: Paul Johnson, A History of the Jews, Harper and Row, 1987

we must expand upon these values to fight against injustice and discrimination toward all minorities; be they gay, disabled, or of other races and beliefs.

PART TWO

INTERNATIONAL TRAVELS

The Rudels Travel Destinations

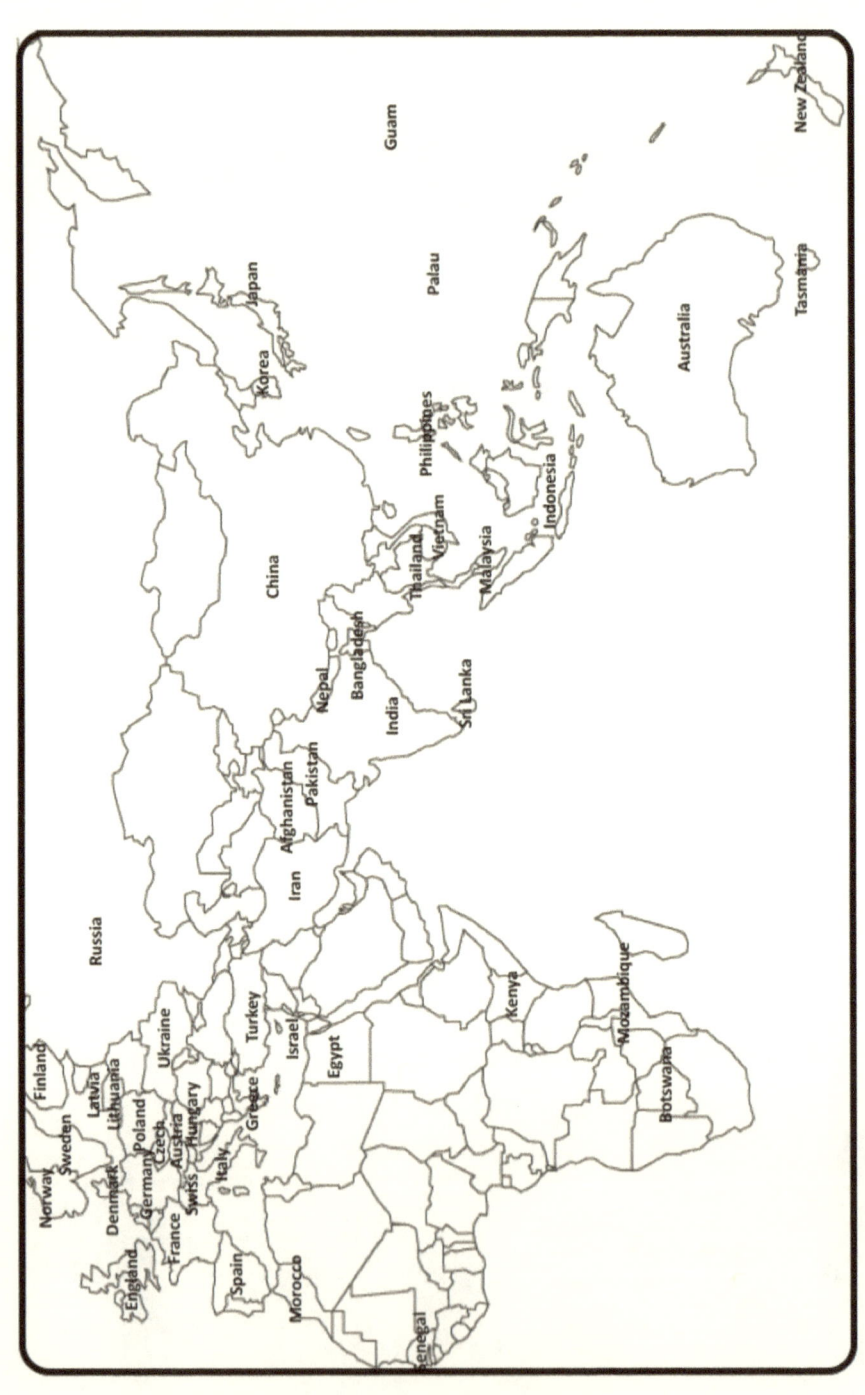

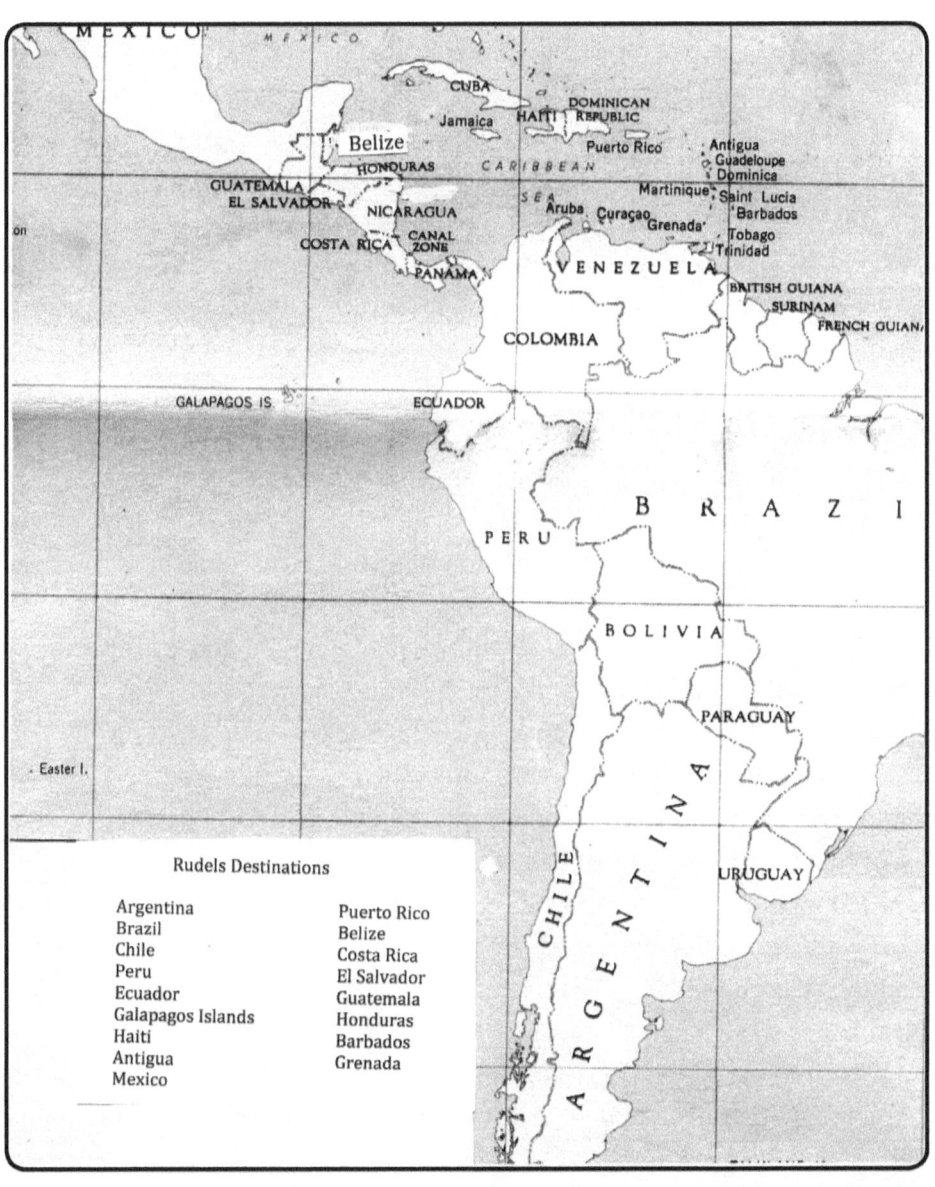

Rudels Destinations

Argentina	Puerto Rico
Brazil	Belize
Chile	Costa Rica
Peru	El Salvador
Ecuador	Guatemala
Galapagos Islands	Honduras
Haiti	Barbados
Antigua	Grenada
Mexico	

OUR FAMILY HAS PACKED a lot of travel into our lives since Joan and I married in 1962. Even before that, I myself had journeyed across many borders. As a child, at the age of eight, I escaped from Austria through Italy and France to find safe haven in the U.S. After completing college, my military service exposed me to Japanese culture during a fifteen-month posting in Sasebo and Gifu between 1953 and 1954. Within two years of beginning my government service, in 1957, I was assigned to an evaluation team and traveled around Iran for two months. In 1960, there were another two evaluation assignments to Europe, one to Belgium and another to Holland; each involved a month of travel. Finally, leading up to the initial formation of the family, I was assigned to our aid mission in Ankara, Turkey in 1960.

Those however constitute only the bare beginnings of our travels. Our children's travels began in 1965 with my five-year posting to the AID mission in India. Subsequently, for me, there were several short-term travel assignments, including those to Vietnam, Korea, Peru, Indonesia, Austria, and France, prior to my retirement from the Foreign Service in 1980.

Volume One describes, in depth, my assignments and travels to Iran (1957), Belgium and Netherlands (1960), Turkey (1961–1962), India (1965–1970), Palau (1981), Pakistan and Egypt in (1988).

It was after retirement that the really heavy travel scheduling began. Annex eleven of the first volume to this memoir lists thirty-seven overseas assignments I performed in the twenty-two year post-retirement consultancy phase of my international development career. All of these voyages were sponsored by an international economic development agency such as USAID, the World Bank, the UNDP or one of the UN specialized agencies.

Chapter four of this volume presents six additional trip reports selected from these consultancies - Thailand, China, Mozambique, Sri Lanka, Latvia, and Bangladesh. I have also included the story of a harrowing road trip taken in 1969 from New Delhi, through Pakistan, Afghanistan, and Iran, to Turkey in a 1938 Buick limousine.

In chapter five, I relate several trips taken by Joan and me to the Czech Republic, Austria, and Ukraine in search of our respective roots and to revisit the escape route my mother and I took through Italy and Croatia in 1938.

Additionally, we traveled quite often for the sheer pleasure of it. On some of these trips, the entire family went; other trips Joan and I made alone. A few of these stories are included in chapter six.

As our family expanded, through the marriages of our children and the birth of our grandchildren, with Ruthann relocating to the Boston area and David to the San Francisco Bay area, we made efforts to schedule at least one week each year to assemble the family at an attractive watering hole. Earlier in our marriage, these gatherings were held at our home in Bethesda, Maryland or at our farm in Pennsylvania. But then, as the school calendar became the determinant of family free time, we drifted towards spending the Christmas holidays in tropical settings such as Belize, Costa Rica, Puerto Rico and the southern U.S. Frequently, after the younger family members returned home, Joan and I remained and travelled locally in that country for the rest of the winter.

Joan and I undertook many trips to explore distant parts of the globe and learn of other cultures and peoples. We visited Argentina and Chile, the islands of Bali and Sumatra in Indonesia, Machu Picchu and Cusco in Peru, the Galapagos Islands off the coast of Ecuador, Australia and New Zealand, France, Italy, the Scandinavian countries, Finland, Germany, Alaska and Hawaii, as well as some Caribbean Islands (Granada and Barbados), plus destinations in Central America (Honduras and Guatemala.)

Then there is Canada, our jolly neighbor to the north. Joan and I were attracted to Canada during our camping expedition in 1981. The scenic beauty of the Pacific Northwest, including Vancouver, Banff, Lake Louise and Jasper lured us back to explore British Columbia, particularly its river systems. Subsequently we toured Nova Scotia and found a different kind of natural beauty in the Atlantic Maritimes. The further north we drove in

Nova Scotia, the more beautiful it became. The Cape Breton area opposite Prince Edward Island and the plentiful supply of sea food persuaded us, in 2006, to buy an eighty acre farm and house in New Brunswick, just a few miles north of Shediac, the lobster capital of the world. We settled on a particularly charming Acadian community along the shore of the Northumberland Straits. That became a frequent destination for us as we made several trips around the Maritimes and Quebec. The Gaspe Peninsula held a particular fascination for us. Stories of some of our travels in Canada can be found in chapter seven.

Finally, this compendium of travel stories would not be complete if I did not describe a few of my flights on small aircraft, often with myself in the pilot's seat. See chapter eight. There is nothing quite as thrilling as defying Isaac Newton's laws of gravity by piloting an aircraft.

The reader is invited to supplement the reading of all these travel stories by simultaneity viewing my photos, which have been uploaded to the Internet.

Our travels were usually lengthy and rarely seemed rushed, such as one tends to experience when squeezing tourist travel into a vacation window. We always made time to explore the cultural aspects of the society -- from historical sites and museums that displayed local antiquities and collections of art, to the concert halls, opera houses, theaters and other centers for performing arts -- in our quest to understand the many components of national character.

Recently, someone asked me what travels I wanted to undertake prior to my demise, the content of that famous bucket list. What part of the world do I crave to visit, absent which I would consider my life to be less than fulfilled? As I searched my mind to select a place I had not already visited that was important to me, I was reminded of the joke about the man who said, "Last year I took a trip around the world. This year I want to go somewhere else!"

4

PROGRAM DESIGN/EVALUATION: WORK RELATED TRAVELS

VOLUME I, *MEMOIRS OF an Agent for Change in International Development*, contains descriptions of eight assignments that required extended international travel. These include those in Iran, Turkey, India, Holland, Belgium, Palau (Micronesia), Egypt, and Pakistan.

In this chapter, I present stories involving work related travels to six additional destinations: Thailand, China, Mozambique, Sri Lanka, Latvia and—my very last consultancy—Bangaldesh[5]. Most of these stories take the form of letters I wrote to members of my family during the period of the consultancy. I have minimized the subsequent editing so as to preserve the freshness of the reports. However, in certain instances, I have obscured or changed the names of persons with whom I had contact and conversations in order to maintain their privacy.

---

5 Other assignments, not described in detail here, took me to Brazil, El Salvador, Barbados, Haiti, Morocco, Botswana, Kenya, Maldives Islands, Indonesia, Pakistan, and on several occasions, India.

BANGKOK, THAILAND - MARCH 1985

Dear Children

Sunday:

I'm sitting by the hotel pool, having skipped breakfast and done ten laps. Nice start, but what will be my endurance? I'm thinking your mother will have arrived in D.C. about five hours ago. Also thinking I never gave David a nickname. The sun is strong enough that I'm sitting in the shade. This afternoon I go to a meeting that will be followed by dinner, to prepare for the formal review (on Monday) of the Science and Technology project on which I have been working for the past four months. I will bring a copy of the project paper home with me. I'm sure each of you will want to read every word of the 250 page document (to be followed by a quiz). The remarkable thing about my experience this time is that virtually every idea, suggestion, comment and criticism I made was taken seriously. Almost all were adopted. Have I gotten smarter or is everyone dumber?

Bob M. and I have "double teamed" here, and in my humble opinion, turned what had the makings of a sow's ear into a silk purse. This is a $50 million project to make Thailand less dependent on foreign technology by building up their own science & tech capabilities (Universities, research labs, engineering institutes) and creating linkages by which the results of research by these institutions gets commercialized by the private producers. Bob did the economic analysis; my job was to figure out how to involve the private sector in determining what subjects the academics will research, and then to get the results of their work into the production process. The development buzzword for this is "linkages".

Wednesday:

I'm in my room at the hotel, having had two beers and a ham sandwich made myself with fresh French bread I bought on my way home from the office at 7 pm. A Japanese department store across from the hotel features excellent French cheese bread. Richard K. and I stayed late to help two secretaries make 20 copies of version III of our master opus so it would be ready for distribution tomorrow morning. I guess we didn't have to, but had nothing to do tonight anyway and Rich, who is married to a Thai woman that I have not met, is just a sweet guy. We didn't want to abandon the secretaries to all that drudgery.

Rich is a former Peace Corps type who likes Thailand and decided to stay. He has been here for ten years, speaks Thai and claims his family in the U.S. has given up on him. He really is not sure what he wants out of life and knows he is "drifting". He is a local hire contract employee for the AID Mission, likes development work and does good work.

It was odd that the chief of the Project Design effort, a former dean of a US Agricultural college, went home at 5 pm. It was also odd that his project development officer, a former Pakistani, now a permanent AID foreign service officer, also went home at 5 pm. If you had been charged for 15 months to design this project, and the final draft was being put together so it would be ready for tomorrow morning's sign-off, would you have gone home at quitting time? One of them said he had been threatened by his family; that he had to come home on time tonight because he had spent too many late nights at the office recently, and he was in great fear of disobeying. And suddenly, I realized this had never happened to me. I always set my own schedule. I came home when work permitted and no one at home had the audacity to question me or criticize. Well, that's interesting. So, I figured I'd better get back to this incomplete letter. Without making judgments, I thought I would share some of the thoughts that pass through my head – especially after two or three beers.

I'm reading John Updike's "Bech is Back". This may surprise you because I hated reading "The Coup". But this one is great. He describes the confused thoughts of a fifty year old writer – so he's writing about something he understands. Updike's command of English is marvelous.

Thursday:

The newspapers are full of stories about the Vietnamese army crossing into Thailand in an effort to surround the last Kampuchean stronghold on the border. They are also carrying stories about the "Killing Fields". I wonder what sorts of attitudes prevail on US college campuses today about that scene. It is difficult to tell the heroes from the villains. The Khmer Rouge, which caused the havoc in 1975 and killed off about 20% of their own country-persons, including every Western educated Kampuchean, are now part of the coalition being attacked by the Vietnamese army that, with Russian aid, has invaded and occupied Kampuchea. One thing is clear. The Thais hate the Vietnamese and think the US had it exactly right in its Domino Theory. They like the US and believe Vietnam would long ago have attacked Thailand were it not for US support for the Thais. They are perhaps the only country in the world that thinks the US was right in 1968 to 1974, with respect to the Vietnam war. Sorry about that, Jane Fonda!

I think the reason the Thais are so receptive to the project design has to do with a feeling of trust about the US. They are also pretty serious about not falling behind their local competition

(Singapore, Malaysia, Korea) in the economic development and trade area.

But there are other reasons too, for their favorable attitudes toward us, and they seem to be cultural. They like our music (rock and roll; country western). It is played on the radio, in stores, bars, etc. all the time. They like our clothes and our lifestyle. They are a happy-go-lucky, individualistic group. Those that visited the US or studied there, return with positive feelings. They enjoy us. Yet a large part of them adhere strongly to their Buddhist traditions. They don't seem to be pulled apart by the conflicts. I think they are not blind to our problems and shortcomings but they find an affinity with our approach to life.

This is the country of smiling people. It is a reflex with them. They never show anger openly. They do not raise their voices to each other but they are plenty capable of anger and violence. If the driver gets lost taking me to an appointment or tied up in traffic he laughs about it. I try to laugh about it too – but it does not work. Everyone is friendly to everyone else, especially to Americans. Inquiries are always politely and fully answered.

And then, of course, there are the women. Bangkok is the sex capital of the world. A man cannot enter a bar alone for a drink without immediately being met by a "companion" who will keep him company, listen to him, talk, drink, massage and in every way try to please him – for a price. It is a very large and well organized industry but there is little stigma to the participants even though it is not part of the traditional culture. Thai women, especially those educated in the West, tend to complain that Thai men never pass beyond adolescence, keep on running around to massage parlors and take "minor wives" (a Thai word that really means "mistress"). There is an absolute double standard. Non-western educated Thai women don't seem to mind.

Saturday:

On Thursday I gave a presentation of our project to the directors of "The Association of Thai Industries". This organization is about 25 years old, has a membership of 1,600 of the largest companies in Thailand and will be the implementing agency for two of the activities included in the project. I set up the meeting and when I told my betters at the AID mission about it they all wanted to come. I said fine. Nobody from the mission showed up. I made my presentation. It was well received. One of the directors, a man named Mr. V, did a lot of talking for the group. He is well educated (in England – then lived 8 years in the US) and clearly well connected. He is married to the daughter of the owner of several major companies. The guy looks to be 30 years old but actually is 47 and is a handsome devil. I went back to the hotel, took a swim and met an American, Josh T, thirty years old – more about him later.

I went to sleep around 8:30pm to be awakened by a knock at the door at 10:30pm. No. It was not a young lady – it was the bell-hop and he chose that moment to deliver the shoes I had custom made. Oh well …. Five minutes later the phone rang and it was Mr. V. Good thing I was awake! He told me he had important things to discuss with me and invited me out on Friday night. Oh boy – I had reached the upper levels. Watch me make policy!

Friday after work I took my swim and there was Josh T. again – doing his thirty laps. I do ten and am glad to get through. We started talking and he tells me he is from a family in New York that has a perfume business that makes $6 a cake soap and has exclusive retail outlets, etc. He worked at the family business for five years, hated it and has been traveling for eight months trying to "find himself". He really wanted to talk but I had to leave for dinner. We agreed to meet Saturday morning for breakfast.

Dinner with Mr. V. was delightful – good seafood in garlic, vegetables and rice. He told me the project we were proposing was
brilliant, repeated back to me all the things I said in my presentation
and said he will talk to the "Minister" to urge endorsement of the
project. Then he tells me he owns a consulting firm. Did I think he
and his firm could be selected as the organization to manage the
new project? He could run the project since he and I were in such
substantive agreement on everything – right? Well – so much for my
superb powers of persuasion. Anyway he paid the dinner bill.

This morning I met Josh and we had a long talk. In fact, it was
so long I finally invited him along on my excursion to Chinatown
to pick up four pair of slippers for Joanna ($2.10 a pair). Also a little
gold Buddha charm for your mother. It is a crazy world when a Jew
buys a Buddha for his Catholic wife. Well – here is the heir apparent to a major deodorant producer who does not see his calling in
life to make the world smell better. He is a jazz musician but hardly
mentions that in his conversation. Most of the time is spent describing in great detail the family business and the various functions he
performed (inventory control, marketing, raw material purchasing,
franchising, etc.) He is contemplating going back to school to get
an MBA so he can do a better job. And why did he stop working
and take this long holiday, you ask? Need you ask when you know
the answer. Of course, - he had a nervous breakdown. Yesterday he
called his father to wish him a happy 77th birthday. His father and his
81 year old uncle still run the business.

So we talked. I found myself telling him that he must know what
gives him enjoyment, what turns him on. Can he find a way of making a living, doing those things? Well – yes – but not the style of
living he likes and has gotten used to. So, there is the trade off. Do
something you hate doing to live in high style, or do what you like
doing and starve. Is there a middle ground? I told him what David

Thomas said – that this generation suffers from too wide a range of choices available to them. Earlier generations had their ways of earning a living picked for them by necessity, interrupted by an opportunity or two. He liked that. I talked about the three of you – how differently each of you were sorting out your interests and life styles. And I confess to having discouraged him from returning to the family business, which his brother seems to be happy to manage. I asked if there might be another kind of business he would like to run. Maybe his family would stake him to do that. I don't think that ever occurred to him.

The sad part of it is that there was continued evidence of self-deception in his conversation. He described himself as artistically inclined, uncompetitive, a pacifist, gentle and non-combative. Only an hour earlier he had complained to the tour guide office that his visit to the snake farm had been disappointing because the fight between the two snakes was not real. Apparently the tired old snakes simply put on a show. He wanted to see a real cock fight and, when he was told they were illegal, and not available for tourists, he finally bought tickets to watch Thai boxing. So much for his pacifism.

I had told him I thoroughly enjoyed my career in the business of international economic development. It was exactly what I had wanted to do when I got out of college. He asked me if I had to make my career selection decision now? Had I just finished college, would I make the same choice? I was surprised to hear myself say, no. The next thirty years don't look as promising for this field as were the last thirty. He seemed to be searching for a career that would be seen to be legitimate by his family. I asked him about that and he denied it – said he wanted to "make a statement" with his life. I wondered to myself why it is that the most confused minds always want to make a statement, when they should really be asking questions.

Sunday:

Last night Dan C. from the aid mission and a professor from Indiana University (Bloomington) named Milt something or other joined me for dinner at the Oriental Hotel. As we sat on the terrace along the river we saw a fire break out on the other shore. As you can imagine, fire fighting in a city like Bangkok is primitive. You can barely get through the traffic with a car. Soon the other shore was a raging inferno. The fire was out of control all the time we sat there. It made quite a scene – the city's affluent, sitting on the terrace of the Oriental, munching on their barbequed meats while watching the show across the river. I wondered what it would take to make the blaze into a firestorm. Probably not much. It was the second major fire I had witnessed close up in Bangkok these last six months. The other fire was a roller skate rink just around the corner from the AID mission. It broke out while a skating session was in progress and the manager tried to stop the skaters from leaving until they returned their skates. Fortunately, no one got hurt that time.

Friday:

A long Friday. I'm on the PanAm flight from Tokyo to New York. We will cross the international date line and so Friday will go on for a long while.

The last week was a bore. I had completed my work and was being kept around to give aid and comfort to the AID Science &Technology types as they negotiated the details of the project with the Thai government officials. But then I sensed a change of mind. The total dollar value of the project was fixed. The details that were under negotiation dealt with the division of these spoils among the participating Thai institutions. I had cranked the private sector into the equation and that left less for the government sector.

I think they excluded me from the negotiations because they did not want me to see them cave in on every significant issue. The "development game" in which we are engaged involves trying to change things. We are change agents. We want to change certain practices in the society that we believe is causing that society to remain poor and underdeveloped. If we thought their present system worked fine, we would not have to design elaborate projects. We could just write a check and let the present system allocate these resources (as we do for Israel). Therefore, negotiating a project gets tricky because the Thais have to agree to change things, so that the resources can accomplish their intended purposes. Eventually I got the feeling I had been used to build some gingerbread on the previous project design so they could satisfy AID Washington's demands to involve the private sector. But they were not sincere in negotiating the strict details to make it work.

So, I hung around until Thursday, with not much to do, waiting for time to pass. Tuesday I flew to Udon Thani, about 25 miles from the Laos border on the Mekong River near Vientiane. An Israeli technician is stationed there under a UN project and his work is relevant to some ideas I cranked into the project. It is an interesting town – lots of refugee camps nearby. I spent the day with this Israeli. He has four children, all in the Israeli army reserve. One is a paratrooper. In the course of our private lunch he said he worries about their safety. They get called up all the time. But then he said something that blew my mind. He would like to get them out of the clutches of their military obligation; maybe leave Israel. "No war is worth dying over."

That crystallized a deep problem on my mind. That morning's headline read, "Sihanouk – Guerillas Can Fight Vietnamese Indefinitely". Translated from rhetoric to reality, this meant, as long as the Chinese give me support and guns I can send young Cambodian boys to attack Vietnamese troops and get themselves killed over my cause, while I am chauffeured around in my Cadillac and enjoy French food and women, indefinitely! The present war between Iran and Iraq falls into the same category – young kids being sent to the slaughter because some zealots think they have a just cause. But, the Israelis? Is there no just war? Is there never a reason to fight and die? I grew up during the Second World War. Should the world have allowed Hitler to take over? I served in the Korean War. Should the US have allowed North Korea to take over South Korea? I cannot say my views are clear to me on this any longer. Maybe yours are.

In flight I am reminded of the young Japanese girl who sat next to me last January, on my way to the Orient. She is a pianist who had been studying at Peabody Conservatory for years and said she often accompanied Ruthann's clarinet teacher, Sidney Forest's students, at recitals. She is very memorable to me because I could see she was quite troubled. Eventually I learned she had lived most of her life in the US and was returning to Tokyo to marry a yuppie Japanese executive from a very traditional family. He had never traveled out-side Japan. She is an accomplished pianist and wants a career. Neat conflict, eh? At least she selected her fellow herself; it was not an arranged marriage.

Well, I'm running out of paper. Also ideas. Also time. Therefore, I'll send this letter to each of you in the hope you will understand.

Love, Dad April 1985

About one year later, in 1986, I had occasion to return to Bangkok to attend a conference. I stopped by the USAID to pay my respects and learned that the S&T project had been approved in AID Washington as prepared by us, endorsed by the Thai government and submitted by the USAID mission. But, when I asked about all of the innovations I had introduced into the project to gain private sector participation, there was nothing to be seen. It finally dawned on me. Once AID Washington had approved the project, the Thai government and the AID mission reverted back to the original project document, scrapping the changes I had introduced. That was why I had gained such quick acceptance to all of my "brilliant" new ideas. There had never been any intention to implement these private sector initiatives in the first place.

FIRST CONSULTANCY IN CHINA - 1991

A wonderful consultancy opportunity arose for me in 1990. The International Science and Technology Institute of Washington D.C. was asked by the UNDP Central Evaluation Office in New York to perform a thematic evaluation of fifteen research and development (R&D) institutions in China and India where it had funded thirty eight technical assistance projects with a total UNDP contribution of sixty four million dollars over the previous ten years.

A common characteristic of these institutions was that they were each to be the national focal point for a set of sophisticated technologies needed by the production sector for modernization. UNDP had found that the technical assistance projects were well implemented and the science and technology (S&T) research capabilities of these institutions had been enhanced. However, this new technology capability was not passing to the local industries. Well then, why was the link between these institutions and the industrial producers not working? Why were the manufactured products produced in India and China not benefiting from the R&D capabilities of these technical institutions, each of them operated by their respective governments?

The UNDP administrator at that time was William H Draper III, an American investment banker who had been nominated for that position by the Reagan Administration. He had served from 1981 to 1986 as president and chairman of the U.S. Export-Import Bank. He had been appointed to the UNDP position in 1986 for a four-year term and was a strong supporter of Reagan's pro-private enterprise philosophy. This thematic evaluation had been his idea. He understood the natural bias within UNDP (and many other international aid agencies) toward enhancing the public sector. He wanted to find techniques by which to reorient UNDP's efforts to focus more on private sector development.

I was assigned as team leader of the evaluation program. Each country would provide staff to work with me but only for their own institutions. I would travel first to India for four weeks to examine their projects and then proceed to China for an additional four weeks.

I was very sympathetic to Draper's objective. In 1962, when I returned from my two-year assignment in Turkey, the bright new appointees of the J. F. Kennedy Administration had evaluated our work under the Eisenhower Administration. New legislation had transformed the old ICA into USAID. I was shocked and annoyed to hear the "best and brightest", like Walter G. "Nick" Farr and Paul Furstenberg criticize our "anti- private sector" bias in places like Turkey, from where I had just returned. I dismissed the criticisms as unfounded. In 1981, when Reagan became president his new appointees quickly leveled the same criticisms at AID. Much against the wishes of the AID bureaucracy, a separate office, headed by Elyse DuPont, was established to shift AID's focus to greater private sector involvement. I performed several assignments for that office such as the one in Thailand described above.

By 1990, I came to realize that these criticisms of AID had, all along, been well deserved. They apply to agencies like UNDP as well. Aid programs funded with official development assistance (ODA) are administered on a government-to-government basis. Those who manage them, both in the aid recipient countries and in the donor countries, for the most part, are bureaucrats and think in terms of their own experience and skills. This bias may not readily be apparent, even to these well-intentioned managers, but it exists. An example of this was described in the earlier story about my design effort for the S&T project in Thailand. It is simply easier for well-intentioned bureaucrats to design aid projects within their professional comfort zones without attempting to elicit private sector participation.

The assignment to China had another very interesting aspect. Less than two years had passed since the Tiananmen Square incident. One may recall that, on June 4, 1989, the Chinese government ended the first major spontaneous civil protest action since China's 1949 revolution. The military had brutally attacked the students that had occupied Beijing's Tiananmen Square at the entrance to the Forbidden City. Following that, foreign visa applicants were carefully scrutinized before being allowed to travel in China. In the aftermath of the crackdown, the government conducted widespread arrests of protesters and their supporters, quickly quelled other protests, expelled foreign journalists, and strictly controlled coverage of the events in the domestic press. The police and internal security forces were strengthened.

A friend of ours who had been stationed in India with us during the late 1960s, Bosley Wilder, had returned to the U.S. from Beijing shortly after the Tiananmen Square crackdown and gave Joan and me an eye-witness report of the incident. Bosley had been teaching the English language at one of Beijing's universities and some of her students had participated in the protests. She told us she asked some of them to explain what exactly they wanted to happen from these efforts. The students said they wanted "freedom and democracy." When Bosley pressed them to be more specific and to describe the freedoms, the students had great difficulty in formulating their thoughts. She asked for examples of actions they felt they should have a right to take. The students then came up with statements that demonstrated a lack of understanding of personal and social freedoms, such as the kind taken for granted here. For example, they wanted the right not to go to class if they did not like the instructor or if they had something personal to do that conflicted with class time. When emerging out of a strict, authoritarian society with no history of political and social freedom, developing an understanding of the broad concepts of freedom takes time.

What was happening in the world in 1990? Big things! The Berlin Wall had come down on November 9, 1989 and Gorbachev had introduced reform measures that led to the break-up of the U.S.S.R. Czechoslovakia had its Velvet Revolution in 1989 and Poland held its first presidential election in 1990. In China, even though there had been the crackdown at Tiananmen Square, the government adopted the "four modernizations" (economy, agriculture, scientific and technological development, and national defense), and had earlier announced an ambitious plan of open-ing and liberalizing the economy, beginning with agriculture.

I was thrilled to learn that both the Indian and the Chinese govern-ments had agreed to hire me for this evaluation. I also secured agreement for Joan to join me for the China portion of the trip. Even the weather cooperated with the timing of this assignment. I would be in India at the very end of winter, when the weather on the sub-continent would be at its most desirable. We were scheduled to arrive in Beijing on April 9, 1991, Joan traveling from the U.S. and I from India, just in time for the cherry blossoms.

We were met at the airport by Xie Fudzan, a bright, bilingual, up-and-coming Communist Party member in his thirties who would spend the next four weeks with me as we performed our visits to the R&D institutions and government bureaus. He took us to the Kunlun Hotel, a very modern skyscraper of perhaps one thousand rooms, where a spacious room had been reserved for us. Later, we learned—it was an open secret—that the hotel was run by the Chinese intelligence agency and was used as a train-ing area for their agents to learn how to mix with Westerners. We also surmised that our room was bugged because Fudzan would be reluctant to speak freely with me when he was in our room.

My work in India during the previous four weeks had given me a chance to structure my thoughts and the approach I would pursue in China. This was despite the fact that while China's industry was still fully inside the public sector, India's industrial base was mixed—certain sectors were in private hands while others, the commanding heights of the economy, were state owned and managed. But I had observed the behavior of managers at the R&D institutions that had received UNDP funding, which were either industry-wide non-profits or government organizations, or some combination of the two. The work of these institutions was not demand driven; the managers and the scientists chose to work on whatever interested them. The institutions usually received stipends from the Indian government. They were not anxious to respond to the industry's requests but, instead, pursued what I then called "Nobel Prize" winning types of research. Meanwhile, industry moguls were unwilling to share with the researchers any of their own technical knowledge and discoveries for fear it would be leaked to their competitors.

Dear Reader, I will shortly describe the touristic part of our four-week stay in China as well as our general observations about life in China and about local values and common behavior. It was a truly unique experience for us as we began to learn something about this ancient culture and civilization with over six thousand years of recorded history. But before we get into that, allow me to discuss with you our substantive conclusions from the work that had been commissioned to me. Here is an extract from our thematic evaluation report, as submitted to the UNDP Central Evaluation Office in May 1991. In reading this summary of our findings, you will note that the situation I found in China was consistent with my findings in India.

Summary of Findings: [6]
Findings at the Institutional Level - Both Countries:

a. **Technology Transfer and Indigenization** The vast majority of the 15 projects succeeded in establishing and enhancing institutions in China and India to become the centers of technological knowledge for a specific area, thereby at least temporarily sewing the two countries perceived need of freeing themselves of dependence on foreign technology.

In virtually every UNDP funded activity that was reviewed, (with the exception of Salt Brine biotechnology in China, and Pesticides technology in India), the transfer and indigenization of the intended technology to the target institution was successfully completed by the UNDP activity, although the time frame for accomplishment may have taken longer than originally anticipated, and the level of resources required was greater than originally contemplated.

In a number of instances, it later transpired that the technology that was transferred remained relatively static and did not keep pace with further global development. See paragraph B.1.c. below.

b. **Technology Diffusion to the Productive Sector** The underlying assumption of these projects was that the technology, once available at R&D institutions in India or China, would be disseminated to the users in the productive sector. Regrettably, this assumption did not prove to be valid in the majority of instances. All of the institutions provide important testing, calibration and measurement services to their respective industries. Many provide training services to their industry. But, particularly in India, their respective roles in performing problem solving R&D for their clients, and facilitating the technology commercialization process, was shown in the case studies

---

6 Extract of pages viii and ix - Executive Summary - Thematic Review of High Technology Assistance in India and China, prepared for UNDP Central Evaluation Office, New York, by Ludwig Rudel, International Science and Technology Institute Inc. Washington DC, May 1991

to be rather limited. China's recent policy shift to eliminate public funding for R&D institutions, thereby requiring each institution to sell its services to user clients, has tended to encourage the creation of linkages between the R&D institutions and the producing units.

c. **Demand for Technology by the Producers** There are indications that, until recently, the Indian and Chinese productive sectors did not have the maturity, nor the human/technical resources to seek problem solving help from local research laboratories which, in any event, did not command their confidence. Instead, producers tended to purchase know-how from abroad.

Normal levels of investment in R&D in developed countries runs from 1% of turnover for mature industries to 9% in rapid growth industries. On the other hand, in India, even progressive companies like Tata's TELCO, invest less than half of one percent (.5%) of turnover on R&D.

Throughout the developed world, investors in the organized capital markets seek to buy the equity shares of companies that are known to invest heavily in high tech R&D because they know that the return on such investment will be high and the company's share price is likely to appreciate in value over time. Why then, in China and India, do enterprise managers tend to undervalue technological innovation and the results of R&D when it is virtually offered to them on a silver platter? Why are they so reluctant to adopt new technologies which offer productivity increases? And why do they prefer strongly to acquire hardware over software, and imported technology over a domestic source?

There appear to be a number of factors that contribute to these behavior patterns, as this study reveals. These factors are discussed in detail in the main text. In brief, these are:

1. Lack of competition due to product scarcity conditions;
2. aversion of investors to risk and uncertainty;

3. fear of criticism and absence of reward for innovative manage-
    ment; and

4. lack of sub-contracting modality arising from fear of loss of pro-
    duction control.

One is reluctantly led to the conclusion that return on R&D investment in India and China is too low to attract industry interest in such
investments or to sustain R&D efforts under present circumstances without special efforts to stimulate demand for technology. UNDP assistance at the company level might have helped to break through that
resistance.

d. **Sustainability of the Results** With only one exception in India
    (ARAI), the Indian institutions do not appear to have any prospect of
    becoming financially self- sustaining in the foreseeable future. Nor
    is there any prospect that these institutions will generate adequate
    revenues to upgrade or replace their equipment without continued
    governmental support. In China, the recent policy change has forced
    R&D institutions to become self sustaining. At this point, however,
    only minimum cash requirements to meet operating costs are being
    generated. It remains to be seen whether these R&D institutions will
    be able to meet their equipment depreciation schedules (including
    their obligation to repay the UNDP assistance to CICETE) and earn a
    reasonable rate of return on investment, thereby providing adequate
    incentives for innovation.

e. **Maintenance of Technological Currency** While the UNDP assistance
    may have brought these institutions close to an international state-
    of-the-art level of competence by project end, it is unlikely that the
    institutions will be able to keep up with the international process of
    technological change without continued UNDP assistance or a major
    change in the recipient government's willingness to increase foreign
    exchange allocations to the institutions.

Neither in India, nor in China have adequate 'foreign exchange resources been made available for technologists to stay abreast of the continuing process of technological change. This derives from a misconception, which prevails in many developing countries, that R&D institution building involves construction of some sort of container which, once filled with technology, will remain forever a continually yielding cornucopia of up-to-date technological information.

Indian Governmental regulations and procedures place arbitrary and severe restrictions on the use of laboratory income and other budgeted funds for technological interchange by attendance of scientists at international conferences. For example, CEERI, with a professional staff of 200, is authorized funding for 5 trips per year, which works out to travel for each engineer once in 40 years. Similar restrictions are evident in China.

f. **Role of Women, Environmental Impact and Private Sector Development** In both countries, the Team found that UNDP efforts to facilitate indigenization of available high technology was gender neutral, although it appears that the expansion of R&D facilities allowed for greater participation of women in the higher skilled work force. There were no indications of adverse environmental impacts from the transfers of technology that were included in the review. Indeed, a number of projects contributed to significant reductions in environmental deterioration. The most important of these projects were automotive emissions control (ARAI), and recovery of spent liquor from pulping of tropical hardwood (Central Pulp and Paper Research Institute). Numerous projects contributed to the provision of important support services needed by industrial producers, such as instrument calibration. However, none of the projects included in the case study sample had an easily discernible, direct obvious positive impact on the expansion of the role of the private sector.

My work would take four weeks and I had added a week to our flight schedule to allow us time to travel around China on our own (Xian, Suzhou, Hangzhou, and Shanghai) before returning to the U.S.A.

Getting to China wasn't easy. D.C. to Chicago took us two and a half hours, Chicago to San Francisco over four hours, San Francisco to Tokyo ten hours forty minutes, and finally Tokyo to Beijing five hours. You add it up. Joan doesn't remember it being grueling. But then again she was younger and smaller. Moreover, in 1991, flight attendants were far more accommodating.

We found this land of 1.1 billion people fascinating, of course. Here, one could find a mix of beauty, squalor, richness, color, drabness, joy and sadness. Some of what we saw and learned was expected, but there were many surprises, mostly happy ones. There was tolerance for critical expression of individual opinion, although not in the press. There was the search to adopt western modernity inside the ancient culture.

The first order of business was a taxi to Tianamen Square. This is the heart of Beijing, a vast area of paving and photo booths, a creation of Mao, and a scene of major rallies during the Cultural Revolution. We were concious of the drama that had unfolded there less than two years earlier. Our first sight-seeing day also included the Lama Temple, Bamboo Garden Hotel, and a restaurant specializing in Peking duck.

The Lama Temple (also known as Yonghegong) is one of the most pleasant temples in Beijing. It has gardens, frescoes and tapestries. It has a complex history and is the most renowned Tibetan Buddhist temple within China (outside of Tibet). The Bamboo Garden Hotel, down a little alley (called a hutong) was a wonderful surprise of exquisite gardens, beautiful courtyards, and an upscale restaurant.

The biggest tourist attraction, the Forbidden City, so-called because it was off-limits to commoners for five hundred years, is remarkable. It is the largest, best preserved cluster of ancient buildings in China and was home to emperors, their wives and concubines, and their court eunuchs. The City burned several times and most of the buildings we saw in 1991 were rebuilt post eighteenth century. The Palace includes eight hundred buildings with nine thousand rooms. Our granddaughter, Emma, traveled to Beijing in 2009, and became lost in the Forbidden City when separated from her school group. It was hours before they found each other.

The primary mode of transport in Beijing in 1991 was bus and bicycle (isn't that what the U.S. is trying to accomplish?). There were few cars and those belonged to the government. Rickshaw and taxi were also available but out of reach for ordinary Chinese. Cars and buses have the right-of-way. Neither stop for right-on-red. Pedestrians beware! The buses are overstuffed. At the time of our visit, there were about a hundred and forty bus and trolley routes, making navigation confusing to us. It was not possible to see out the windows of the buses due to the crowding so you never knew where you were and, of course, we didn't speak Chinese. It took us three hours and two bus rides to buy tickets for a chamber music concert. We found the English speakers on the bus would try to move close to us, so anxious to practice their English.

We rented bicycles. The streets were full of them. It was a ballet of moving bicycles and beautiful to watch. Everyone appeared to be going at the same speed and was very courteous. Joan bicycled extensively for several weeks in Beijing without incident. She parked her bike in the Kunlun Hotel garage. This took a bit of doing since the garage was meant for cars.

Beijing had no visible beggers, drunks, or homeless. Everything was swept -- streets, sidewalks, construction sites. Litter existed but was picked up by sweepers, usually women wearing white caps, blue uniform, and face masks.

All workers had uniforms (often to compensate when salary increase is not possible). The uniforms were a variety of colors, all the same design. Footwear was the flat black Chinese slipper. My colleague on the evaluation team, Dr. Wu, wore a suit and sneakers and had studied at MIT.

Toddlers would have an open seam in their clothing between their legs for easy potty stops. School children were well dressed.

The diet included lots of rice, deep fried food, and sweets. Delicacies included birds on a skewer, sea cucumber, eel, jelly fish and sheep stomach. The markets in April had lots of bananas and great watermelon but only storage oranges and apples; the garlic greens and vegetables were beautiful. The snake soup was actually quite tasty.

At the time, Beijing had a collection of ugly Russian style buildings. There was block after block of worker housing. Most apartments had no bath. Baths were taken at work on appointed days. Children were bathed at daycare and also received three meals. Some apartments had no toilets even. Honey buckets and public toilets, which were numerous and fairly clean, served. Due to the One Child Policy, most couples had one child, which meant one bedroom, a very small sitting room and a kitchen. Public toilets were a positive experience. The fee would be approximately three cents. Three people are employed to collect the money and dispense the toilet paper. There would be a long trough over which you squat simultaneously and together with others doing the same business. If there was a door, it was a low one. It was an efficient operation as the women standing in line (there is always a line) did the unbuttoning and pulling down before reaching a position near the trough.

Beijing had about twenty new hotels with an occupancy rate of about twenty to forty percent, poorly trained staff and food prices set high by the government. A fifty cent coke cost two dollars and twenty cents in a hotel. Our hotel, the Kunlun, with its large staff, had an employee or three standing on every floor, at every elevator, at every front door, and at the entrance to every restaurant. Staff hovered over you as you read the menu. Your plate would be removed the second it was empty, and sometimes before.

Most tourists were overseas Chinese from Taiwan, Hong Kong, and Macao followed by the Japanese. A non-Chinese tourist did not feel comfortable taking photos of the local scene. Some Chinese seem happy to have their picture taken, some get very angry. Joan had an experience in Tianjin. She wanted to take a picture of a six-foot pile of shrimp on the sidewalk. No person would have been in the photo. A woman came out of the shop yelling and screaming, waving her arms at Joan. Perhaps thirty people gathered around Joan who put the camera away and just stood there. Other people did likewise with no expressions. Joan turned and walked way. End of story.

There are wonderful names used in China, especially in the Forbidden City -- Hall of Supreme Harmony, Hall of Middle Harmony, Palace of Heavenly Purity, Hall of Mental Cultivation, etc.

We experienced Beijing at a beautiful time of year. The multitude of cherry blossom trees budded, then were in full blossom, then gradually eased into their green leaves, changing daily. There were beaugenvillia in pots five feet in diameter all over the Kunlun Hotel. It was a time perfect for lots of pictures. Almost all the Chinese had cameras and took pictures of each other one at a time. Old men with birds in cages gathered at the park. The cages would have blue denim zippered cage covers. Tai Chi groups were present in every park.

Once, the day after we attended a great banquet given by the Textile Academy, my team mate, Xie Fudzan, and his family packed a picnic lunch with leftovers, mainly duck, from the previous night's banquet and we were off to see the Great Wall and the Ming Tombs. The construction of the five thousand kilometer-long Great Wall had begun some two thousand years ago, and took over a hundred years to complete. The wall never really functioned as a defense. It did serve as a highway though, Today, it is an important tourist attraction. The section at Badaling (seventy kilometers northeast of Beijing) was restored in 1957 and was the first to be opened to tourists. Every year, people come to picnic; they throw their litter over the side of the wall, and everyone is very jolly.

The approach to the Ming Tombs is through a valley surrounded by mountains. The seven kilometer "sacred way" leads to thirteen mausoleums- each holding the body of an emperor, his wives, his concubines, and his treasures. We remember seeing just one tomb excavated and open.

One Sunday, Fudzan and family took us for a picnic lunch to the Summer Palace, an immense park with buildings and a lake. The buildings were gutted during the Opium War and the Boxer Rebellion. A major renovation took place in 1949. The original palace was used as a summer residence for the Forbidden City, an escape from the heat of the city. The main building is called the Hall of Benevolence & Longevity. You've got to love it. One becomes aware of the long, rich and continuous history of this very sophisticated culture, and our own ignorance about it.

During the first three weeks, while I was engaged with my colleagues on the evaluation, Joan traveled around Beijing on her own. She would take the number hundred and ten bus to Temple of Heaven, a beautiful example of Ming architecture that has come to symbolize Beijing and appears on tourist literature. It was there that the emperor would perform the major ceremonial rites of the year. Commoners were not permitted to view the ceremonies and remained cloistered inside.

Another day, Joan bicycled to the Great Hall of People viewing the five thousand seat banquet room where Nixon dined in 1972 and the two thousand seat auditorium with the familiar red star. She also visited the Mao Mausoleum.

On April 29, I made the final two presentations of the team's findings, one to the UNDP resident representative, the other to the office at the Ministry of Foreign Economic Relations. That completed the team's work. We were then free to travel on our own for the last week of our stay in China.

The next day, we were to leave for Xian, home of the terracotta soldiers, but spent the day at the airport because our 11:35 am flight was delayed by a sandstorm.. At about noon, Joan bought a cup of noodles for ten yuan; when she found the hot water dispenser (a person), she got annoyed enough to point out an intruder who was then sent to the end of the line. Later, food boxes and drinks were handed out to holders of boarding passes. Mayhem ensured. People were not nice to each other and there was a lot of shoving and pushing. There was no systematic procedure--the one who pushed hardest, shouted loudest and had the longest arm at the end of which was a boarding pass got the food first. We observed a man, holding three styrofoam boxes which the crowd squashed against his chest, the rice and meat dripping down his front. He showed no recognizable emotion. Those who did it to him appeared to not even notice. There was no emotion to be seen on anyone's face; everyone was simply stoic.

There was a time when Xian was in the running to be the greatest city in the world. It became an international center for trade and had a population of two million by the eighth century. Architectural sites in and around the city are a reminder that it was once a booming metropolis. Today the chief attraction is the tomb of Emperor Qin Shihuang and his army of terracotta soldiers. The tomb has not been excavated but is reported to contain palaces filled with rare gems and equipped with crossbows which automatically shoot intruders. The terracotta solders were discovered in 1974. Excavation uncovered thousands of life-sized terracotta warriors and their horses in battle formation. Each soldier has unique facial features. In 1976 two other vaults were discovered and excavated, but were then refilled with soil to protect these treasures until China had developed the capacity to research them properly.

In Shanghai we stayed at the Peace Hotel on the Bund overlooking the Huangpu River. Shanghai is known as the Paris of the East. It is also known as the Whore of China. In 1991 the municipal area of Shanghai had a population bordering on twelve million. It accounted for fifteen percent of China's total industrial output. It receives many large foreign investments and is a political hotspot. It was the center for early Communist activity, the beginnings of the Cultural Revolution and the Gang of Four had their power base there.

We arranged for a tour guide and taxi. The guide was poor, uninformed and uninterested -- a misappropriated fifty-two dollars. So we toured on our own as best we could in this wild and noisy city, visiting the old Jinjiang Hotel with its wood paneling and iron chandeliers and the elegant Garden Hotel.

Having spent a couple of days in Shanghai, we managed a taxi to the railway station to buy "soft seat" tickets to the city of Suzhou; we also bought "hard seat" tickets to Hangzhou. There happened to be a tour group in our soft seat car with its light blue chairs like those one might find "in Mabel's living room". We were served tea, which was all very pleasant. We traveled through some of the richest most developed area of China-- lots of water, canals, truck farms, large two-storey farm houses with upper balconies. We were told only one family could live in these large homes. In contrast, in Beijing four to five people would live in one room.

Arriving in Suzhou, we took a public bus through the city, but then started walking. In that town walking was a pleasure. Suzhou is known as the Venice of the East. It has elegant gardens, a network of canals and silk production facilities. The bridges over the main moat served as impromptu markets and were abuzz with barge activity.

On the train back to Shanghai, it was a Saturday night and all the hotels (mostly government-built during the European concessions period) were lit up in a most beautiful way. The Peace Hotel, where we stayed, was outlined in Blue Neon. Welcome to Shanghai, the New York City of China--noisy and crowded with a touch of class.

On Sunday we were to leave for Hangzhou. The taxi our hotel arranged was not around. We eventually found a taxi, and got off at the train station. We found our car, a sleeping car, with three Chinese men, no English. They were very kind, encouraged me to the top bunk, Joan to the bottom.

They refused to spread out, even at our invitation. I noticed that when they thought we were both asleep, they reached for the magazines we had left on the table, *Aviation*. They were delighted to know we come from the U.S. Joan offered them cookies - the jolly one sitting in the middle was about to reach for one but his friend motioned to him to not take it. Joan and I drank a lot of tea and ate a lot of cookies. A large thermos of hot water was on the floor of our compartment. Hot water was always available in railway stations and in airports.

We were met in Hangzhou by a taxi that took us to the Wanhu Hotel. We had lunch across the street--steamed prawn noodle soup; sounds so good and it was. We wanted to walk, but it was raining. So we bought rain ponchos. Hangzhou is like any other Chinese city with streets of shops, food stalls, walkovers crossing busy streets. There is one big exception: West Lake, the most beautiful garden we had ever seen. We walked along the lake and took a boat to a small island. The gardens were large and a feast for the eyes in any direction at any turn. There were pools, ponds, bridges, but the trees and shrubs, especially the "Oriental" red maples, were exquisite. Each view was a work of art. Of Hangzhou it is said, "Above there is heaven, on earth there is Hangzhou." With more rain predicted for Hangzhou, we decided to say good bye. Imagine our surprise when our hotel bill showed an unexplainably low rate. We said nothing and departed for Beijing and, upon arrival, immediately attended a Mozart concert being held at the Kunlun hotel lobby. We are assigned exactly the same room we had previously occupied, convincing us that our room was "bugged" by the intelligence folks

Of our journey from Beijing to Dulles, Joan is fond of telling the story of the airport shuttle. On Wednesday morning she reserved a 6:00 am shuttle to the airport for Thursday morning. We were to meet at the duty manager's desk. The same day, she asked where we could find the duty manager's desk. We were told there was a schedule change; the shuttle would now depart at 7:00 am. That would have been too late for us to catch our flight. We pleaded for reservations for 6:00 am The assistant manager agreed to reverse the schedule change. That evening, at 8:43 pm we got a call from the travel department saying the shuttle would depart at 7:00 am. We told him to talk to the hotel manager. But then we got another call from the travel department saying the shuttle was scheduled to depart at 7:00 am. We protested. Finally the manager agreed the shuttle would leave at 6:00 a.m the next day.

The next morning at 6:10 am we were off to the airport in the shuttle accompanied by five adopted babies and ten very proud parents on their way back to the U.S.

A few months after we returned to the U.S., Xie Fudzan was selected to enroll in Princeton University's International Studies program. We had a few brief encounters with him and hoped our friendship with him and his family would continue. Sadly, we lost contact.

Some General Observations

The Chinese time horizon is far longer than ours. They are conscious of their long history, their many dynasties each with its own characteristics and values. Some achieved their goals through military conquest; others were passive and allowed the arts to flourish. At the time of our visit the Chinese were engaged in a socialist experiment. But the middle class was growing. Economic development was leading many to prosperity. Dogmas will adapt as conditions change and the middle class does not feel the need for socialism. They see themselves with a nationalistic ferver, on a path to restore their high place among world powers.

In 1991, there were restrictions on internal migration. A permit was needed to move out of the rural areas into cities. The government feared losing political control in the cities. One of our team members had been raised in the rural areas. He had joined the bureaucracy and moved to Beijing. He was assigned to the UN office in Sri Lanka where he learned to speak English. He was approaching retirement age. I asked him if he planned to move back to his native village and he looked totally confused by the question. Then he said, his village had no indoor plumbing or electricity or paved streets. Why would he give up his right to live in the city?

Results of the Thematic Evaluation

Once our report was submitted to the UNDP Central Evaluation Office, it seemed to disappear into a large void. I was never invited to New York to discuss the report or to make a presentation of my findings to UNDP staff. It seems that, with Administrator Draper's departure and his replacement by Mark Malloch Brown, there was little interest in this report. In his carefully documented history of the UNDP, published in 2006, Craig N. Murphy has little positive to say about UNDP's evaluation efforts. No mention of that function appears in his forty year history of the UNDP. Murphy ends chapter three of his work as follows:

> (T)he peculiar "patrimonialism" with which Owen built the UN's global development network ensured that, when UNDP did begin a concious programme of advocacy, UNDP's culture, the values shared by its staff over more than a generation, would largely be a reflection of Owen's own. Advocacy of democracy and of egalitarian principles, more broadly, would come naturally to the Programme's staff while other goals, such as promotion of the private sector, would be treated with scepticism and misunderstanding.[7]

However, I have the impression that our report was well received by the Chinese government. The Chinese take these evaluations more seriously than other aid recipients. I would like to believe the report contributed in some small way toward the government's decision to shift away from public ownership of industry. It perhaps also led to a

---

7   Craig N. Murphy, *The United Nations Development Programme: A Better Way?* Cambridge University Press, 2006. page 81.

subsequent UNDP project to assist in reforming some of China's major industrial enterprises to prepare them for privatization, by selling company shares on the Hong Kong stock exchange. My second consultancy in China in 1998 to evaluate that project is described in the next section. That consultancy revealed to me the Herculean measures the Chinese government had to take to make these companies economically viable.

SECOND CONSULTANCY IN CHINA - 1998
Letter to my Daughter, Ruthann,

Principessa Divina!

What an interesting trip to China. That society has a lot going for it. Not that I would want to get crosswise with their police. But I think there is every likelihood that they will become a powerful, yet responsible society within the next 25 years. They seem far less doctrinaire now than I had found them during my travels here in 1991.

My colleague, K T, a Cambodian economist, teaches at Johns Hopkins School for Advanced International Studies and has retired from the IMF. He sounded a bit pompous at times but he had several things to be pompous about. He is President of a Cambodian professionals association, His entire family (except for K T, who had gone to France in 1953), were killed by the Khmer Rouge. He is well connected and had dinner with Sihanouk on the last evening we were in Beijing. The Chinese don't forget those that remained their friends in time of need. Sihanouk supported the Chinese when they were the global pariah in 1967 and so they built him a palace in Beijing and now fund his very lavish lifestyle. Anyway, K T was a useful person to have on the team, along with two Chinese economists, but he kept wanting to show me his medals. "I was on the board of directors of 20 major organizations; my students are all famous. I studied with three Nobel prize winners. I had students such as Einstein in my class. I have traveled to 100 countries. I was chairman of so many conferences" On and on. Still, he did good work.

The two Chinese were both excellent. They were highly qualified econometricians who had been visiting scholars at US Universities. One studied with Larry Klein at University of Pennsylvania. One of them is coming to the US next week and will be visiting us. His sister lives in Potomac. They served as a window to help me understand what is really going on in China.

We traveled to Manchuria. While in college, I had taken courses on Imperialism and European history of the 19th century. The behavior of the European powers in China is a real scandal, particularly the Russians in Manchuria. The Japanese learned from them very quickly and then moved in themselves to do them one better.

The story of imperialism is closely linked to railroads. Berlin to Baghdad; India; and, of course, the Trans-Siberian rail link to Vladivostok. The Russians decided that they would like a short cut to take 1,000 miles off that distance by going through China, and so they built the Chinese Eastern Rail line through Manchuria. They looked longingly at Port Arthur (now called Dalian) as a warm water port and also built a rail spur to that city. The key city was Harbin, where the line to Port Arthur joined the line to Vladivostok. Harbin had about 50,000 Russians living there around 1900. Two of them were our neighbor, Reva Jolovitz grandparents. Reva's mother was born in Harbin in 1907. She is still alive and when she learned I was going to Harbin she asked that I try to find some old Russian buildings and take photos. So I did.

Now, you may not be surprised to learn that the Chinese have little, if any, nostalgia for that period, since they were very much subjugated at that time. Nevertheless, they accommodated my request to visit "Central Street" in Harbin which still has these old buildings built by the Russians during that period. The street is still cobble-stoned and they allow only foot traffic there. The approaches to that street are guarded to fend off traffic. Our van drove to the closest point where parking was restricted and when a guard tried to stop us from entering the parking area, the driver yelled a few words and the guard quickly pulled back to let us pass. I asked my Chinese colleague what the driver said and he told me "This is a government car with foreigners". The double whammy!

I suppose you wonder if I did any work there. Yes. It was fascinating to get into the inside of the government's privatization program as they shift from a communist, centrally planned economy to one that is open market driven. This was a gem of a project, to assist them change large State owned enterprises to operate independently. I visited and met with the senior management staff of about 10 enterprises that received help through the UN to modernize, separate ownership from government control, issue stock on the Shanghai and Hong Kong stock exchanges and operate on a competitive basis to respond to the markets. Then we talked to the policy formulators who were also getting help in building a legal framework within which these enterprises were to operate. The idea behind the project was to serve up to the policy people, the experiences of the enterprises so they could take these into account as they formulated the regulatory system. It worked well.

The privatization of State owned enterprises into independent companies that will be responsive to market conditions is fraught with difficulties. Imagine a company that has been making widgets for a couple of decades. The widgets are now obsolete. Still, the Ministry has been telling the management to produce them. When the company can't sell them and needs cash to meet its payroll, the Ministry tells the nearby government owned bank to advance a credit line to the company. Most of the State owned companies are so much in debt to the State owned banks they are insolvent. If enough companies are unable to pay their debt to the bank, the bank becomes insolvent. Then, there is the matter of pensions for retiring employees. Until the Chinese Government undertook this privatization effort, it was the government that funded the employee retirement obligations of the company. Now it falls to the company to pay for these pension benefits even though no fund has been established for this purpose. The Chinese now want to sort out these problems and then sell common share stock of the company on the Hong Kong stock exchange to private investors.

Here is one of the major conclusions the team presented in its report:

"One of the major 'changes in the mindset' of SOE managers and government officials resulting from this program, is a recognition of the importance to domestic and foreign private investors, of **openness and transparency** in the access and flow of information about SOE operations, and about government laws, regulations and policy affecting their operations. This recognition is only in the beginning stages. The Team believes that its importance to the success of the economic reform effort urgently needs to become better understood and implemented. The experience in other countries tells us that if unpleasant news continues to remain partly hidden, market forces will not allow for rational and optimal resource allocation."

One final word about China. On my last evening, at dinner with the Chinese members of the Team, I finally found the courage to raise a question about Tiananmen Square. I asked the Chinese members to help me understand what was going on there. The first response was that there were a few radicals that challenged the authorities and they demonstrated on the Square. There were very few demonstrators on the Square. I said that I understood that. But, what about all the thousands of people in the side streets who seemed to be supporting the demonstration? Who were those people? That question was followed by a long silence. Then, one of the Chinese slowly said, "Well, one of those was me!"

I asked why he was there? The answer was that there was widespread dissatisfaction with the corruption that was prevalent in government at that time. He also said there was a sense of fear about the shift in economic policies and the impact this shift might have on the government employees retirement benefits. There was limited support for the demands for "freedom" by the demonstrators but these two grievances caused an outpouring of the public into the streets. He said, after the suppression of the radicals in the Square, the Party then acted quickly to address these two grievances by instituting major reforms. He was satisfied these problems now had been adequately addressed by the government.

So, now you have my report from China. Your mother is less than pleased that I left her behind. She will not let me get away with that again.

I look forward to your visit at Passover. We may try to organize a family get together in August in Washington. For your information, we plan to be in Aspen from July 6 through 15. Jul will be performing Verdi's Falstaff at that time. We will do a bit of sight-seeing the week before and the week after. You are welcome to join.

Dad   - March 10, 1998

MOZAMBIQUE - 1992

Some background with respect to this assignment: Graciela Machel, the widow of the former president of Mozambique, had visited New York after the untimely death of her husband. The aircraft in which he had been flying on return from South Africa, piloted by an inebriated Russian, had flown into a mountain. The conspiracy theory that prevailed in Maputo at the time was that the Israeli Mossad had moved the ground based aircraft navigation beacons, thereby causing the crash. (Some years later, Graciela went to South Africa and married Nelson Mandela.)

During her visit to New York, Graciela met Peggy Dulany (whose maiden name is Rockefeller) an activist philanthropist. Ms. Dulany urged Graciela to set up a foundation in Mozambique, patterned after the Rockefeller Foundation, to undertake economic development projects. When Graciela asked how to raise funds for the new entity, Ms. Dulany put her in contact with USAID and lobbied on her behalf to allocate PL480 generated local currency to Graciela's Foundation. The PL 480 program allowed us to sell surplus U.S. agricultural commodities, such as wheat and corn, for payment in the local currency and then to grant that local currency to local organizations for economic development projects The USAID folks did not think well of Ms. Dulany's idea, since these PL 480 funds had been committed to the Mozambique government. But one does not turn down an idea presented by a Rockefeller without due exploration. My job was to explore this idea on the spot and make a recommendation to USAID.

I addressed my letter to our first-born grandson, Wolfgang. He had been born two months earlier.

Dear Wolfie,

Happy Sadie Hawkins Day from Maputo!

This extra day every four years should be put to special uses. Ask your father to explain Sadie Hawkins day to you. It is an important detail of one of his many special interests. I'm glad they don't practice it here in Mozambique; although, having been away from your grandmother for three weeks... who knows. The women here get to look prettier with each passing day. Don't puzzle too much about that last line, Wolfie. You will soon enough know how these things work.

It is 6 am and the day is just beginning... and it is raining. Today is the first day since my arrival that we had rain. The southern part of Mozambique, where Maputo is located, has drought conditions. This rain came too late to do much for the crops in the ground, but it is some relief for the water supply. It is also a relief for me that I finished my work yesterday and that my colleague, Mr. P, who is best described as a large hemorrhoid, is on an airplane out of here. There exists a 35 page report, it has been turned over to USAID and the client, The Community Development Foundation of Mozambique; my team mate and I made presentation to the local representatives of the aid donor community and to the Board of Directors of the Foundation, and I had a private meeting with the Finance Minister to give him the word that it was going to cost him a cool $15 million.

Last fall we saw a Saroyan play at Arena Stage. One minor character who drank his way through the first two acts had only one line that he repeated, every time someone asked him for a comment; "No Foundation!" That line kept running through my head as I examined Graciela's Foundation. More about that later.

What was the most remarkable part of this visit, you ask? Well, it was the trip to Pemba, a port city about 1000 miles north of Maputo. It is a 3 hour flight by jet, and there was no drought there. One really has to experience a tropical rainstorm to understand it. We drove about 25 miles out of Pemba to visit a village. During that short ride we hit a rainstorm. By the time we got to the village, the water was so deep, and rushing through the ruts and ravines, that the driver of our 4 wheel drive Landrover would not take that car off the hard surface road. So we turned around and went back.

Next day we decided to try to get to another village by boat. Pemba is located on what, I'm told, is the third largest bay in the world. Our hotel was a series of cottages right on the beach and, for perhaps, the first time in my life, I enjoyed the beach. The cottage was air conditioned, the beds were clean and we ate fresh seafood (mostly grilled shrimp) all three days we were there. You could walk the beach and swim any time because the water was warm. And the jellyfish do not sting.

Meetings were conducted on the veranda, lots of beer and a very casual, non-belligerent demeanor among the people, including the Governor of the Province of Cabo Delgado, who came in his Mercedes to have dinner with us.

Pemba was the area where the Portuguese finally put out the last resistance to their colonization in 1920. It was also the first area to make an organized fight by FRELIMO, that led to independence in 1974. In the intervening period the Portuguese conducted a brutal control mechanism. The governor with whom we dined was a prisoner who actually was required to dig his own grave at one point, but somehow miraculously survived. I saw the now abandoned headquarters of the secret police, located on a cliff overlooking the harbor, where many were taken and never heard from again. I was also told that the main cathedral in Maputo was built by prison labor, in chain gangs.

All of this is just the setting. It was the boat ride that was clearly the highlight of this entire Mozambican odyssey.

The hotel has two very modern fiberglass boats, each equipped with twin 70 horsepower Yamaha outboards. The hulls were of a catamaran design so these boats could really move on this large smooth body of water, the bay. We took one for the 10 mile ride across the bay to the village. In the boat was the driver, his copilot who also doubled as bearer when we landed and walked ashore to the village. The man who arranged all this, Antonio Carvalho N. is a story all by himself. He is now a paid employee of the Foundation. But he started out as a Marxist revolutionary in 1969 when he completed high school and joined the

FRELIMO movement for independence from Portuguese colonialism. He is a pure Portuguese. There is not a drop of black blood in him (or his wife, for that matter). We shared the cottage at the hotel and had lots of fun discussing political economics. He is still a Marxist, thinks the debacle of the previous Marxist government was due to the fact that there really wasn't a true Marxist among the elite. I told him the trouble with Marx was he never read Freud.

On our way back, having visited the village (of which I have lots of pictures), cruising midday in the bay, we suddenly noticed some dolphins rolling and frolicking. So we went closer for a look. There must have been 50 or 60 of them, and when they saw they had an audience, they performed. Of course we stopped the boat, turned off the engines, and watched. Eight or ten would do rolls and then breaches, with the snouts coming straight out of the water, an eye turned to the boat, and then a flip on to the back. The water was clear enough so we could see them swim under the boat and up the other side. What a show.

Eventually, we got jaded even of this wonderment of nature, and decided to proceed back to the hotel. We started the engines and slowly picked up speed, not wishing to disturb them or possibly injure one with the props. Two of those rascals decided to race us. They swam under the boat and surfaced right in front of the bow, not more than 10 feet ahead of us. There they stayed, swimming in the same direction just in front of the boat, flipping their tails at us right on the surface. I panicked, fearful of hitting one of them and told the driver to slow down, which he did, though he knew full well that those fish could easily out swim the boat at full throttle. When we slowed down, they just peeled off with what I interpreted as a look of disdain that we gave up so quickly.

The other highlight of this trip occurred just two days ago when I got Oma's letter, delivered courtesy of Celia D. Boy-o-boy this a remote place. I will not come back here without my own satellite dish. Oma is very thorough. She wrote you weighed in at 11/6 on your month birthday. Did she complain about your belly too? Good idea, giving Oma a rose for Valentine's Day. Now she has another man in her life. I was so pleased to receive the letter, I took Celia out to dinner on Friday. She has huge breasts. I think you would like her, Wolfie.

It is probably a sign of the aging process, but I find myself having little interest in Africa. I keep looking for something that would turn me on to the local cultures, but nothing has yet done so. Not the art nor the music. I have not seen any dance. Not the value system which allows lots of room for exploitation and corruption. Lots of thievery and crime. All windows with iron bars. Park a car and a bunch of urchins run up to ask for money to guard it. Don't pay and your car is guaranteed to be in worse shape when you return. Government functions are capricious and mismanaged.

One thing is clear. However primitive some may believe these people to be, it must have been really degrading for a black to have lived in a colony, where the whites ruled by virtue of their skin color. I can understand their desire for independence at any price ... and did they ever pay a price. Without question, these people are worse off economically (and maybe also politically, in the sense that the juridical system, from law making to law enforcement, is unpredictable) than they were under the colonial administration. All ministers (and there are lots of them) ride around in chauffeur driven white Mercedes. But they were emancipated. This same thing is going to happen in South Africa.

The Foundation is a group of elite who want to help the rural villagers become aware that it is in their power to become masters of their own fate. I doubt that they understand their own village mentality. (Not that I do either.) There was lots wrong with their plan but, amazingly enough, they seemed very receptive to our suggestions for changes in their approach. For example, the project near Pemba (Matuge) that I insisted on visiting, calls for cement construction of seven six-room schoolhouses, one for each village. We asked how the nature of the project was determined. Carvalho said the villagers themselves decided what they wanted when Grace Machel visited them. I asked him if he found it surprising that the villagers, standing before the former first lady who for 13 years had been the education minister, would ask for schoolhouses? Surely they would be deferent to her and would want to say what she would want to hear. Would he expect them to ask her for a football field?

I saw that each village already had a school built out of the same materials villagers use to build their own houses, but the schools were in disrepair. I then pointed to another building in the village in excellent condition and was told that the building was the FRELIMO Party headquarters. Then I reminded Carvalho that John Dewey defined a school as "a teacher, a student, and a log" and asked if cement walls were really going to make a difference to life in the village. Or was this a manifestation of the "edifice" complex of the do-gooders?

I suggested that theirs was a "top down" approach and proposed that the Foundation simply make available to local village groups small amounts for materials that the villagers would have to match with their labor to do whatever was on the list of eligible activities. Instead of a very few expensive and intensive projects administered by the Foundation, they would fund many small projects managed by the village groups themselves, thereby giving the villagers a sense of empowerment over their own destiny. The Foundation could serve the villagers' interests by exposing them to new technology that villagers would not know about, such as solar powered cool rooms to store perishables where there is no electricity. They could use mass media to run education programs.

And they took it. Maybe we were being stroked but it sure felt good.

This letter was interrupted for about 4 hours while Reinhard K. came by to visit and lunch.

I found him at the dinner with the Governor at Pemba and I think he is the first German I like. He is sufficiently anti-Nazi even for me, (and said so before he ever knew anything about me), has a Peruvian wife and has spent a lot of time in Mozambique over the last 12 years helping build up a farm implements plant in Maputo with his own money. He is in Maputo now, having paid his own ticket and just took me on a tour of the plant. It is made up of three shops, including a substantial forge shop. It is fully run by local blacks and is in better shape than any I saw in Pakistan (except the Honda plant of course). It's impressive. Maybe some of the economic problems will lift with the end of the fighting.

After visiting the forge shop Reinhard invited ourselves to visit the home of the forge shop manager, a 31 year old engineer named Joao C, trained in the Ukraine from 1983 to 1988. He came in first in his engineering class. Earlier, we had driven past the refugee camps on the outskirts of the town. They look better than the shantytowns of India but not by much. Now we went to an area where Joao was building his new house. It was not finished and Joao was obviously reluctant to let us see it but Reinhard was not to be dissuaded. At first it seemed presumptuous of us but later it turned out that Reinhard knew what he was about. He really had built a close relationship with Joao and his family over the years, had Joao visit him in Germany (at Reinhard's expense) in 1990 and was his professional mentor. I think Reinhard, who has been technical adviser to the plant over the years, probably trained Joao to become the plant manager. In that position he is paid $260 per month.

We stopped at an open market near the house and suddenly a black woman spotted Reinhard, shouted and ran up to hug him. It turns out that she was the first woman to be hired by the plant while Reinhard was the adviser in 1982. I think he had a lot to do with breaking the sex barrier. She definitely had not been hired for her looks. Her smile could shatter crystal as the wind whistled through her teeth. Reinhard explained that now there is almost equal employment opportunity but at first it was the married women who had been rejected by their husbands and had to earn money to repay their dowry, that took the factory jobs.

Joao's house was built of fired clay and cement block, had a cement facing which was painted white. Joao said to me in a straight face when he pulled his truck up to the house, "My house is white but my wife is black!" Other than that, the house could have passed for a refugee hut. It had corrugated sheeting - that did not quite meet - for a roof, a cement floor, three rooms of very small dimension, and an earthen/sand pit in the back yard where people sat and talked. Windows were all barred and a heavy door and lock were evident. He placed his only chair for Reinhard and a loose cement block for me, and the rest of the family sat on the ground around the pit. A small table was brought out from the house and placed in the center of the pit, glasses and beer were placed thereon, and we had a party in two and a half languages. Reinhard speaks Portuguese and German, with a few English words, Joao speaks Portuguese and Russian, with some English words, and I struggled in German with a few English words, with Reinhard doing a lot of translating from Portuguese to German and back.

Before breaking up, Joao asked me what my reaction was to this visit and to what I saw driving up to his house. I said a lot of polite things but was surprised to hear myself say that I had the sense that the people in the community, his neighbors, seemed to be supportive of each other, were friendly and not envious. He was quick to agree and I think there is something about that feeling I experienced which may provide a clue to the Community Development Foundation's approach. I suspect there is more camaraderie in these villages than is obvious. So go explain the war, then.

I suppose you are waiting for me to tell you what I thought about setting up endowments in Africa, modeled after U.S. endowments, as is being pushed by that nice lady in New York, Peggy Dulany. Well I shall not disappoint you. Here is a little something I came up with one morning when I could not sleep:

ELEEMOSINARY IN AFRICA

It has been said that behind every truly large family fortune lies a major crime. Many times the crime is a personal crime. But it is often a social crime; the illegal imposition of power by one to the detriment of another. There are ample examples of ill gotten gains by some through the exploitation of associates, be they workers or coal miners, competitors, consumers or perhaps partners and shareholders.

And after the crime is successfully accomplished, to assuage their guilty consciences, to perform penance and, incidentally immortalize their name, the perpetrator becomes a major benefactor to social development. They have been referred to as the "Robber Barons". Some names - Mellon, Carnegie, Rockefeller - come to mind. And to facilitate these philanthropic efforts, the U.S. tax code has been structured to provide attractive benefits to those who choose to follow this course.

It is said that this practice has created an entire non-governmental sector of institutions in developed countries which serves the larger interests of society. This group has taken note of their own valuable work and sees opportunities to apply these lessons to their less fortunate colleagues in developing countries. They have taken on the task of replicating themselves. Often they are prepared to provide seed money to get the process started.

It should work better than it has so far. Looking around Africa, we can see the necessary ingredients. Certainly there are ample examples of ill gotten gains being made by rulers who, if and when overthrown, will need assets abroad as a safeguard. Who knows; these people too, may want to immortalize themselves by becoming social benefactors. (How does "The Idi Amin Trust" grab you?) If a way can be found to provide social insurance to these persons, a flow of cash from Switzerland to Africa may result.

Perhaps a role for the old line Foundations in developed countries might be to provide iron clad guarantees to these rulers and former rulers that adequate funds would always be provided to them in case of their need, if they were willing to make their ill gotten gains available for recycling back to Africa for developmental projects. Some sort of international investment guarantee program, based on actuarial ratios, might be a cheap means to mobilize hard currency resources.

Perhaps the U.S. Government might facilitate such an effort by using debts of the least developed nations, which it is about to forgive, as a source of funding for the guarantees.

With love and good wishes on your arrival to this world, Opa - February 29,1992

SRI LANKA - 1992

This letter is just a bit of fluff. It does not describe who sent me to Sri Lanka, nor what I was to do there. Still, it provides a brief glimpse of a developing nation trying to resolve internal social conflicts dating to the second century BCE.

Dear Wolfie,

Happy Easter Sunday from Colombo, Sri Lanka, or, what used to be called Ceylon in the good old colonial days. Until 1948, the British treated this place like their favorite watering hole; vacationing on the beaches, enjoying the tropical climate along the coast, and the cool of the mountains in the interior of this island. At that point in time, these quaint brown people who had inhabited this island for 30 centuries decided that enough was enough; they wanted their independence. Then they changed the name of their country from Ceylon to Sri Lanka.

It is 7 pm and I have just come back to the Oberoi Hotel from the verandah of the Gall Face Hotel, across the street. The verandah faces the beach towards the west and so it is the "in" thing to watch the sunset there. You order a beer and some chips, sip the beer and keep the crows from stealing the chips, swat flies and try to observe the sunset without going blind. But it is an awesome sight. The trouble is I like the local beer and that comes in a large bottle, more than I'm used to drinking. It is ideal for two. Moreover, I have always found it more pleasurable to experience such a beautiful sunset with a sympathetic person. So where is your grandmother when I need her most urgently?? I ask you that. Probably painting the bedroom.

If you get there around 5:30 the sun is pretty low on the horizon. There is a crescent of palm trees and, if you manage the right seat, the palms block the rays until the sun is low enough to look at without going blind. Sometimes the low clouds sit on the horizon and you can only see the sun disappear behind the clouds. That's still OK because the pyrotechnics really begin after the sun disappears, with its rays shining upwards from below the horizon at the clouds and sky over your head. But today I could see the sun dip right into the ocean, deep red and orange as it touched down. What followed was really a show. The whole sky above just played its colors from heavenly blue to white and yellow and crimson, offset by some deep grey shadows of clouds. Soon the palm trees turned a deep dark green, and then black as they silhouette against the multicolored sky. It's only then that you notice the breakers rolling into the shore. When the sun is up, its reflection on the water seems to flatten the surf. You hear it but its motion does not strike you until the sun sets; then the perpetual motion of the waves catches your eye.

The Gall Face Hotel was built on the beach in 1864 to allow for accommodation of royalty for some important celebration. Its lobby is right out of the colonial period, hugely spacious, full of marble, with high ceilings and punka fans, real arches and columns and statues. The doors are intricately carved and stained. The wooden chairs and tables have to be a hundred years old. And at the entrance is a stone plaque giving the names of about 50 of the more prominent hotel guests over the past 120 years. The Queen of England is there as is the Maharajah of Baroda. The list is in alphabetical order so Mark Tully's name (a colleague of ours from our India days who has been the BBC correspondent in India the past 30 years) appears just above Kurt Waldheim's. I must remember to tell him that.

Well, if you really want to know all the good things that happened after the British left and the people gained their independence in 1948, you may be disappointed. It's not like the fairy stories where everyone lived happily ever after. Actually it's a bit like the story I wrote to you from Mozambique. Things have been pretty rough these past 40 or so years, what with the Tamils (who are Hindus) and the Singhalese (who are Buddhists) fighting each other.

But we should not be so sanctimonious about it since our race seems to be on a similar self-destruct path. Ask your Dad to tell you about the IRA in Ireland or the Israelis and the Arabs.

Unfortunately, there are many other examples. Gandhi once was asked what he thought about Western Civilization and answered that he thought it would be a very good thing.

But the country is beautiful. It's getting polluted and the population is growing too fast, and there are lots of poor people; but it has a wonderful potential; it could be a paradise if they let it. But the fact is that this world has seen a lot more of dictatorial and repressive societies than it has of free societies. Maybe we, who have had the benefit of living both an affluent and a free life, are just spoiled and unwilling to admit that it is our living condition that is the unusual one. This train of thought can easily lead one into policies of isolationism, and that's impossible now that modern technology can make a small dictator into a big threat, even to a country like ours. But I have the feeling that, even in your long lifetime, this world will not become free of even the more extreme economic and political inequities within and among societies.

I spent last week in Indonesia but will not write much about that because I know so little about that country. It is a big country, with a population of 180 million and the islands spread over an area 3000 miles wide. It seems to have a very small but rich upper class and a large population that is unbelievably poor, but I was told that there is a growing middle class and people are becoming better off. I do not understand that society at all. It appears terribly corrupt but there seems to be a flow of these funds both upwards and back downwards. Who can tell. There are lots of five star hotels, as good as any in the U.S., and many Indonesians stay there and eat there.

Actually, I was a little down in the dumps last week. You know how that is, Wolfie, like when lots of people smile at you and try to get you to react in your usual charming way, and all you want is to be left alone?? Then you start crying, and then these people try even harder to change your mood. Well, I didn't cry, but just sat sullen in the airplane and dared anyone to try to talk to me. Fortunately all my various seat mates must have felt the same way because no one said one word to me, all the way to Jakarta. Except for one United Airlines hostess who has been with the airline more than 20 years. She is grateful to the management for keeping the company solvent but still cannot quite accept the CEO paying himself wages of $18 million last year. I think she has a point. Her husband is the Harbormaster in Bar Harbor, Maine and. she commutes to Chicago to fly with United. (I don't think she goes home for lunch.) She painted such a beautiful picture of Bar Harbor (in the summer) that I'm ready to take us all up there to see it. Not in May or June because that's the fly season.

Maybe being depressed gets me dreaming the wrong dreams. Last night I had a very disturbing one in which something really bad happened to your Grandmother and some other members of the family. It was so powerful that I woke up and looked to see if the message light was on.

So you see, I think a goodly amount about you and the folks back home. And I gaze at your pictures a lot. I think about all the witty remarks I'd like to make to you all that I can never think of when the occasion arises. Remind me to tell you the story about the kid who would always answer a question by saying "It depends".

If something interesting happens in the next few days, before I start the trip back, I'll add to this letter. Otherwise, see you soon, and keep smiling.

Opa   - April 19, 1992

RIGA, LATVIA - 1993

After the break-up of the Soviet Union in 1991, the World Bank was asked to provide financing to the Baltic countries. In the past, their economy was planned and managed from Moscow. Now, they wanted to break their ties and move to be independent. The World Bank offered to help Latvia establish a planning unit to prioritize their investment strategies. I served on a team to do this.

Dear Wolfie,

This trip has taken me to Riga, Latvia, an ancient city that still has structures (city walls and towers) built around 1200, when the Knights of the Sword established the "Livonian Order" and extended their control from Riga over this area along the Baltic Sea. These people had been dominated by stronger neighboring countries throughout the middle ages, including Germans, Swedes and, eventually the Russians after Peter the Great. Riga's claim to fame rests with its port, since it is the most northerly port on the Baltic sea that never freezes in winter.

After World War I (1918) Latvia received its independence from Russia but in 1939 the Russians (then called the U.S.S.R.) occupied it. In 1941 the Germans attacked and drove the Russians out. At the end of World War II (1945) the U.S.S.R. again reoccupied Latvia (and also neighboring Estonia and Lithuania) and continued to control these countries until the break-up of the U.S.S.R. in 1990. Russia imposed a communist system of government on the Latvians, eliminating private ownership of property and putting all power into the hands of the government. Now Latvia is attempting to reestablish its economy along democratic and private enterprise lines, and to maintain itself as an independent nation. I'm here as part of a team sent by the World Bank and the United Nations to help them restructure their government policy decision making process so that they will be able to get maximum benefit from the resources being provided to them by international aid donors, and incidentally, also from their own tax revenues.

The trip over was unnerving. Because of the thunderstorm that hit Washington on Sunday at 3.30 pm, the incoming flight was diverted to Richmond. That delayed our departure for 2 hours. I had only a little more than that in London to catch my connection to Stockholm. I prayed that the pilot would make up some time and indeed he did. But when we approached London, the pilot announced that London approach radar was out and we would have to hold. So we circled and circled... When we landed, I had 5 minutes to make the Stockholm flight. I raced to the gate and, miracle it was, got on the flight. And there we sat for another hour because the departure radar was also out. When we finally left London it was obvious I could not catch the next connection in Stockholm for Riga. I did not know if my luggage was on board. I was hot and sweaty and without sleep.

In Stockholm SAS decided that the way to get me to Riga was to send me back to Copenhagen (halfway back to London) to connect with another flight to Riga. Finally, at 8.30 pm Monday we landed in Riga... and no luggage. No one spoke English or German so filling out the lost luggage form was fun. But the last blow was yet to be delivered. I got into the car that had been sent to pick me up, checked into the Eurolink, a 5 star hotel and subsequently discovered that there was no hot water to be had, and there would be none until June 4!!!

It seems that the previous government came up with the brilliant idea that it was wasteful for each house to have its own hot water system. And so, they built a giant hot water enterprise to supply an entire section of the city with hot water. This system was now down. I had no luggage, so no shampoo or hair brush. And no suit or clean shirt or tie to go to my scheduled meetings.

First things first. I took a cold shower. Then I ran to the department store and found a suit made in Finland for $65 that actually fit me. It is a size 44 but the lining is a size 64. And it was made for men with extremely small hands if you can judge by the pockets. When it rains (fortunately we have a drought just now) I will find out what material it is made of. A shirt and tie set me back $11 and $15 respectively but the store did not have any narrow black belts in stock just now. "Come back next month...." The principal of consumerism is... buy whatever you might need in the future, when you come across it in the store.

Actually, the store was well stocked, prices were in hard currency, had a large staff of sales clerks that earn about $50 per month, and lots of people looking at the merchandise, but no customers. Nobody was buying. I tied my wide belt over the loops of the Finnish pants (which I am proud to say are too big for me) and went to my meeting.

For the next two days I took cold showers. I also pestered people to search for my bag. By this time my hair was getting a bit matted and the entire neighborhood was beginning to smell pretty ripe. So I marched myself down to the Metropole Hotel, which, rumor had it, has its own hot water system and is every bit as nice as the Eurolink. Lucky they had a room. In between meetings I pestered about my bag some more. SAS got replies from Copenhagen, London and Stockholm that the bag was not to be found. Finally, someone had the good sense to call the airport in Riga. Yes indeed the bag was there. Did I want it?

One of the men who works at the U.N. as a driver (actually he is a trained medical doctor - a urologist) took me to the airport to pick up the bag. I asked him why he is not practicing medicine and he said that there is a surplus of medics in Latvia, about three times as many per 1,000 population as there are in Germany. He can't get the money to set up a practice. Besides, he said, most urologists are Jews and,"... since their noses are shaped one way and mine is shaped another, I will not be able to fit into the system."

Quite a few Latvians escaped to the West since the end of World War II. Their children seem to be coming back here, some to stay, but at least to assist in the reformation of the country. These are bright, optimistic and hard working young people and they work at translating new laws and assisting at the Parliament. Some came back even before full independence was achieved. There was a party at the U.N. office and one such young woman who was there (she lived in Chicago and now holds a fairly senior position at the Ministry of Foreign Affairs) told me how they used what are now the U.N. offices as the meeting place for the resistance groups during the August 21 coup attempt when the Russian Black Berets were attacking the Parliament building, only 3 blocks away. The party, by the way, was such a simple affair. Some wine and cakes, a lot of singing of folk songs, and a warm feeling of camaraderie. The doctor led the singing.

This old town is marvelous. The river flows right through it. The church spires make a great skyline. The old architecture is wonderful. As I walk down the narrow, cobblestone streets I think I'm entering a time warp and will meet some 18th century dressed characters around the next corner. Riga has been known for its architects throughout the ages. I'm told Serge Eisenstein, the film-maker came from Riga and his father was a famous architect. There are sidewalk art shows and even the art intended for tourists is pretty good work.

When you cross the large bridge over the Daughava, you would be able to see the main square where the church spires rise up in their splendor, if only the Russians had not built the most awful mon-ument to themselves to block out the view, many think deliberately.

Today is Sunday. I walked along the cobblestone streets and around the town squares. At one such square, where the Dominican church stands, a couple of fellows, one playing a bass and one a trombone, were performing a concert. Gentle, soft music; nothing great, but a relaxing mood. I bought a beer, sat in the afternoon sun, looked at the array of multicolored two hundred year old houses, listened and watched the other people. It was sufficient to make up for all the trouble of getting here. And, for a brief moment, I felt the presence of your Oma. It was 10 am Washington time and I realized she was probably in her church. I was in mine.

The assignment has its interesting aspects. On the surface, my job is to examine the governmental organizational structure to see where technical assistance could be provided that would facilitate the policy making functions and investment decision process of the government. In a democracy, the elected politicians are required to make decisions about policies and how to spend money. They need a. professional staff that can analyze the various alternative actions, and after calculating the costs and benefits of each option, provide a reasoned analysis that will allow the politician to make a decision. We try to understand how they do things here, and then suggest ways to organize things and to train and equip staff to do the professional work.

The problem is that the old socialist mindset has not changed, particularly among the ministry staff. They still want their ministry to continue to control the economy, some say to get pay~offs. They do not want to have personnel assignments on a merit system; rather through personal contact as they did these last 46 years through the Communist Party apparatus. And there is huge corruption. The officials are selling off any asset the state owns that is not nailed down. Forest timber belonging to the state is sold off and petty bureaucrats of the Forestry Ministry who earn $100 a month are driving around in Mitsubishi 4 wheel drive vehicles. Boatloads of sugar are being smuggled in without customs duty payments, On and on. It is not clear whether the police are part of the problem or part of the solution. I don't know how technical assistance will solve that.

On June 5th, the day I'm scheduled to complete my work and return to Washington, there will be a national election. The new government will take office July 6. They want our report to be ready for the new government when they take office. I'm trying to make the report useful to the "good guys", if I can find them.

A couple of days ago, I visited the Prime Minister's office. I was waiting to meet with one of his advisers, but his reception area is worth describing. It has a central European regal splendor. From the matched parquet floors, the gold painted friezes and moldings on the high ceiling and the dull brass chandelier hanging in the center, to the large double windows and the make believe marble columns embedded every six feet in the walls, it was a throwback to the Tsarist court. There were gold moldings in the shape of panels on the walls between the columns. The walls were painted a fine shade of green.

In the center of the room, under the chandelier, was a large desk, behind which sat a large woman, her dark blond hair coiffed perfectly into a severe Cleopatra style. Her green polyester dress was the identical shade of the walls, and stated firmly to all who entered, "I belong here".

It is Thursday, and I just returned from a wonderful performance of La Traviata. Somehow, the cultural life of Latvia has not been neglected. These artists, both the singers and the orchestra, are exceptionally well trained. The dance choreography was a little sloppy, but the rest of the performance was first class. I never realized how timely that opera is; it's about long-term health care.

The opera house is under extensive renovation, and so the performance was held in a smaller hall, with only 200 seats. My hotel is located just down the street from the opera house and I can see the construction. It is expected to be completed in 1994. I was surprised to find that this very expensive project was one of the first things the new government funded, even though they are strapped for cash and all the aid donors are telling them to finance only the highest priority development projects at this time. In fact, the whole purpose of my trip here is to set up a process for ranking the many projects they need to undertake in some priority order based on return on investment. So I sat in the auditorium during intermission and made some mental calculations.

Here was this orchestra and about 25 vocalists performing for 200 people. I bought the best seat in the house and paid 70 rubles. That means the gross revenue through the door tonight was less than $100, about the price of one ticket at the Washington opera. Now, how do you suppose the renovation of the opera house would be ranked against other development projects if we did a rate of return on investment calculation?

June 5th has finally arrived, and I'm ready to depart. Yesterday I took the train to Jurmala, the beach community on Riga Bay. What a wonderful area. The beaches are beautiful but the water is polluted. The entire Baltic Sea is said to have four feet of sludge and industrial waste at the bottom. Still, people fish. But I did not put my hand in the water. The ride on the very old and very hard ride commuter train took 30 minutes and cost 15 cents each way. A lot of Russian retirees live there, and they have no voting rights or citizenship here. We, in the U.S. do not quite understand ethnic attitudes in other parts of the world.

Well, Wolf, I think I'll deliver this letter to you personally, since I'm about to get on the airplane to go home. In all, the visit to Riga has been pleasant. But I have the sense that, as charming and reasonable as these people appear on the surface, as victimized as their past has made them, there is a primitive aggressiveness and a manipulative, scheming mind underlying it all.

During World War II the Finns fought the Russians; the Danes actively resisted the Germans; but the Latvians served in the SS. I would not be comfortable to find myself in a situation in which I were in their power or in need of their help. Minorities here should take care as they walk between the raindrops.

Love, Opa   - June 1993

BANGLADESH -2002 – MY LAST CONSULTANCY

In 2000, the World Bank provided a loan to Bangladesh for export industries diversification. That credit covered funding for an analysis of the constraints impeding the growth of exports. Much work had already been done to identify these constraints. In 2002 I was hired to analyze "the nature and magnitude of those constraints to growth and diversification of exports in Bangladesh and to recommend appropriate measures to improve the situation." I was puzzled that yet another study was needed to do this since so much was already known about these impediments. Nevertheless, I took the assignment.

Here are my e-mails to Joan during that assignment.

Dear Joan:

At 5:25am this morning I was awakened by the call to prayer of the muezzin. I don't know where the mosque is, but the loudspeaker must be directly outside my hotel window.

Things are OK here. This hotel is clean and adequate with CNN on the television. The 5 star hotels downtown are little luxury islands in the midst of squalor. We are in the diplomatic area and the security here is better than most places. The US Embassy is 2 blocks south. The American International School is 2 blocks west. Roving local patrols by the Embassy run through the streets. It is easier to walk around here than downtown. There is a park about 6 blocks away with a walking track. (Three loops to a Kilometer).

The office hired a full time car and driver for me so I am mobile. I will try to join one of the clubs here to get access to a swimming pool. The hotel has none, nor an exercise room.

And now, the local scene! The office is downtown, a 40 minute hair raising ride from the hotel. There is a rhythm to the traffic but I could not drive in these conditions. The city has 12 million inhabitants and they are all on the move. Cycle rickshaws are ubiquitous, some loaded like a pickup truck. It is hot in the sun but the mornings, when I do my walking, are glorious. The flowers are magnificent (lots of zinnias and bougainvilleas). My walks in the park on the walking track are fun. Most wear street clothes (I wear those famous shorts and a tee shirt). This morning I was passed by a small veiled woman wearing a full-length black burka. I'm sure she was beautiful!

A full American breakfast is included in the room rate. This is my undoing. How can I turn down two fried eggs on toast, fresh squeezed orange juice and instant coffee. For a while, I ignored the jam which was put on the table, thinking it was going to be too sweet. Then I tried it. It is imported marmalade, and just wonderful. I ordered pancakes, which turn out to be made very thin, like crepes, and, what do you know - I had made my own palatchinken. The head of the dining room is a Bangladeshi who spent 14 years working for the Sheraton in Saudi Arabia, after attending hotel school. Now, the Saudis have developed an allergy for Banglas after one killed his master in Jidda in 1998. So these folks can't get their old jobs back there any more and are available in the local work force.

When he saw my Herald Tribune he almost salivated on me and then asked to read it.

There are 52 cable channels, including VOA, BBC and CNN. Also channels from India. "If it bleeds, it leads!" It is absolutely frightening, all the outbreaks of violence around the world. Colombia, Zimbabwe, Israel and West Bank, India. It is quiet here in Bengal. And a good thing too - I have no confidence in the local constabulary. Everyone is on the take.

(One day later)

No "black burka streaker" this morning. But there were others who were just walking - in their black flowing burkas and their veils, which they keep up until there is a man in view, at which time it is flicked down.

And who can blame them, there hardly is a day that passes when the paper does not report an acid throwing at a woman by some disgruntled man whose overtures were spurned. Or a gang rape of a teenager who somehow, conveniently commits suicide over the shame. Today's paper has a story about a married woman who was raped by some politically connected man. I quote from the news story:

"Later, the housewife narrated her ordeal to the villagers, alleging that Bablu had raped her at gun point. On March 3, a village court accused the housewife of engaging in immoral activities. She admitted in writing that Bablu had raped her and prayed she should not be ostracized from society. The Village court fined her 1,500 Takas and sentenced her to 25 lashes with permission to continue living in society. Papers relating to the incident and the judgment were sent to the Miapur Islam Samaj, a socio-cultural organization seeking action against the offender."

So, I ask you, would you not wear a burka here? I would.

To Joan

Not only am I not able to even boot my laptop but now the desktop that they gave me for use in my room is causing problems. So is my memory. I no longer remember what I sent to you because I have started to write several emails only to have the power go out and therefore I lost them. It may happen again but here goes.

Did I tell you I found the Dhaka Flying Club? Not cheap! $100 per hour for the 182; $75 for the 150 (a 2 seater). I was thinking of flying to Chittagong for a couple of meetings but the regular airfare is only 20% of what it would cost me to fly myself. I will do some joy riding anyway.

The worst part of being driven around in the downtown area is the beggar women with the babies. I know they rent them but also I see the baby's condition as they show them. They seem almost dead, surely they soon will be. I'm told they deliberately deform them to make it more sympathy evoking. They are all over the place. There are 400,000 cycle rickshaws and they are driven two shifts. That makes 800,000 rickshaw peddlers in a city of 12 million. The level of poverty is worse than Delhi as I remember it. The five star hotels are islands of opulence planted in this sea of squalor. I'm glad I'm not staying in one of them.

The hotel is clean. I had them remove the carpets from my room because they were not clean. I have been fighting with my intestines which are producing a looseness. My morning walks are performed every second day. I delude myself into thinking I'm getting fresh air but the local traffic cops wear nose masks. I have swum only once at the International club. But it is a fine watering hole. Beer is a buck a can.

I bought a book of poetry written by Kazi Nazrul Islam translated from Bengali to English. My professor partner said he is a very famous poet (died in 1976) but the translation loses something. He is supposed to have followed in the footsteps of Tagore (who died in 1941).

The work is OK. I think I have figured out how I can be of use to this place. I don't expect to have much impact but will follow the first rule of the Hippocratic oath - do no harm. Nobody is impressed by aid donors around here. The World Bank staff that designed this activity must have been a bunch of well meaning but arrogant fools.

Well my dear. This computer has behaved itself for a change. I'll try to send this off tomorrow. By the way, I am not making things up to impress you. The story about the woman who was raped is a direct quote out of the newspaper, 25 lashes and all.

Love, Lu

- March 11, 2002

Dear Joan and Family!

Well, how nice to receive three (count them three) emails from family at once, not to mention a joke from fredssssss.

Now I'll tell you how things are going here.

My driver. He is a very cautious driver. Frankly I like it that way. But he has a way of always getting into the lane that stops. But there is such lunacy on the road here that I guess it's ok too. He negotiates through a sea of cycle rickshaws scooters, and trucks each operating at a very different speed. I laugh at that too, particularly when some other driver cuts in and out and gets no further with that technique than my driver. But there are times of tension in the car. Today, after some really harrowing encounters (we were never in danger but it was a miracle we did not kill someone). I said Allah must be really looking after the people in this city. It's a wonder they don't get killed in this traffic. Shaker actually laughed out loud.

D H, the chief of Party for this activity has a Sri Lankan wife and two beautiful daughters (13 and 9). He is a Brit but his home now is in southern France. She teaches English at the Japanese school. He has lived in developing countries a long, long time! He plays the tenor sax and is part of a Japanese jazz band. He is very good as are the other Japanese musicians. Last Friday he invited me to a concert and it was great fun. We hit it off quite well.

The Ministry of Commerce. My first meeting was with the Joint Secretary, who carefully looked me over. This project is not tops on their priority list of interests. I had to hide my own doubts about this assignment by implying that I would put something together for them that they could use. Somehow we began to work up the line and they took me in to the Secretary. He looked me over as well, I made my pitch and he seemed to go for it. Then he spoke about two sections attached to his Ministry (the Register of Companies and the Insurance Commissioner) and said he would like me to look in on them. He would like to have them emerge from the 17th century to do something useful. I agreed, visited each of them the following day and wrote a one page memo to him on each section about how I thought it might be done. No response!

But, just today I was told that the Secretary would like me to present my findings before I leave. That was no surprise, but then he said that it would be at a formal meeting with 50 guests and chaired by the Minister. So now David has gone out to hire a hall at a hotel here in Downtown Dhaka. I think this will be like a Bar Mitzvoh. Please express mail my Tallis.

Actually, I started to pull a few ideas together for this project and tried them out on David. He liked them and I suspect he passed them on to the Secretary.

Now I'll tell you the story about the poem. My first meeting of that day was with the Managing Director (another name for the title President) of a large bank. His name is T. U. We had a very candid and useful chat and, when it was time to leave, he asked me if I read poetry. Shaker, who had worked with me in my hotel room and saw that I had purchased an English translation of poems by Nazrul Islam, then allowed how I have an interest. This banker then said he writes poetry and pulled out a copy of a book of his poems called Fathomless Deep. He read one poem which seemed OK and then he autographed it for me, addressing it "To My Friend Lu Rudel." I was touched.

I felt pretty good about the day, but then met with the Chairman of the Dhaka Electric Supply Agency. That was my undoing. He was hopeless. Thus this poem.

A Cry for Change in Bangladesh - 2002

What is to be said about the spirit of co-operation,
Between aid donor and recipient, locked in an interminable relation,
When one finds senior officials with no sense of obligation,
Toward their own wretched poor; lives mired in degradation,
Desperate for sustenance, absent adequate sanitation.
These poor hear yet again, what had been promised to the previ-
ous generation,
And believe again the new promises for poverty alleviation.
Yet, our senior official remains idle at his station.

But promises for improvements are not made in the present tense.
Problems are huge, the population growing ever more immense.
The senior official demands immediate personal return.
Follows his imperialist mentors' model; can't seem to unlearn
Behaviors demonstrated to him by the old ruling classes.
Where is his sense of social responsibility to the masses?

The aid donor, in his role of "change agent",
Has been cautioned to be ever so patient.
"But time is the enemy, it is running out,"
The change agent wants to scream and shout.
Trifle with your people's basic demand
And risk retribution, if – no, when -- things will get out of hand.
Reread Nazrul's description of "The Rebel" if you dare.
You'd best fear his destructive force when he, his teeth, will bare.

There were two senior officers who inspired me to write that poem. But a lot of the other people I met seem to want to get things done. The Secretary of Finance (Harvard Law school) seems quite sharp and he now wants me to see the governor of the Reserve Bank because I tried out a couple of ideas on him and he liked them. So, maybe this is not a total loss!

They are constructing center barriers on the major roads in town. That is a good move because otherwise people would travel abreast as wide as the road permits, each trying to pass the other. But then, they decided to plant trees to beautify the setting. The barriers are about 18 inches wide and have holes about 6 inches square into which seedlings were placed. I asked David if they did not expect the trees to grow and what they thought would happen to the barriers in 5 years. He shrugged as only a Frenchman can.

So now to respond to your lovely message Ruthann. Please tell your son Ezra he cannot impress me with diarrhea at this point. I can outdo him in a split minute! I am looking for someone to change MY diapers. But wish him a speedy recovery.

Well, that's the story from "Lake Dhaka," where all the men are sweaty, all the women are beautiful under their black Burkas and veils, and all the children pee in the streets.

Love to you all, but specially to Joan.

Lu/Dad/Opa

- Mar 14, 2002

Dear Family: Hello from Opa:

How wonderful to receive your newsy email. I got it this morning, which is yesterday evening for you because we are 11 hours ahead of you across a date line. No matter how much you hurry, I will, each day, see the sun rise before you. In fact, it will be setting here when it is rising where you are.

I loved the story about your weekend at the farm. Wish I could have been with you. I look forward to eating the ice cream you left for me. Thank you for your prayers.

This morning I delivered a "Discussion Paper" which will be printed and distributed to 80 people that will attend my presentation on April 2, 2002. Now that is when I will really need your prayers. I am saying a lot of things that people here do not want to hear. The day after I arrived there were newspaper articles in every paper about a World Bank economist who said a lot of things that people did not like. He was truly roasted! Well, it is part of the job, I guess. Then, after my presentation, which will be chaired by the Minister of Commerce (a rather decent fellow), I will take D H and his family out to dinner and, next morning, get on my horse and ride off into the sunset!

Wolfie, you want to know what my room looks like. It is on the 4th floor and has a balcony that allows me to look across a large street that runs to the airport. My room is about the size of your parent's bedroom. It has a very large and well appointed bathroom attached. Lots of ceramic tile on the floor and walls in the bath. It takes about 5 minutes of running the faucet to get hot water in the morning but the water is good and hot once it arrives. And the shower is as good as the one you have used at our farmhouse.

The room has tiles on the floor but I think they are vinyl. Ceilings are high but there is no punka fan. The drapes are drawn all the time because the sun is so strong the a/c would not be able to keep up otherwise. There is a huge double bed, a closet, some tables and chairs and an air conditioner and a TV with 52 channels (many different languages French, Italian, Hindi, Arabic, and of course English). All the tables are covered with my papers. (No surprise there) And there is a desk on which I have placed a desk-top computer on which I am typing this message. The room also has a small refrigerator in which I keep water and soda. I have fruit (bananas, oranges) on the table and also what remains of a bottle of Irish whiskey (Jameson's). There is one picture on the wall; a close up of four flowers, I do not know what kind but maybe they are zinnias. If you drink enough Jameson's the number of flowers double.

Looking out the window I see a lot of flat land that is just being developed. It is waterlogged, like most of Bangladesh because it is so flat and low and there is so much rain. Dhaka is 27 feet above sea level. Chittagong is the seaport; it is just about as far from Dhaka as Washington is from New York. Chittagong is 5 feet above sea level. There are no hills between.

Somewhere on the other side of the street is a mosque that I cannot see but I know it is there because they have loudspeakers set up and five times each day, starting at 4:45 am, they chant their prayers. The loudspeaker is so powerful it would make YOUR loudspeaker system blush with envy.

About every other day I get up at 6 am and put on my shorts and go to the park about 5 blocks away to walk on the track. That is the best moment of the day in terms of weather. It is cool and the air is about as fresh smelling as it gets around here. My room boy also runs in the morning at the park where I walk. He takes good care of the room. It is kept quite clean.

In the lobby there is a restaurant and I eat breakfast there every morning. The waiters there take good care of me. There are no women working at this hotel that I can see. Also in the lobby is a "Business Center" which has computers, copy machines etc. and access to the internet.

The mode of transport for the masses (I have a car and driver) is the cycle rickshaw, a three-wheeler that carries enormous loads and is powered by a very scrawny man with powerful legs. He will not be able to read or write.

There are 400,000 cycle-rickshaws and they are operated in two shifts. If the driver is lucky he will earn about $3 per day and then pay the owner of the rickshaw 70 cents for the use. They probably come to the city from a village to earn some money. Their family will remain in the village. This is a level of poverty that most people in the U.S. do not even comprehend. These people wake up in the morning and face each day that way, knowing there will be no change in their life style.

It is amusing to see how the traffic flows. If you hesitate, you will be there forever, so everybody moves and inches forward. No one gives anyone else a break. The horn is a tool of driving because everyone uses it but it has no effect because no one pays the slightest attention to it. Allah must really take care of these people or they would surely all get killed.

I flew to Chittagong last Thursday in the cockpit of a 50 passenger turboprop twin. The pilot taxied to the runway, started rolling, got to takeoff speed, rotated and about 100 feet above the runway, shifted to the autopilot. Then we sat there in the cockpit and swatted flies until it was time to land.

All my love to you all,

Opa

- March 27, 2002

Dear Family:

Yesterday, after completing my work on the study and hand-ing in a printable Discussion Paper for distribution to just about everybody in Dhaka, I had a meeting with the Governor of The Bangladesh Reserve Bank, the Allan Greenspan of Bangladesh. The Central Bank building is as ornate and pretentious as anything in Dhaka can be. And of course it is well decorated with works of art. I looked very hard for signs of women in this facility but the only ones I saw were in the paintings on the wall. Not even the cleaning force!

Actually, he is a rather thoughtful and reasonably candid man and gave me as good answers as the material allowed him to give. I had caught one of his senior staff in a lie and he was not as defensive as I expected when I pointed it out.

Then, after the meeting, I went to - are you ready for this? - a rock concert! Actually, it was not quite a rock concert. It was a British Council affair. They brought in a trio from London: Susheela Rahman, the vocalist, originally from Madras, a guitar player whose uncle was the previous World Bank rep in Dhaka and a tabla player with roots in Gujerat. They seem to meld south Asian music with popular (Beatles type) music. Some songs sounded like they might have been sung by the likes of Joan Baez but they definitely had an eastern flavor to them. In the final number they invited four local artists (harmonium, sitar, tabla and flute) to play with them and it was quite a jam session.

The musicians were staying at the same hotel as I. We had met in the restaurant yesterday and they invited me to the show. That vocalist, in fact all of them, had great musicianship and boundless energy. The egalitarian elements of our family will be pleased to know that I got my driver a ticket so he would not have to sit in the car outside, waiting for me. This morning, I saw them get ready to check out and, boy were they dragging. They must have partied all night. Then Susheela could not find her cell phone and a big search was made. Her partner found it in her suitcase. Then she misplaced her plane ticket. But these are happy people!

So now I am preparing some hand-outs for the presentation.

I just got a hair cut in my hotel room. The barber was nowhere as cute as you, Joan. I could not see his legs but, well, you know just not as much fun as usual. So the haircut went rather badly because I caught him using thinning shears.

Just so you will know what I'm eating, last night I had pizza at the International Club, the night before was Donner Kabob at a new restaurant called Topkapi. The décor was magnificent, the service was great and the food in each case was ordinary. I asked the Maitre d' at Topkapi just who was Turkish and he said the chef was. He will arrive in about a month!

Tomorrow I will be having dinner with the pilot of the flight to Chittagong at his home. I had invited him for lunch the day after the flight and we had a good conversation. He had lived in the U.S. for about 6 years but then returned to Dhaka. It promises to be an interesting evening.

I look forward to seeing all of you soon on my return.

Love Dad/ Opa

- March 28, 2002

Hello Family:

My presentation to the assembled government authorities did not go well. They did not care for my analysis of the constraints under which exporters were operating and my criticisms of the government's procedures and regulations. Somehow, they expected me to tell them which products they should be making that would be easily sold abroad under existing conditions. The World Bank office in Dhaka did not even send a staff member to the presentation.

I drafted a transmittal letter for my betters to send along with the report but doubt they will use it. No point in antagonizing the client. Here is an excerpt from my proposed draft transmittal letter:

" … We have searched in vain to find any guidance or references in the Terms of Reference (TOR) for this study to give cause for the expectations described above. Please note that the section on **Problems to be Addressed** of the TOR asks the study to address "…the causes for the relative lack of success in diversifying exports…" and propose "…appropriate remedial policies and actions…." The **Objectives** section limits the Part II study to "…the data and findings of the enterprise survey in Part I of the study." The **Scope** section asks the study to, "… examine in particular, (a) supply side constraints and (b) policy, procedural and regulatory constraints. The broad subjects of institutional and infrastructure constraints will be examined in general terms from the exporter's point of view…. The different types of infrastructural constraints may be identified and prioritized for possible detailed further study."

Having said all that, we agree with the thrust of your comments that additional work needs to be done (although not as part of this report) to help the Bangladesh export community identify where their comparative advantage lies and into which international markets it should focus its efforts. In fact, I direct your attention to the first of the "Overarching Conclusions" of the Part II study (page xx), the last sentence of which states, "…Commodity surveys need to be undertaken to develop a plan to bring about diversification for these sectors." At the end of the April 2, 2002 discussion, our consultant, Mr. Rudel, made that very point.

Annex xx to this report provides an outline for such commodity surveys which was developed by Mr. Rudel, in the course of his work in India some time ago. I also attach to this letter, for your information, a letter written by Mr. Rudel that describes the magnitude of this undertaking in India. That program was executed by about 10 Indian consulting firms over a five year period, each study receiving assistance from expatriate experts.

I hope it will now be possible for the Ministry of Commerce to take the lead in considering and, if found useful, implementing the recommendations contained in this study even though, as was stated repeatedly at the presentation, many are not new to those who have long been involved with Bangladesh exports.

Should you require anything further from us, please do not hesitate to contact me.

Sincerely,

The big bad wolf!

5

Travels in Search of Our Roots

Five travel stories are presented in this chapter, all related to my family's search for links to Joan's and my ancestors. The first story is of the only trip that took us behind the Iron Curtain, in 1979, long before the Berlin Wall came down ten years later. We traveled by bus from Vienna through Bratislava and Prague, to the Bohemian regions of what was then Czechoslovakia to visit the villages from whence Joan's great-grandparents departed for the U.S. in the early 1850s.

The second tale describes a large-scale family trip, organized by Julius in 2002, to take us all back to Vienna, Salzburg, and Paris--following the trail of Julius' 1938 escape. The third recounts our trip during 2009 along the Dalmatian Coast from Dubrovnik towards Trieste, tracing a portion of my own escape route. The fourth tells of our trip to Cernivtsi (formerly Czernowitz) in Ukraine during the summer of 2010, where my parents and grandparents lived prior to World War I, before they moved to Vienna. The final travel story describes a recent trip (2014) Joan and I made to Austria and northern Italy. The differences in national character between the Austrians and the Italians are noted, even though there are no longer border restrictions between them. They now have open borders as members of the European Union.

Czech Bohemia – Behind the Iron Curtain - 1979

The state of Wisconsin was formed and brought into the Union of the United States in 1848. To attract immigrants the state set up a land grant program, offering settlers a parcel of land if they would clear it and cultivate it for some period of time. The state also established an office at the Bowery in New York City to encourage immigrants arriving by ship to move to Wisconsin. Joan's eight great-grandparents all migrated from the Bohemian part of what was then Austria-Hungary to the United States in the 1850s, crossed the Allegheny Mountains and settled near Green Bay, Wisconsin. They cleared their land parcels of trees, planted crops, and became dairy farmers. Joan's parents married in 1934 and she was born soon thereafter.[8]

There is no recollection among Joan's side of the family of any Wisconsin family member having returned to visit Bohemia since the migration of the 1850s. In 1979, I was assigned to the U.S. delegation to attend an international conference in Vienna. Since I would be traveling on a diplomatic passport, it would be easy to arrange for travel behind the Iron Curtain into Czechoslovakia after the conference ended. We secured visas for Joan and me to travel to what was then a part of the U.S.S.R.

Thus in August 1979, we departed Vienna by bus for Bratislava, then by train for Prague. Our route to Bohemia took us to Plzeň and Domažlice, then Mrákov and Kaut, the villages from whence Joan's ancestors came.

We were to spend our first night in Prague. We had made hotel reservations through Intourist, the official state travel agency of the Soviet Union. On arrival late at night, the desk clerk claimed he had no reservation in our name. We assured him the reservation had been confirmed but he could not be moved until I placed a U.S. ten dollar bill into my passport and slipped the passport to him through the protective screen on his window.

---

8 Joan has prepared an unpublished family history, reconstructing such information as she found to be available, covering the period 1850 to 1949 for Denmark, Wisconsin. See Annex 2.

I then asked him to check again. Well what do you know? He found the reservation! That was our introduction to the "Workers' Paradise".

We stopped at the Prague Jewish Museum and at the synagogue. We saw the children's drawings made during World War II while they were being held in the concentration camps awaiting shipment to the gas chambers. We also visited the Saint Vitus Cathedral with its magnificent stained glass windows. When we tried to get tickets to that evening's performance at the Opera House, there too, we found a small racket was in process. Before we could reach the ticket window, one of the custodial employees approached us and offered to provide us with two tickets to that evening's performance. If we could just come to the performance someone would be waiting with our tickets. We agreed to do that and did not buy tickets at the sales window. Later, when we arrived, the same woman was waiting for us and escorted us to prime seats in the orchestra. We paid cash and no tickets were provided. Soon thereafter, another opera house staff person rushed to our seat to tell us that they had made a mistake and escorted us to two other, equally fine seats, a few rows away. As we seated ourselves in the new location, we saw two well-dressed men being led to the seats we had just vacated. It seems the deal was this: prominent communist party functionaries would hold reserve seats at these performances but rarely show up. The staff would "sell" these seats to tourists and pockets the money. If the functionary showed up, the tourist was moved to another seat.

We took the train to **Plzeň**, the heart of Bohemia, and spent a day trying to locate someone who might be genetically linked to Joan's family. Looking through the phone book, we saw two numbers listed under Joan's maiden name, Fogltanz, by the old spelling of Vogeltanz. We phoned one of those numbers and there was an immediate offer to help. It was fortunate that I could still negotiate a bit of German because nobody spoke English. The man had just come home from work at the Skoda Plant, was embarrassed to receive us while still in his work clothes and virtually swooned at the thought that we were from his long departed family that had moved to America many years before.

However, it soon became clear that there was no family link between Joan and him. Nevertheless, he was eager to help us in our quest. He told us that the Vogeltanzes came from the village of **Mrakov**, located near the district headquarters of **Domažlice**. That was very helpful because Joan's relatives in Wisconsin did not have a clue from where their ancestors hailed, other than the general area of Bohemia. We then planned the next phase of the trip; a train to Domažlice.

Meanwhile we were beginning to take notice of our surroundings. The farmlands appeared to have poor and stunted fields of grain, with very short corn stalks. There were no animals to be seen; they were kept inside the barns and not allowed to forage. The farmlands had been taken from the farmers and turned into collectives. The farmers were then hired by (or became members of) the collective as workers just as though the big farm was a factory. Plum trees along the roadside had signs nearby that informed passers-by that the trees and their fruit were state property and it was against the law for people to pick the plums. It was a system that did not provide incentives for farmers to exert themselves.

We found it easy to strike up conversations with people once they knew we were tourists although the language was a problem. Hardly anyone spoke English. Our conversations would pass through four levels. First everything was beautiful and wonderful. Once a bit of confidence built up, there was curiosity about us. From which country did we come? How is it there? Where were we going? Once it was established we were not dangerous to talk with, there came an outpouring of complaints about life dominated by the Russians and their local stooges. Finally, there would be the invitation to change money.

Conversations with people in the parks or on Sunday picnic grounds suggested that the lowest paid worker received not less than one-fourth the wages of a top paid worker. In comparing the wages of, say, a taxi driver and a doctor, that four to one ratio seemed to hold. However, since doctors were very important to the life of a family, it had become customary for patients to bring the doctor valuable gifts just to be sure the doctor would do a good job. For the physician, clothing of choice was a pair of imported jeans, worn by those who were willing to pay a hundred dollars apiece. That practice certainly had an impact on the theoretical four to one ratio of earned income. Most of the locals had some sort of way to game the system. So far as we tourists were concerned, the food was excellent; beer was cheap as well as delicious, and hotel rates were reasonable.

Our train ride to Domažlice was uneventful except for the fact that life at the train station at 6:15 am was a lot busier than we expected. We wanted to get some coffee and entered the station's large dining room only to find maybe fifty men sitting at tables sipping their beer and eating cold speck for breakfast.

Domažlice has a very small town square, sort of like a set design for a *Wizard of Oz* play. The staff of the District Commission tried to be helpful in opening to us the birth records. But it turned out that there was a twenty-year gap in the records for the period of 1820-1840, the very time frame for which we were seeking information. The local staff confirmed that Mrákov was the principal village of the Vogeltanz clan. They also identified **Kaut** as the town from whence the Schleis family, Joan's mother's side of the family, would have come.

We decided to visit Mrákov first. It was a three-mile walk. There was a well-marked trail through the forest that took us past a cemetery. We peered through the fence to see wall-to-wall graves of Vogeltanzes. There were no older gravestones – from the 1800s; it looked like the cemetery had been layered. Once they ran out of space, the next graves would be set on top of the previous layer. Onward we marched on the path. Soon the small village of Mrákov appeared. The promontory of the town was the church. We entered and found the priest, a jovial, roly-poly, smiling specimen of peaceful humanity who spoke very respectable German. He was delighted to be of help to us in our quest to find some of Joan's family linkages. He immediately walked down the short street to a house and introduced us to an eighty-year old woman named Vogeltanz. I took one look at her and immediately saw a resemblance to Romy, my father in law. But the priest then pointed out to me that Vogeltanz was her married name. Her maiden name was not that and she did not even come from the village.

While it was interesting to see this village and speak to its inhabitants, we were no closer to finding family links than before we arrived in Czechoslovakia. As we began our farewells, the priest gave us one enormous kolatch, a famous Bohemian pastry filled with cottage cheese and fruit. We offered to pay for it but he would not accept any remuneration. Joan said we would like to make a contribution to the "poor box" but he refused that as well, telling us to enjoy the pastry on our trip back to Domažlice. Finally, we asked if there was something he would like from us that we could give him to show our appreciation for all of his kindnesses. He then smiled and said, "Please remember us at Christmas. Send us a Christmas greeting card. We would so enjoy receiving that." When Joan and I returned to Wisconsin and told the family about our trip, we provided the international mailing address of the priest in Mrákov and asked Joan's relatives to send a Christmas greeting to him.

VIENNA, SALZBURG, PARIS – CHRISTMAS 2002

Dear Family:

It is now almost two weeks since our return from this remarkable trip; enough time to have absorbed the bumps along the way and to allow the truly outstanding experiences to stand out. So here is a rundown of the events.

First, you have to know that your mother's description of the trip (wonderful) is quite sincere and accurate. She loved every moment of it, notwithstanding the cast on her broken wrist. She was particularly struck by Paris, and wants to spend a lot of time there in the near future. But she really appreciated the trip as a whole, and also each one of its parts. My pleasure index is somewhat less, say at the 90% level, but still well into the positive range.

We met Jul, Tony, Kristy, Rebecca and Susannah at the Paris airport, boarded the flight to Vienna; met Jeff, Madeleine, Christopher and Emily at the Vienna Airport at noon on Dec 23. Transport was standing by and we were quickly ensconced in the huge Intercontinental Hotel. (An enormous, luxurious breakfast served to 900 people daily). A quick trip to the bank by Jul, Tony and me to withdraw Euros and we were ready to go. Jul took his role as tour director very seriously. Baton in hand, he led us through the entire trip, including his selection of favorite eating places. Occasionally there was resistance from one of the grandchildren and, only to these protests, did he make serious accommodation.

The schedule was as follows:

Dec 23 -A walk through the Rathousplatz Christmas market and then through downtown area to dinner at The Griechenbeisl (unremarkable) and early to bed.

Dec 24 - Breakfast on which we gorged ourselves; train to Schonbrunn (magnificent opulence as the Kaiser's summer palace). A walk through the old Jewish section (Judenplatz) and marvelous soup at a Schtube just before they closed for Christmas. Christmas Eve seven course dinner for 11 in a private dining room at the exclusive hotel "Konig von Ungarn" with some really remarkable wine. A walk through downtown Vienna back to the hotel.

December 25 - Another enormous breakfast. Walk to the Hoffburg Chapel to do Christmas Mass, listening to the Vienna Boys Choir do the Haydn. Then, a streetcar ride to the Cemetery to visit our father's grave and that of grandmother Sonnenblum. The

Statsoper to see Magic Flute followed by dinner for 12 at the Café Mozart.

December 26 - Breaskfast as usual. Visit to Leopold Museum. Afternoon Private bus tour to Jul's old Vienna haunts, including the Prater and a ride on the Riesenrad, the apartment buildings where our parents (and Grandparents) lived from 1918 to 1927, before our parents moved upscale to 16 Kandlgasse. Then by private bus to Kaltenleutgeben and finally to Grinzing for a great meal.

December 27 - (Friday) The Grants leave for Italy. The rest go to 16 Kandlgasse. A walk around the neighborhood. Then, photos for the article Tony is writing about Jul. Dinner at a restaurant that serves the largest Wiener Schnitzel in the world.

Dec 28 - Train to **Salzburg**. Rooms for seven at the Sacher Hotel. A walk through this fairy tale town; dinner at Eulenspiegel followed by Kaiserschmarn but no Salzburger Nokerl. This was then followed by a very difficult night for me and Joan. This one-armed wonderful wife of mine had to clean up after me. If you have to get sick on the road, it is best to do it at a five star hotel.

Dec 29 - Exploration of Salzburg by all but me. All but Joan and I go to visit Marcel Pravi, the 91 year old Austrian who arranged for Jul to conduct "Kiss Me Kate" at the Vienna Volksoper in 1956. Jul sends a portion of Salzburger Nokerl up to Joan in the room.

Dec 30 - The Maurice Ravel train to **Paris**. Rooms at the Scribe Hotel one block from the old Opera. Dinner at another superb restaurant.

December 31 - Walk to La Madeleine, the Louvre, lunch at Goldberg's deli in Marais district. Joan and I ran into Jackie Boehm on a street corner (small world). New Years Dinner in a private dining room at another great restaurant. This time it is Rebecca who gets sick.

Jan 1 - Exploration of Montmartre, The Sacre Cour, and the Eifel Tower. Another dinner, this time at a Brasserie.

Jan 2 - The New York Rudels leave early. Joan and I walk to Place de la Concorde, across the Seine in brilliant sunlight, the Louvre again and back to the hotel. We return to Washington.

And now, the highlights:

There are many memorable highlights from this wonderful trip. Walking at night across the lighted bridge to the Sacher hotel in the Fairyland called Salzburg; window-shopping along the Boulevards in Paris; looking out of the cabin on the Riesenrad at the city of Vienna; eating a wurstl with mustard in the cold while standing in the snow covered streets of Vienna; entering the railroad stations that must have been our departure point from Vienna in 1938. But the most significant experiences were these:

The apartment at 16 Kandlgasse - Not much changes in Europe. Here it is, almost 65 years later, and the shop selling coal and firewood (where we were customers in the 1930s) is still operating on the street level of our apartment house. The cobblestones which were on the street 65 years ago have been evened out and placed there again, perhaps laid on another of their six sides. And the apartment, which now has central heat, looks very much the same. The cabinets, the doors, the windows - pretty much the same. It is now occupied by a Greek woman and her daughter, working for a Greek Travel Agency. They were very gracious, served tea and cookies and made us feel very much at home. That apartment is where I spent the first 8 years of my life. I could still visualize how it looked then. The piano; the dining table, the small table in the anti-room with the needlepoint and crochet table cloth hand-made by my mother that is now hanging on Joanna's wall. My crib and Jul's bed. A place for our toys such as the matador set.

Kaltenleutgeben - About 30 km. out of Vienna where we summered for two years. The sanitorium where my father recuperated from his first operation is now an apartment complex. As our bus drove through the town we asked a passing woman that was probably in her 60s if she could direct us to the sanitarium. She boarded the bus to direct us and we told her why we were there. She said there were photos dating from before the war that were used to make a calendar about the town and offered to collect these photos for us. I gave her some money and my mailing address and asked her to be kind enough to mail them to me. The next day, there was a call from hotel reception that the woman had come to the hotel to deliver the pictures. I rushed down and spoke with her and accepted the pictures. She offered to return the money and I told her to give it to someone who is needy. I don't think I would have done as much as she did to meet our request, for someone else under the same circumstances.

The Opera - What a magnificent structure! And what grand acoustics. The production staging was too far out for me but I thought the music and singing was good and said so to Tony and Jul. This got me a lot of "egg on my face" because they were highly displeased with the whole show (except for Mozart). So much for buying 11 tickets at $160 per. Then off to the Café Mozart around the corner from the Opera for a magnificent meal.

So now, the editorial commentary:

As you know, Joan and I were Jul's guests on this trip and he was very gracious. Tony was so solicitous of Jul's needs that I thought he might suffer a heart attack.

Both Jul and I recognize that, had there not been a Holocaust or Nazi annexation of Austria or World War II, our lives (and, I guess yours too) would have been very different and most assuredly less affluent. Our migration in 1938 to the U.S. provided opportunities for economic and social betterment that would simply not have been available to us in Europe. Jul thinks he might have been a music teacher. I do not know what to think about my own career there. The risks posed by historical events (World War II) were very high for us. We could have been turned into bars of soap. Instead, we won the lottery and wound up as citizens of this country.

Both Jul and I have it in our minds that we have an Austrian heritage. Jul was born in Vienna in 1921. I followed in 1930. So all that Viennese stuff is in our blood. Right? Well, maybe! Taking the long view, our ancestors came from parts of Poland that, at the time of partition in 1793 or shortly thereafter, fell under Russian domination. The Russians were notoriously anti-Semitic. Our ancestors migrated out of those areas to a province of the Austria-Hungarian Empire called Bukowina (located near the Ukrainian border) where there was far greater tolerance of Jews. They thrived there until the end of World War I (1918) when the Austro-Hungarian Empire was dismantled and Bukowina was given to Rumania. Again they picked up their things and moved to Vienna. Three years after my parents arrival in Vienna, Jul was born. And we left Austria in 1938. So how deep do our ancestral roots run in Vienna? Don't we better fit the mold of the "Wandering Jew"?

That view allows one to appreciate that Jews have found refuge and opportunities in a variety of "Empires" throughout history. None of these has demonstrated a capacity for permanent dominance. Many of us have now found a home in the U.S. But we need to understand that this country also does not have a permanent lock on world dominance. Things can and will change. There are some lessons here.

With love, Dad February 2003

RETURN TO MY 1938 ESCAPE ROUTE: CROATIA, RIJEKA, OPATIJA AND THE DALMATIAN COAST – 2009

The Dalmatian Coastline along the Adriatic Sea is one of the most beautiful parts of this planet. It has a rich history, including the period following the Spanish expulsion of the Muslims and Jews in 1492. The latter, fleeing the Inquisition, sought and were granted refuge in cities like Dubrovnik, Split, Zadar, Trogir and Hvar.

Joan and I flew into Dubrovnik, a marvelously well-preserved ancient city with an illustrious history. We drank beer in the main square, walked along the ancient wall of the city, heard a quartet play Mozart, ate well and explored the old parts of the city. The synagogue was erected in 1652 but the Jewish community's presence dates back to 1492, when the Spanish refugees were given land in the city and invited to settle.

Today, we see that the entire city is organized to separate the tourist from his money. We noted that the pedestrians make no eye contact with strangers and seem rough around the edges, unlike the Austrians who appear to be more polished. The men are usually muscular and macho in body language. Strength seems to be valued as with the "knights of old."

Leaving Dubrovnik, we traveled by bus along the coast. Stopping overnight at Split we went to a double performance at the opera house (*Sister Anjelika* and *Gianni Schichi*). We then proceeded by ferry to Hvar to celebrate our forty-seventh wedding anniversary.

We loved the Dalmatian coastal towns, the scenery, the touristic attractions and the ease of life enjoyed by the native population. But our principal destination was further up the coast: Rijeka, once called Fiume prior to World War II while it had been occupied by the Italians.

My mother and I had escaped to Rijeka from Vienna by train in June 1938 (see volume one) and were taken into hiding in the nearby town of Opatija, then called Abatzija. Ruthann had been scheduled to attend a conference in Europe and agreed to meet us in Opatija for a few days in search of family history. We arrived in Opatija on May 26 and met up with Ruthann. The next day, we traveled back to Rijeka and located the synagogue, which was closed, it being mid-day on a Wednesday. We were able to contact a member, Filip, who willingly came from his home to meet us. It seems to be the practice to meet wandering Jewish tourists who have an interest in seeing the synagogue and give them a tour in the hope of eliciting a financial contribution.

When Filip began his presentation, I interrupted him to say I had a story to tell him. And then the fun began. I related our escape and the help we received from one of Rijeka's Jewish businessmen in finding a hiding place. I asked him whether he might know how I could find out the name of the person who had saved our lives. He then led me into the synagogue and pointed to a tablet mounted on the wall listing four hundred and one names. It was a complete list of every Jew who was a member of the synagogue before the war. All had been killed. Filip asked that I write to him and send him the story. Here is the message I sent to him:

> Subject: RUDEL VISIT MAY 27, 2009
> June 9, 2009
> Dear Filip:
> Thank you for taking the time to show me the synagogue in Rijeka last week and also for listening to my story about my escape from Austria in 1938.
> I promised to write about my escape, and the help my mother and I received from someone in your community at that time. This message is in response to that promise.
> Here is my story.
> The German ANSCHLUSS with Austria occurred on March 12, 1938. Treatment of Jews in Austria got worse and worse over the next few months and it culminated with Christalnacht burnings of every synagogue in Vienna in November 1938.
> My father died at end 1937 and so my mother, at age 43, found herself to be a widow with two sons, one age 17 and one (me) age 8. I was no longer allowed to attend my neighborhood school after the Anschluss and was supposed to travel daily to a school in the

Jewish section of Vienna (Second District). My mother thought it too dangerous for me to do so and she made arrangements with a tutor to come daily to our apartment (16 Kandlgasse in the 7th District) to teach me. In June I went to that special school in the second district one day to take an exam to complete my class work and obtain my report card.

My mother managed to send my older brother out of Vienna to the USA on June 1, 1938. Then, she packed up what she could and we left Vienna by train in late June for Italy. When we crossed the border and were checked by Italian immigration, they informed us that Jews were not allowed to enter Italy. Since we left Austria illegally, being sent back would have been the end for us.

They took us off the train at Udine and put us on another train back to the border. Fortunately, that train was a local and it went to the border but did not cross over to Austria. We were taken off the train and put under guard, awaiting the next train that would take us back into Austria.

My mother then bribed the guards (she had some jewelry in her purse and also Austrian cigarettes that were better than Italian cigarettes) and persuaded the guards to let us proceed to transit through Italy to France. We assured the guards that we would not exit the train but take it to France. Actually, we took the train out of the station and then changed to a train to Fiume.

She wanted to get to Fiume because she had been given the name of a Jewish businessman there. I should also explain that she had been successful in obtaining visas for us to enter the USA but these visas were not valid until October 1938. We needed to hide out until October. It was only late June.

When we arrived at the train station, we placed our luggage into the "left luggage" window and walked to the businessman's work address. I do not remember the name of the person who helped us.

He asked if we had registered at a hotel and we told him that we had not done so. He said that if we had registered at a hotel, we would have been required to fill out a police record card which is sent to the police the next morning. He then said that the only place where we could stay would be at a Sanitarium because the people who register to stay there are not reported to the police. He then made some arrangement on the telephone and took us to pick up our luggage and took us to Abbatziya. I think the story was that I was recovering from whooping cough and needed rest. We stayed at the sanitarium for 6 or 7 weeks until my mother was able to obtain a Swiss visa.

During our recent visit to Opatija I think we located the sanitarium where we stayed. The Opatija Hotel has been remodeled but the old front entrance, which is no longer in use, looks like the place where I stayed. Perhaps my story could be confirmed by examining the admission records of that sanitarium. My mother's name was Josefine (Pepi) Rudel. Her maiden name was Sonnenblum. My full name is Ludwig Rudel. If you want to know more about me, you can Google me or my brother. His name is Julius Rudel and he is a musician (conductor).

Our stay at the sanitarium was marked by being careful and not being exposed to view too much. I think an 8 year old does not like to be kept out of sight and so I probably caused my mother some unhappiness as I insisted on leaving our room. I think the staff was not trusted to know that we were fugitives.

I believe that the help we received from the businessman in Fiume in June 1938 saved my mother's and my life. I wonder who that businessman might have been. Perhaps the Jewish community of Rijeka might have some record of actions taken by their members to help fleeing Jews at that time. You showed me the names of the 401 members who themselves were killed during the Holocaust. Perhaps it was one of them. Probably there was a Jewish doctor that was associated with the sanitarium. The businessman might have consulted him about admitting me there.

That is the story. My mother and I were very lucky to have survived. In situations like that, some people will risk their own safety to help someone in need. The Jewish community in Rijeka should take pride in what some of their members did in those days.

Many thanks for your kindnesses during the visit of my wife and me last month. I would appreciate hearing from you as to whether the information in this story can be confirmed by any records to which you can secure access. And also whether the identity of the businessman can be discovered. If you can think of any additional information I might provide, please let me know. If you have any success in learning any more about my experience in 1938, please let me know.

Lu Rudel

We spent another day in the area and then traveled by train, for nine hours, back to Vienna to give Ruthann a tour of the city, including the various haunts where I had spent my childhood. Too soon, it was time to return home.

BUKOWINA: UKRAINE, AUSTRIA– SEARCHING FOR DEEPER ROOTS– 2010

Hello Children and Grandchildren:

Hope you are well. How does your new life style at Pratt Institute suit you, Wolfie?

If you wish to follow our travels on the map, here is a summary of our route. We began our travels in Vienna, Austria and enjoyed 5 days in the city where Uncle Jul and Lu were born. Then by train further east to Krakow, Poland, a beautiful city that had not been damaged by the fighting during World War II. Four days wandering around and learning about that wonderful city with our friends, the Rosners who met us there. Then, east again by train and bus, to the Ukraine and the city of L'viv, formerly called Lemberg. (We will describe that day of travel and border crossing in detail - it was an experience of a lifetime.) After a weekend in L'viv, a taxi ride for 200 miles southeast to Cernivtsi, formerly called Czernowitz during the rule of the Austro-Hungarian Empire until the Empire collapsed in 1918 after the end of the First World War. That was our primary destination. Finally, a trip to Odessa, on the Black sea and then the return flight to Vienna.

As you might remember, the purpose of this trip was to come to Cernivtsi to search out my "roots". Both my mother and father (the grandparents of our three children) were born in Bojan, a small town about 7 miles from Cernivtsi along the Prut river. And my father's parents and his great-grandparents are buried here. But the trip was all the more fascinating because we could see the differences in the cultures and the behavior of the people as we moved eastward.

I wanted to see the landscape of the area around Bojan and Cernivtsi to better visualize the scenery my parents would have seen and the community in which they grew up. I always wondered what life was like for them before they moved to Vienna during the First World War.

We have often spoken to you about Vienna so we will be very brief about our stay there except to say we went to the opening of the Vienna State Opera season by buying standing room for the performance of Wagner's Tannhauser. Four and a half hours on the feet! But the young kids around us were lots of fun to speak with. This was Joan's first time seeing Tannhauser and she loved it. The singing was very good and the music, even though Wagnerian, was very melodic. We also attended a Mozart concert in a beautiful concert hall – all gold and highly decorated. The musicians and singers wore costumes and everyone was quite mediocre. Walking back to our pension after the concert we pass a bar and one of the customers was singing an aria. He was better than what we heard in the concert hall. Do you think it is possible to walk by a bar in the US and hear someone singing an opera aria???

We visited the cemetery on the outskirts of Vienna, as we usually do, to visit my father's grave (it is your great-grandfather's grave if you are one of "the eight cousins"). We spent about a day and a half at the Belvedere Museum which is made up of two palaces and large gardens that had been lived in by Prince Eugene in the 18th century. We attended a mass, featuring Mozart's Ursuline Mass.

———⊶⊷———

Krakow, Poland: After a 6 hour train ride from Vienna to Krakow, we met our friends, Lee Rosner and Kay Chernush. Our hotel was very central, just a few steps from the large and beautiful city square. We spent half a day in the old Jewish section of the city. At one time Krakow had approximately 68 synagogues and many Jews, but of course the synagogues were destroyed by the Nazis (and Poles) and the Jews were killed. We spent a lot of time in the remaining "old synagogue" which has been turned into an excellent museum. We ate in student restaurants as well as upscale restaurants. Saw a good performance at the local music school.

———⊶⊷———

Lee Rosner's mother was born in a small town in eastern Poland. His father was born in a small town near Cernivtsi. He wanted to learn about these places, just like me. We left Krakow by train at 8 am and got off in a town called **Lancut** (pronounced "winset", … go figure!) about 4 hours later. At the train station we stored our luggage and hired a taxi to take us to Lee's mother's village (**Zolynya**). After visiting Zolynya we toured around Lancut, had lunch, collected our luggage and got on a train at 3 pm going further east to the city just before the Ukrainian border.

Off the train with our luggage. Joan with her big pack on her back and her small pack on her front! I with a small pack on my back and pulling my suitcase on wheels along! We caught a 22 seat mini-bus to the border. After we had boarded the bus, the driver just sat there, without starting the engine. After a while, I asked why we were not moving and the driver motioned at the three empty seats, unwilling to proceed until he had a fare payment for each seat. We gave him the fare for the empty seats and then he began the short drive to the border. Again we loaded up the luggage on our backs and began the long hike to the border control building. First the Polish exit control, then through "no man's land" and to the Ukrainian arrival control. A lot of standing on line, waiting. Finally we were admitted and walked a little more to another bus (about 30 seats plus a lot of standees) that would take us to L'viv in the Ukraine. It is the city where our friend Eric Griffel was born. That ride took 2 hours. By the time we arrived at the Grand Hotel, one of the top hotels in L'viv, and turned the luggage over to the door man, we were really tired and smelling plenty bad!

This way of crossing the border is the cheapest way to do it. Most people who use that route are students or are quite poor. We got to talking with a man who clearly was something of an intellectual, perhaps a professor at a University, and he knew enough English to give us some useful directions in the course of our border crossing. We were modestly dressed and he thought us to be quite poor, as we are sure he was. When we got near L'viv he offered to help us find a cheap hotel. When we told him we had reservations at the Grand Hotel, he just burst out in laughter. These crazy Americans!

We only stayed a couple of days in **L'viv** and found it to be a thriving, beautiful city. It is very difficult traveling in the Ukraine. No one speaks English and all the street signs and writing is in Cyrillic. But the weather has cooperated and so we have very little to complain about. The four of us went to the L'viv Opera House to see Fledermaus. It was a respectable performance even though it seems to have been Ukraine-ized to change the behavior of the characters from that depicted in the opera.

Departing L'viv by private car with Andre, our driver, at 8 am on September 13, we drove east and a little south in the direction of Cernivtsi, the city where my parents were born in the 1880s and raised prior to World War I. We also scheduled stops at Ivano-Frankivsk, Kolomya and Kosiv, enroute. The driver spoke no English but was in contact with Natasha, our multi-lingual guide with his trusty cell phone so we were able to communicate easily via Natasha. The car was comfortable, Kay and Lee were excellent company and we thoroughly enjoyed the ride, except for the pit stops which were smelly and less than sanitary.

Ivano-Frankivsk is about halfway to Cernivtsi. Andre did not know the city and we wasted a bit of time driving around looking for the Synagogue, found it to be locked, walked around the pedestrian mall, saw the old buildings of Hapsburg architecture and then moved on. Before 1918 this area was part of Austria-Hungary. Not much to report.

In **Kolomya** we stopped at the synagogue (run by Lubavitchers) where morning prayers were in process with only seven Jews participating. A "minyan" of 10 is supposed to be the minimum for a service but that did not seem to deter them (as Lee said, "they do the best they can"). The synagogue was set up with a separate section behind a wall for women (none were in evidence) and this image did not sit well with Joan and Kay. The synagogue had been rebuilt and the interior was quite modern. We went to the town center, ate a picnic lunch at the square and moved on.

The stop in **Kosiv** was to let Lee view his father's place of birth. Lee's father left Kosiv as a young boy to immigrate to the USA around 1909. There we found a spot on a hill (after Andre inquired of some pedestrians) with a commemorative plaque in Hebrew for the atrocity committed there. Apparently the entire Jewish community of Kosiv was rounded up by the Germans with Rumanian help in 1940 and were killed there. It was a solemn moment for us. Later, we drove to the Jewish cemetery in town. It had a fence around it and the grave sites were under heavy foliage and weeds. There are no survivors to tend to these graves. Still, someone was trying to keep paths open around the grounds. Lee and Kay climbed over the fence and explored the cemetery for several minutes while we respectfully kept our distance.

———∞———

At 6 pm, after a long day, we arrived in **Cernivtsi** at the Magnat Lux Hotel – pleasant enough, shiny silky sofa and bed covering, no shower curtain, one reading light. Natasha was waiting for us. We checked in, washed up and went to dinner with Natasha at the nearby Knause restaurant to enjoy local beer, eat some pyrogi and plan our visit. Natasha made an odd impression. She is short, stout, has a round smiling face with good blond hair and speaks excellent English. We had no trouble communicating. She was an excellent guide, referred to us by someone who is active in the "searching for roots business", Ed Hauster, of the Netherlands. But still, in the first day of our stay, she had followed her set routine for conducting tours. We had to bear with a lot of explanation of the touristic wonders of the city (the buildings of the city square; the university, etc.) before we could plan to make our first trip to the cemetery.

Both of my parents were born in a small town about 7 miles outside Cernivtsi called Bojan. I thought that the Bojan cemetery would be the place to look for my great-grandparents' graves. Nevertheless we went to the Czernowitz cemetery as well because, as the old joke goes, that was more easily accessible. Surprise! The records of that cemetery did reveal some interesting things. The original "Rudel" who was sent by the Galician Rabbis with a wagon driver, to get him out of the Cholera epidemic area in 1833 (named Leiser) seems to have died in 1914 and is buried in Czernowitz. We have a certificate but that name showed up as Leiser RUBEL. Then, we found another grave very close to Leiser's, with what looks like the name RIVKA RUDEL, probably Leiser's wife (and the wagon driver's daughter.) My father's parents are also buried in the Czernowitz cemetery. The records show that, and cousin Rita in Israel confirms this, but that section of the cemetery is overgrown. We could not find the graves.

There are about 200 Jews still living in Cernivtsi today. We visited a synagogue and spoke to the Rabbi. He has been Rabbi here for 18 years and is a native of Ukraine but had little information for us. The old Jewish section of Cernivtsi was next to the Turkish section. The mikve was turned into a Turkish bath and is active today.

We then visited **Bojan** (pronounced Boyan). The town is located downstream from Cernivtsi along the Prut river and is quite close to the border with Moldavia and Rumania. There is nothing "old" there. It is now a modern town with new, lavish, quite ugly, single family homes that Natasha explains are being built with repatriations from overseas workers. I suspect it is more likely to be the result of smuggling profits. There was nothing to identify any old sections of the village where my parents were born. We stopped near a house to take photos and the owner (Greshia) came out to find out what we were up to. Natasha translated and we learned that there were no Jews living in Bojan now. Greshia became very friendly and offered to show us where the Bojan Jewish cemetery was located. It was high on a hill, in agricultural and currently tilled land. He came with us (we never would have found it otherwise) and it revealed nothing. It was heavily overgrown. Indeed, a new wall had been erected by some international volunteers who have devoted themselves to preserving Jewish cemeteries in these remote areas. It has kept farmers from cultivating the land. (We found evidence of plants that had been harvested there before the wall was erected.)

Greshia also took us to the Prut River. It was a lot farther than I thought, based on my mother's comments about the area. The Prut empties into the Danube before the Danube enters the Black Sea.

I was disappointed in the visit to Bojan. There was nothing left to see of the "old" town, and the "new" town was truly depressing. The main industry there is a soft drink factory to compete with the likes of imported Coke.

I try to imagine my parents' and grandparents' mindset before and during World War One. On my mother's side, the Sonnenblums were reasonably well to do, upstanding citizens of Bojan and my grandfather had owned the town granary which was burned down during the war. He and his six children see the Hapsburg Empire implode. The protections that Jews enjoyed under the Hapsburgs for centuries, would have now seemed imperiled. The territory probably would have been ceded to Russia if there had been no revolution there in 1917 but now likely will go to Rumania. He decides, even before the Versailles Treaty, to uproot and move to Vienna and start a new life there.

On my father's side, his brother (Nathan) and parents opt to stay in Czernowitz where the elderly grandparents will suffer through the

German occupation, only to die in 1944. Nathan and family survive the Second World War and then move to Israel.

After serving as an officer in the Austro-Hungarian army during the war, my father moves to Vienna in 1918 simply because he was pursuing my mother as a love interest. They marry in Vienna. Julius is born in 1921; I in 1930. One by one, the Sonnenblum siblings move from Vienna to the USA during the 1920s. My grandfather follows them in 1935 after my grandmother's death.

This scenario helps me understand the kind of uncertainty many other Europeans must have felt at the end of the First World War. It goes a long way to explain the events of the 1920s and early 1930s, as societies that had been run by monarchs for more than 300 years, suddenly find themselves compelled to create new governmental systems.

Cernivtsi had such a large Jewish population in 1939 that the mayor persuaded the Germans not to exterminate them right away because the Jews were the only ones who knew how to run the key city services. Today ... Cernivtsi has the feel of a dead city in a remote area of a country that can barely govern itself. Residents of Cernivtsi might well feel nostalgia for the Hapsburg rule of the period 1850 to 1914.

Before departing Bukowina for Odessa, Joan and I took a side trip to **Kamenets Podolski**, about 50 miles from Cernivtsi across an area called Transdniestria - the land between the Prut River and the Dniester River. The bus trip took 2 hours each way and the hotel in Kamenets was quite comfortable and clean once we convinced the manager that we did not want three rooms four flights up in the turret without windows. There was but one other couple staying in the hotel. The sights were something truly amazing. A tributary to the Dniester river makes a sharp, almost 360 degree circle around approximately 300 acres. This virtual island has cliffs of rock

(Kamenets), thereby making it a natural fortress. Over the centuries, various armies laid siege and some, like the Turks, conquered the island and thus controlled the area. The fortress on top of this land is in relatively fine shape and we enjoyed the scenery and let our imaginations wander. Then back to Cernivtsi to catch our over-night train to Odessa, Ukraine.

Odessa is a large city on the Black Sea. The train trip lasted 19 hours. We had no way to figure out the train's route ahead of time so ... what a surprise... the route took us back (northwest) to L'viv and then again southeast on another track to Odessa on the Black Sea. The peculiar train routing results from the fact that the original routing, through Moldova, is now considered unsafe for travelers. Moldova is something of a failed state. We took the top of the line accommodations on the train and that gave Joan and me a private compartment with sleeper. But the toilet (if one may call it that!) was at the end of the car. The equivalent of the old time Pullman porter was in charge of our car. He was dressed in a natty uniform with epaulettes on his shoulders designating his rank and authority. He looked like a two star general to us! And he did absolutely nothing except "control" by taking our ticket when we boarded and returning it to us as we exited. Oh yes. He also made tea (and charged for it). But at least we were secure for the night. There was no dining car but Joan anticipated that and brought provisions, including water.

At nine am on Monday, September 20 the train pulled into Odessa Station, right on time. We walked to our hotel, the "Black Sea", which was only about 10 minutes from the station. It was a rainy, foggy, gloomy day and Odessa looked grim.

The Black Sea hotel was a concrete block with holes in it, made into small rooms. It was a typical Russian hotel and was a little short on maintenance. But it was clean enough and conveniently located at the edge of the center city area on the same street with the Opera House. The hotel service was fine in that they left us alone. There was an excellent Japanese restaurant in the hotel.

We declined to take a formal city tour and did not regret it. The downtown area was small enough that we could walk it with no difficulty. The big market and the old Jewish section was near the train station. We were directed to the bus and tram that traveled along the Black Sea in each direction from Odessa center. We had learned to read the Cyrillic and did not get lost. As for the rest of the city, in the words of the hotel desk clerk, there was "No reason to go there".

Odessa was a city built on the Black Sea at the instruction of Catherine II in early 1800, just as St. Petersburg had been built several years before, as a port on the Baltic, by Peter the Great. St. Petersburg was intended to be a "window to the West." Odessa was Russia's warm water port. Nature reserves and bird watching are to be found outside of Odessa. The rail line and roads run north – south and connect it primarily to Kiev. The city has a long history of semi-independence from Russian micro-management, due to its remoteness. The Tsar exiled intellectuals to Odessa, on the assumption they could not cause much trouble for him from this backwater. As a result, it has a rich heritage of dissidents sent here who made major contributions to the intellectual life of Russia. Their writings are, even now, valued around the world. There is an important "Literary Museum" here which chronicles some of these contributions. A knowledge of Russian is needed to benefit from these original texts. The museum features writings of Pushkin, Babel, Gogol, Chekhov, Herzen. And, of course, the Eisenstein film "Potempkin" about the mutiny in 1905, features the "steps" leading down to the harbor.

The architecture is a mix of Hapsburg and Russian. The old buildings and palaces, many of them restored or in process, makes the more recent construction look bad. The worker's housing blocks and the hotel in which we stayed was pretty awful but the old buildings made up for it.

The Opera House has been fully rebuilt and is beautiful. We saw a very creditable performance of Turandot there (except for the terrible visuals introduced in this production, proving that Ukraine has stage directors that are every bit as crazy as ours) and also a ballet performance of Swan Lake. Then we went to the Philharmonia Hall to hear the local orchestra do Mahler's First Symphony. That was a mistake! But at least they tried!

Food at restaurants is, by and large, good, and features borsht, pirogi or varanishkas, stuffed peppers, potato pancakes and blini. Those restaurants trying to go upscale just could not pull it off. The Turkish culture is ever present here, since that country lies just across the Black Sea. We found an excellent Turkish restaurant near the hotel. The synagogue had been completely rebuilt and had a kosher restaurant in its basement that was open to the public. There is a Jewish community of about 30,000 here in Odessa. We saw no tensions between Muslims and Jews as the orthodox Jews took their evening strolls past the Turkish restaurant sidewalk tables where we ate. Other patrons wore Muslim attire.

The beaches improve as we traveled further from the city. About 10 miles along the coast is Arcadia Beach with good sand. It was reasonably clean. It is a one hlivna (12 cents) tram ride from city center. Many swam although it was starting to get a bit chilly for us.

The city market is about 6 blocks long and features everything from fresh and dried fruits and vegetables to pickles, kraut, wurst and fresh and dried fish. It is truly a sight to see and smell, an uplifting experience for the senses.

Some general comments about Ukrainian life and people. We began the trip in Vienna. The further east we went, the worse things looked. There is a coarseness, a hardness here. These are not gentle people. Very little eye contact on the streets. They seem to push through a crowd in an unfriendly way but it probably is just their way of dealing with each other. The police seem to be of very little help and have an unhealthy swagger of authority in their gait. One has the impression the government gives these uniforms (power) to the wrong people. Yet, most people (not all) will go out of their way to help if you ask. Others will dismiss you and say they do not understand.

Religion is a big item here. There is a mix of Russian Orthodox, Greek Orthodox, Roman (Polish) Catholic, with a little Baptist, Jewish and Lutheran as well. One has the sense these people are strong believers! The paintings, icons and such are quite severe. The value system features faithfulness to family, clan, group and emphasizes valor, loyalty and power.

Information still seems to be held back and used for advantage in spite of the internet. At the rail station in Cernivtsi, one has to pay the information clerk for each question about train schedules for Odessa. We asked 2 questions and paid 65 cents. They want tourism but they do not make information readily accessible. There appears to be no effort to encourage tourism, except from Russia. Using only Cyrillic letters on their street signs makes it difficult for a tourist from the West.

A significant part of the Ukrainian Gross Domestic Product is apparently comprised of illegal and unsavory activities (prostitution, human trafficking, mail order brides, hacking the internet, smuggling, the arms trade.) It would appear one can buy anything and anyone here. The number of high priced cars (BMW, Mercedes) in the big cities is staggering. We ate lunch at an upscale restaurant and saw two men having drinks while three personal security men hovered around them. At the table next to ours – an American man speaking in an animated fashion (selling?) to two young Ukrainian women. I told Joan it reminded me of my land salesmen at Glendale. A depressing scene. There is a big gap between this BMW group and the income level of the rest of the population. Unemployment is high. Jobs are scarce. 29% live below the poverty line.

I realize, as I make contributions to sections on the Ukraine in this message, that I am prejudiced against this country. There is the remembrance of Babi-Yar, the role of the Ukrainians in killings in Bukowina and similar stories that I have to contend with. And yet, there is the contradiction of stories my cousin Rita told me about Ukrainians who hid her from the Nazis in a potato cellar. Also, the contradictions in behavior by Ukrainians who we asked for guidance on this trip. Some went truly out of their way to respond to us, no matter the difficulties and inconveniences this caused; others shun us like we were pests. Yes; I have to admit it. I am prejudiced.

With Love, Dad October 2010

AUSTRIA AND ITALY - A FINAL TOUR - 2014

Joan and I have often traveled to Austria but, perhaps out of a sense of nostalgia, most of our visits had been focused on Vienna. I particularly enjoy the city's parks, the Vienna Woods, Grinzing, the Habsburg architecture, as well as the food and the music. Sometimes our travels incorporate additional destinations and use land routes to connect with Vienna. For example, one trip to Prague was extended as we traveled by train south to reach the Danube near Krems, spending a few days there before proceeding east to Vienna. Another trip started in Vienna but then took us into Hungary and then southeast to Pecs, Budapest and

Debrecen. And, of course, our travels with Julius and family in 2002 took us to Salzburg. But we had never visited the central and southern areas of Austria.

In the late summer of 2014, Joan and I planned a six-week trip to explore that area. We intended to begin in Vienna, then drive west along the Danube to Krems and Steyr, proceed south across the high mountains to Murau, Villach, Klagenfurt and the Wörthersee. We added a short diversion into northern Italy to visit Venice, Padua, and the surrounding area. Our original grand design unrealistically included a visit to Cinque Terre, the five picturesque Italian villages on the coast between Genoa and Lucca. That portion of the trip turned out to be too much distance for a couple of eighty-year old folks. Finally we would drive back to Vienna. Here are our letters to the family about that trip:

—∞∞∞—

Sunday, Sep 7, 2014, Austrian foothills

I'm sitting under a tree having a beer. We don't precisely know where we are although we can find ourselves on the map, having followed the Enns River to this point. This river was the boundary between the Russian and American Sectors in 1945. As you can see from the accompanying photo, our pension is well located; the scene is the view outside our room. As we drove by on the highway, we saw the sign, "zimmer", drove in and now we are the only occupants of this very large, Bavarian-looking pension; three stories, with every room having a balcony and every balcony having red geraniums in window boxes ...how Austrian can you get?

This is day five of our thirty day car tour, before we head back to Vienna. So far, during the past four days we traveled from Vienna in our Skoda (Czech car) along the Danube (where we had bicycled in 2004) to **Krems**, then to **Melk** and **Steyr** and landed here in this empty pension. A tour group had just departed. The owners are taking care of our every want. I keep wondering aloud what I would have turned out like had there been no Hitler and I had grown up in Austria. I delight in this solitude and the pastoral setting.

The weather has been wonderful. The Danube hills are littered with ruins of castles and ancient fortifications. Krems on the Danube, is where we spent the first night. It is in the middle of vineyards and good white wine is available at about $1.50 a glass. The river is wide and fast flowing with some cruise boats, but mostly boats for public transportation. A few miles down the river is the town of Melk which was having an annual festival, the town square filled with hundreds of picnic tables and hundreds of people, lots of um-pa-pa bands, lots of men in strange uniforms who looked like Nazis and huge quantities of food ...pigs heads, bellies, and roasts in smokers. It tempted Joan, but not me. Late night, the live music changed to loud rock bands. Though our pension was just a block away, our room was quiet. Melk is known for its Benedictine Abbey. It had started as a castle which, in 1089, Leopold II donated to the monks (how to buy your way into heaven). Fire destroyed the abbey and it was rebuilt and enlarged to 500 rooms, has its own church and has imperial rooms in which slept Napoleon, etc., with opulent spires, a dome, smirking cherubs, gilt twirls and polished marble. It stands tall and opulent over the town of Melk!

We sign off for now. Time for dinner. I'm on a varied diet ...wiener schnitzel every night! Auf Wiedersehen! Oma & Opa

---

Trip Report #2

It is Friday, the tenth day of our trip and we are in our apartment in **Villach**, Austria. Today was a particularly interesting day. We drove all along the Worthersee (a large lake and vacation center) to **Klagenfurt** approx 25 miles. This is one of the most beautiful areas in the world. The Worthersee has crystal clear water surrounded by large villas and hotels.

One of the lovely towns along the lake is **Portschach**, where I remember having vacationed in my childhood. We had a sumptuous lunch at a first class restaurant on the veranda along the water with a backdrop of high mountains covered with lush green trees. Joan ate Taffelschpitz (boiled beef with horse radish and fried potatoes). This tastes much better than it sounds. I had my usual Schnitzel! - this time with veal instead of pork. Lots of wine. Great coffee afterward. The day ended in heavy rain.

How we got to Villach, you ask? Last Monday we departed that almost empty pension with that spectacular view from our room's balcony and drove over high mountains and through narrow passes next to fast river waters to **Murau** on the Mur river. After spending four hours on the road we arrived at a neat "Gasthof" right in the middle of the old town of Murau, rented a room for two nights and took a walk thru city center. We cannot rave enough about that four hour drive thru the mountains.

My accent when speaking German seems to give me away when talking to other guests at restaurants or hotels, waiters or concierges. My vocabulary is limited but the accent seems to be recognizably Viennese. When I admit to having been born in Vienna and then departing in 1938, the smile never changes - but the subject does.

Cantilever - this seems to be an important concept here in Austria. There is a cafe in Murau (named The Open Space) that juts out of the hill high up and over the Mur river. It is the pride of the town. More important, every toilet we have seen here, juts out of the wall and has no legs to support it from the floor. Moreover, the horizontal platform within the toilet bowl in European toilets allows for display of the output from one's digestive system, whereas American toilets have a bowl of water. Oh well. This focus on cantilever would certainly thrill Frank Lloyd Wright.

We took some interesting walks around the town of Murau along the river and through the Hauptplatz, the main square. A relaxing day reading up about Villach and its surrounding area where we will spend a week.

The apartment in Villach is spacious. The location is right on the Magdalenensee, a small lake located on the fringes of Villach, surrounded by houses fronting right on the lake - as is our Villa Mayr. The only problem is - we would have preferred to be in the middle of town. As it is, we are dependent on using our car to get to Villach and back. We immediately went into downtown Villach to do our shopping for the week. Bought good cheeses, wurst, and other staples of life. Yesterday it rained all day. We stayed indoors and then went to the neighborhood Stubbe (a tavern that serves food) for dinner. Lots of smoking. We cannot get away from it. Most medium and lower-priced restaurants allow smoking, all restaurants allow smoking in the courtyards/gardens.

Maps, Maps, Maps. We pour over the road maps daily to find the most interesting and scenic routes for the next leg of the journey. And ... do we ever have detailed maps!

Then today, was our day for the Worthersee and Klagenfurt, the provincial capital. It and the surrounding area have a long history dating back to the middle ages. Pageantry including the flags of each nearby town continue to be an important part of the culture, even today. Each town's coat of arms is displayed in Klagenfurt's town square. We were surprised to see the coat of arms for the town of Dachau embedded in that stone work. Since Dachau was a notorious "death camp" during World War II, one would think its tourism bureau must have a difficult sell. Image the phrase "Visit beautiful Dachau, you will never leave" as a promotional slogan. By the way, it was raincoats and umbrellas in Klagenfurt's town square, albeit a beautiful pedestrian area.

Next Wednesday, we are to depart our apartment here in Villach. We are undecided where we will go, keep checking the weather. We must get out of this rain. Headlines say there is a sluggish rainy weather system hanging over eastern Europe ...and we are in it.

Be of good cheer. And to all, lots of love. Oma & Opa

——⊶∞∞⊷——

Report #3

Today is Saturday, the 18th day of our 30 day car trip around Austria and Italy. We are in the Italian Alps. Thru our bedroom window and thru the clouds we can see the beginning of the Dolomites. **Belluno** is about 150 miles north of Venice. It is an ancient town. Wherever one looks, one is reminded of how much history has preceded us here.

Our small hotel is in the heart of the old city and the Saturday open-air market is taking place beneath our window. Lots of chatter, mostly from children. Joan went out into the market for about two hours this morning: fruits and vegetables in one square, lots and lots of clothing and household goods in another square ...maybe a 100 stalls. How this was set up during the night without us hearing, we'll never know.

Here in Italy, most people walk around with smiles on their faces (not such dour looks as in Austria) and there is always lively conversation, socializing, going for coffee and lots of laughter. Not much anxiety except when one gets into traffic and the motorcycles vrooom, vrooom ... past us. On the roadways, everything is serious. The speed limit on the autostrada is 78 miles per hour (ie. 130 K) and the cars go much faster. We have never found it necessary to be in the fast lane. We have parked our car for the duration of our stay here in Belluno (as we did in Udine) and walk everywhere. We also enjoy taking city buses to explore and gaze out the windows at the city sights.

Our rental car came with a GPS. It worked fine in Austria, but not so in Italy. In **Udine** we went to a shop that fixed GPS. He could not make it work ...couldn't get a signal, and said it was trash. We are now using the iPad. It has served us quite well considering our amateur iPad status. You should hear Siri - in the US she says "turn right at 14th and P". In Italy Siri says, "turn right at Palazzo Crepadona Biblioteca via San Lucanno AND Palazzo Rosso via dei Battuti" !!!

Joan was particularly taken with the architecture of the buildings at the Piazza Liberta in Udine. It is described as "a shimmering Renaissance epiphany materalizing from the surrounding maze of medieval streets." She really fell in love with it and tried to wish away the construction equipment parked nearby.

Udine was an important part of my "escape story". In 1938, when leaving Austria my mother and I were taken off the train in Udine and sent back to the Austrian border. Now, we explored the train station a bit. Then we boarded a train for a ride to the town of **Cividale** (10 miles from Udine) for a day trip to this small village. It was established by Julius Ceaser in 50 BC and has been inhabited continuously since then. If only those stones on which we walked could tell us what they witnessed since then.

There are three museums in Cividale; two run by the church and one (the archeological) by the government The church (Duomo) museum was small but exquisite, with fine old vestments and decor. One exhibit actually used a light projector to project layers of color on an 8th century stone alter, whose carvings were still sharp edged but whose paint had worn off, to show what it would have looked like. The Archeological museum was a disappointment. Lots of interesting items but the narrative was more self-congratulatory about the process of digging and finding than on its revelations about life at the time.

Lunch in Cividale was at a cafe with tables on the street (since the street was too narrow for sidewalks.) We sat at a table located in a parking spot reserved for cars with a handicapped sticker. So much for law enforcement in Italy. The lunch - always wine - then exquisite pasta with mussels and small clams. Everything, always, with lots of butter ...and we find the butter in both Austria and Italy so much tastier than in the US.

Restaurant food here in Italy is just wonderful, as is the beer and wine. Right now we are in "prosecco country" and can enjoy a glass of decent quality prosecco at an upscale restaurant for about $2. We sampled three of them yesterday.

In the culinary world of Italy we are almost getting tired of prosciutto, a very fine quality ham always sliced very thin. It is cured in salt, not smoke cured like regular ham or speck. This is definitely prosciutto country and it is on every breakfast buffet and every menu under "appetizers". There are 2 kinds of prosciutto: one from the Parma region which is the one we normally eat in the U.S. The other is from a town (near Udine) called San Daniele. It is considered exquisitely sweet. At this point we are not sure we can taste the difference.

We have changed our travel plans. Decided that the whole western area of Cinque Terre, Lucca and Florence would be tooooo much for us to do on this trip. The five days of rain in Villach caused us some grief, Udine and Belluno were not on our original schedule, but turned out to be good choices.

Buonna notte!

Oma and Opa

Report #4

Dear Family:

Today is September 30, the 28th day of our 30 day road trip and we are sad that it is almost over.

Well ... in our last report to you, we had spoken about the inclement weather in Villach, that had persuaded us to shift our trip from the mountains, south into the valley leading down to Venice. Then the weather cleared up and we have enjoyed good weather ever since. It was almost hot in Venice, but the air coming into our room this morning was 62 degrees.

After leaving Belluno (which we dearly loved) we drove south for barely an hour and stopped at **Vittorio Veneto**. Here we arrived just in time for its annual festival. Joan always seems to know where the next festival on our planned itinerary might be. We received an interesting email from Declan that described his own adventures. In our response to him, we described the scene in Vittorio Veneto. I hope Declan will not be offended if we repeat a small section of our response to him, that describes how we reacted to this town. Here it is:

> "Here in Italy, we are in a river valley that runs north and south between Germany and Italy just north of Venice. It seems to have high military value if one wants to invade Italy from the north. The people who live here have suffered badly during World War 1 (1914 - 1918) and then World War II (1938 - 1945). Yesterday we visited a museum located in this village overlooking the Piazza. On the Piazza there was a festival with musicians, jugglers, buskers - all entertaining children and their parents. Inside the museum were art works depicting the atrocities committed during these two wars to the local citizenry by the invading armies. They lived in the wrong place at the wrong time."

In Vittorio Veneto, we stayed in a very modern hotel and were almost the only guests. We explored the surrounding area and Joan drove on the narrowest road in the world, up a mountain and to the Castello San Martino, perched on the mountainside outside the town. It seems to be used as a retirement home for priests. The view was spectacular - a marvelous place for contemplation and serenity. As usual, we also explored the local churches. I am beginning to get tired of churches and we haven't yet hit the areas in Italy of great church architecture and paintings. Mainly, we loved the big square of the old city. It boasted a great little restaurant and we ate there both days.

One evening, as we sat in the restaurant on the piazza, munching our pasta, I looked at a poster on the wall announcing a series of four lectures on the subject of "The Microscope in Literature" to be given by Professor Fabio Girardello next month. The Italians seem to be very proud of Galileo's accomplishments The poster had the good professor's picture on display. He looked a little bit like Leon Trotzky. As we sat there, slurping on our pasta, I noted that there sat a man on a sidewalk table in front of the restaurant who resembled this fellow. We asked about it and, indeed, that was he. It took little effort to get him to join us at the table. It took a lot more effort to understand what he was saying. He had a good laugh when we said he resembled Trotzky. It was clear that he was a professor of literature and would be discussing the impact of the discovery of the microscope on literary writing. We did not offer to buy him a drink and so he soon moved to another table.

From Vittorio Veneto. it was a short drive south to **Padua**. Padua is a city of over 200,000 people. It was filled with a hip student population. It is home to Italy's second oldest university. We visited the university, which was started in 1222. This was a first for Italy because it featured the sciences - astronomy, medicine, etc. Galileo taught there. As Padua was a strategic military-industrial center, it later became a parade ground for Mussolini to deliver his speeches.

We visited the Cappella degli Scrovengni - a chapel built in 1300 to honor Scrovengni's father but, most importantly, its walls are covered with frescoes painted by Giotto, which he did between 1302-1305. Giotto introduced biblical figures as characters in recognizable settings with true human expressions. Access to see this rare treasure is tightly controlled. The tours are scheduled by language about 30 minutes apart. One makes a reservation and you had better be there on time. You are then admitted to a waiting room to watch a 25 minute video, in your selected language, that provides a full explanation of the history of the chapel and gives an artistic appraisal of the chapel's contents. While you are watching this video, the waiting room in which you are sitting has been sealed. Humidity and temperature controls work to bring the group's moisture and temperature to a level that will assure that when the group enters the chapel, its humidity and temperature will remain constant, thereby helping to preserve the Giotto frescoes.

We also visited the Basilica of St. Anthony of Padua. I was "blown away" by its beauty and amount of art it contained. OK! I have been dragged through more Catholic churches than any other Jewish boy in the history of this planet. I have seen acres of art depicting the Madonna and Bambino, not to mention Last Suppers, Baptisms, Crucifixion and Resurrection. But St. Anthony Church in Padua is simply magnificent. The architecture, the art, the way it is laid out for use, the lighting effects as the sun hits the windows - it is truly a jewel. It beats St. Peter's in Rome by a mile.

Our four-day stay at an apartment in **Venice** was truly amazing. It was well located and we explored the city by walking. Walking is all you can do in Venice, and you walk a lot. Yes, there are water taxis and water buses. Taxis are very expensive and water buses, in true Italian fashion, don't always make all the stops listed on the signs at the docks.

The apartment was wonderfully located. The mosquitoes thought so too, and there were no screens! We had a washing machine in our apartment. Of course all the instructions were in Italian. We finally got it going but couldn't get it to spin dry. We hung the wash out the window and used the lines on pulleys ...just like in the Italian movies!

Instead of Schnitzel, our diet shifted to excellent pasta with lovingly prepared pomodoro. Also clams, mussels, mushrooms (it is the mushroom season and there is an infinite variety of them) and excellent very rich sauces in which to bathe the pasta. Many churches, acres of canvas depicting religious scenes, huge numbers of tourists that have debarked from gigantic cruise ships, gondoliers everywhere plus motor boat taxis at astronomical prices. For example, a gondola ride of 35 minutes costs 80 Euros (Euro 1 = $1.39). A water taxi for a less than 40 minute ride from the airport to the city costs 130 Euros. We basked in the knowledge that George Clooney was getting married down the street at a hotel that charged $6000 per night.

We each had a Campari and tonic at a sidewalk cafe on Saint Marco piazza (at a cost of 50 Euros). The cafe had a neat band playing on an outdoor bandstand. That justified the price for this once in a lifetime experience. We also toured the Jewish Ghetto. There were commemorative plaques for the inhabitants who were sent to the gas chambers in 1943 at about the same time the Hungarian Jews were sent. There is a small Jewish community here. It receives special protection from the police.

Even in late September there are many tourists in this city ...on Saturday five enormous cruise ships unloaded 20,000 tourists. We tried to use the ferryboat on the Grande Canal (at a cost per ride of seven euros each) but, once on board, found that they were not going to stop where we needed. We had to get off at the Rialto bridge instead, and then walk.

The Italians are happy people, they talk and laugh a lot ...in spite of a high unemployment rate and a very poor economy and an even worse political situation. It is a bright and sunny country. The big thing we noticed was wonderful design and style. The store windows have gorgeous clothes and leather goods, the Italians buy these stylish items and look great on the street ...you can usually distinguish them from the tourists. It is refreshing after the dour, conservative (but very clean, efficient) Austrians. The Austrians are experiencing a very good economy and a stable government. Go figure.

One more custom we discovered in Venice - the experience of "cicheti" - - it is bar food. You stand at the bar, there are a variety of appetizers already prepared in front of you, you indicate what you want and have a small glass of wine with it ...you eat it standing at the bar of take it outside and eat it on the street in front of the bar since there are no cars.

In Italy and Austria, it is a joy to go shopping in their super markets - great variety: 10 kinds of salami, 50 varieties of cold cuts, 100s of cheeses and a endless variety of pasta.

Our entertainment highlights were with music. We attended a concert of baroque music at the Chiesa San Vidal. But then - we got tickets (partial view) to Il Trovatore at the Fenice Opera House. What a performance! First class voices. The conductor, barely 30 years old, was great! The house has only 1124 seats. I don't know how they make it. The opera house interior is many tiers of gold.

I have had an interest in sewerage systems since building one at Glendale. Therefore, I was not totally surprised to learn that the canal system also doubles as the sewerage treatment system. In Venice, the three foot tide in the lagoon changes a portion of the effluent every 12 hours or so. From time to time a canal is shut down and drained to remove the sediment. When that occurs they also do repair work on the normally submerged portions of the foundations of the buildings lining the canal. Good, sound economic theory would hold that this city is an inefficient, high cost urban system that cannot be sustained for long. In fact, the city has survived under these conditions for about thirteen hundred years. Go figure!

We departed Venice, boarding the waterbus from a dock about five blocks from the apartment where we had stayed. The waterbus brought us directly to the airport where we had parked our car. The airport is small, very crowded with a short runway. We drove to the autostrada, then north into the Dolomites and Austria. We stayed in what was once a 4 star hotel in the town of **Friesach.** Joan believes that no 4 star hotel should have mildew in the shower. Friesach is the last town in Austria to still have walls and a moat around the city center. It dwells on its history, dating to the Middle Ages with Knight's armor on display and signs about the virtue of war to protect the "honor" of someone or something. But I, always the pessimist, remind that they were burning witches in those days!

Enroute from Friesach to Vienna, we stopped at a town named - **Judenburg** - which translates to "Jew Town". It is a charming village tucked away among beautiful green mountains, has a history of containing a large Jewish community dating back to the tenth century and was at one time an important trading center. However, it is now "Judenrein" There is no Jewish population living here now. The town's tourist information person proudly reported to us that the Germans tried to have the name of the town changed during the War but the township resisted and it was never changed. We then proceeded to spend the night in **Semmering** at the Alpenhof hotel, about one hour southwest of Vienna.

Here in Semmering it is raining and so we are taking it easy and writing our report to you. Joan has repacked everything in readiness for the return of the car and the move into the Pension in Vienna tomorrow. It is amazing how much one collects in the car as one travels. Now it has to all fit into 2 small suitcases.

All our love to each of you. And ... since next Friday is Yom Kippur, a Happy New Year to us all.

Oma and Opa September 30, 2014

6

Travels for Sheer Pleasure

Of the trips taken on our own dime, I have previously presented to you five, described in chapter five. In this chapter, I describe nine other major voyages:

- The Buick – Overland from India to Turkey -1969
- Driving the Buick from Ankara to Paris - 1970
- Family Camping trip to Canadian Rockies – 1981
- Australia and New Zealand-- 1994
- Galapagos & Machu Picchu, Peru - 2001
- North Europe - 2004
- Alaska - 2007
- Christmas Travels with our Family
    1 - Costa Rica: Winter - 2009 to 2010
    2 - Puerto Rico: Winter - 2011 to 2012

Joan and I went on numerous other extended trips, in some instances with our entire family, for the sheer pleasure of exploring this magnificent planet. While not described in this volume, our other travels included such destinations as Israel, Argentina, Chile, some Caribbean islands (Granada, Barbados), Hawaii, Belize, Honduras and Guatemala (winter

2007-2008), several trips to Mexico (Cancun, Copper Canyon, Chihuahua, Baja California) plus destinations in the Florida Keys (winter 2005-2006). Our notes for these trips are not adequate to provide a coherent narrative, although some photos can be seen through the web site, www.rudel.net.

– THE BUICK: OVERLAND FROM INDIA TO TURKEY – 1969[9]

As one of my first extended trips of cultural discovery, I offer the story of my 1969 drive from New Delhi, India to Ankara, Turkey, in my 1938 Buick. A reading of that story should demonstrate how dramatically the world has changed during the past forty-five years. It is not possible for an American to make that trip today.

Dear Joan:

As you may gather from this letter, the trip almost whipped me. I found myself so depressed,   shaken apart, unnerved that I could not even talk about it at first. Foremost was the realization that the idea was idiotic and could have resulted in the loss of everything we put in the car and more. Also I realized that this sort of nonsense is great for twenty year olds but not for forty year olds. Perhaps that was the "unkindest cut of all."

But now I find a demand for the story, and it is no longer' painful to talk about it. And it was a fantastic experience, and now that it's over, an exciting memory. In retrospect I was ill prepared for the trip. Yes I had a screwdriver and a pair of pliers, but no wrenches - and you need wrenches. Yes, I had two brand new spare tires, but unhappily none of my tools' fit the nut holding the tires in place. Fortunately, I had no flats.

I lost the screwdriver early in the game, bought one in Afghanistan as a replacement, and bent it into a pretzel the first time I used it.

---

9 This article is reprinted from the March 1970 magazine, *News Circle*, published by the American Womens Club of New Delhi, India.

Also one should not take a trip like this with any time pressure on him. It makes one take chances.

The first three days were relatively uneventful. I had to drive one hour in the dark to get to **Rawalpindi** but that was not too bad. I started for **Kabul** the next morning. That was the easiest day. The car behaved beautifully, and I got to Kabul by dusk. I stayed at the Embassy guest house, rested up and walked around town.

It is 650 miles to Herat on excellent roads. I was out of Kabul before daybreak and drove like mad. At **Kandahar** I stopped and got the spark plugs cleaned. Later I found that they were not properly tightened when they were put back. No great loss, just some reduced fuel efficiency. We must have averaged about ten miles to the gallon for the entire trip.

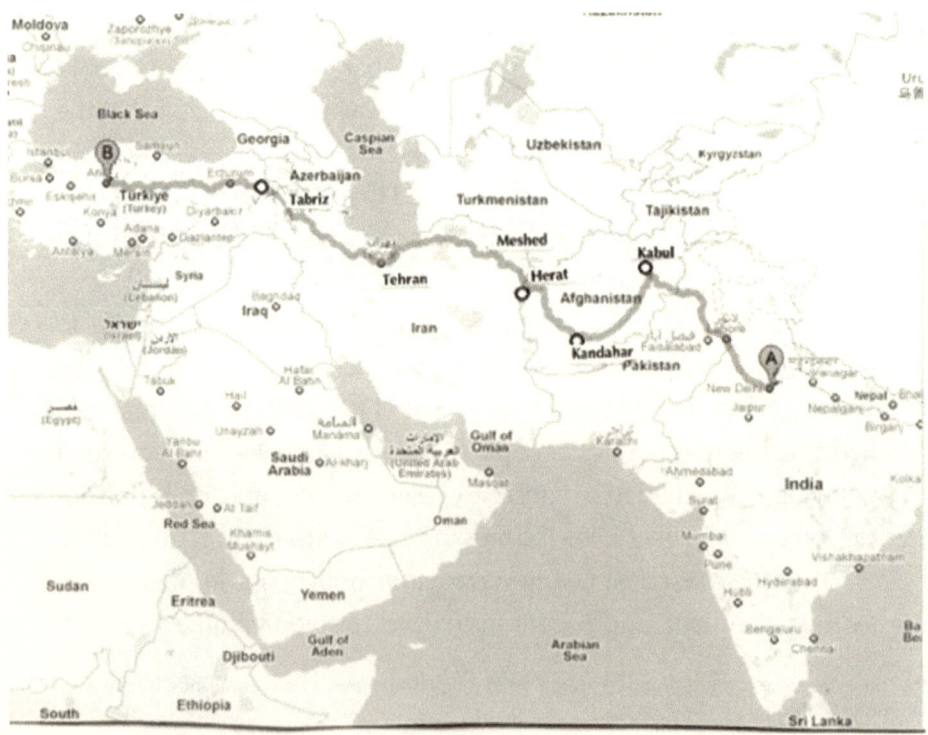

This 1938 seven-passenger Buick Landau was bought from the Maharajah of Jind. It is shown here before restoration. It had been worked on for more than a year before departure. It had been completely repainted, had its interior leather replaced and had many of its engine components rebuilt.

I arrived in **Herat** one hour after dark and I was pretty tired. Tried to see the "night life" but retired early. The next morning I got the car serviced and proceeded to the border.

The Iran-Afghanistan border is probably rated the least prominent assignment for a customs officer the world over. It was here discovered, by an alert Afghan customs official that I had been improperly processed on entry into Afghanistan. It was an even bet that he would send me back to Kabul. Reason prevailed. And he met the challenge by improperly processing my exit. The carnet does not show me going through Afghanistan.

At No Man's Land the road ends. It is like driving off the end of the world. There is a road under construction which I had been assured would be finished by now. Regrettably the culverts were not in so it was useless, albeit picturesque to drive beside. Eventually I got to a little hut flying a yellow quarantine flag.

I walked into the hut, the medical technician got out of his cot, rubbed the sleep from his eyes and stared at my diplomatic passport, medical certificate, the doctor's letter and my letter which I eagerly waived under his nose. It took him thirty minutes to read all that and he finally said he could do nothing but that I could show all this to the Medical Director at the quarantine station at **Tayabad**, twenty miles west.

The Medical Director, an unshaven man with chelo-kebob stains on his vest, took forty minutes to read the papers, then smiled and said: "Rules are rules. You must be our guest for 24 hours." He assured me they would spare no effort to look after my comfort, pointed to the tents, said there were better facilities at the "other camp" and sent a personal escort along with me. The "other camp" was the Tayabad Inn. It was a reasonably well built structure with one large dormitory and four private rooms. As the dormitory was occupied by about twenty hippies, I was able to get a private room.

As a guest of the Shah, I was entitled to free rations. If I did not have anything worth quarantining when I arrived, it seemed I would have it on departure. As an antidote they served antibiotics like after dinner mints. I abstained.

Next morning, without so much as a bon voyage, they gave me back my passport, and I was free to go. In the meantime my car had created some interest among the hippies and I was asked about taking some riders. Since the battery had given out I thought it prudent to do so. From the morass I selected three teachers-a Scottish couple named Stuart and Sheena and their friend Tony (short for Antoinette)-returning from Australia overland to the U.K.

The road to **Meshed** could not possibly have gotten into such disrepair without deliberate sabotage. It was just beside a newly paved road which was complete except for culverts and was consequently of no earthly use except to add to my frustration. It took four jarring hours of driving to cover the 100 miles to Meshed.

I indicated earlier that my battery had gone bad. Unfortunately it did not have the decency to indicate on the testing device that it was bad. Consequently when I had it checked in Meshed, the mechanic insisted that the battery was not at fault but that it had to be something else. So he pulled out the starter motor, the generator and the voltage regulator and tested each of these items separately, only to discover that they were all in good working order.

After reassembling the automobile four hours later, he advised that all was in good repair and that, after an hour's driving, the battery would be charged up and all would be working properly again. This was never destined to be, and the performance was to be repeated daily until I thought I would lose my mind.

I was reluctant to spend $35 for a new battery just a week before putting the car in storage for six months and concluded that it was worth trying to get to Ankara without a battery. Now a car can be made to run without a battery so long as nothing else goes wrong with it. But if a second fault should develop, the absence of a battery becomes very much felt. More about that later.

It was too late to proceed from Meshed that same day, the afternoon having been taken up checking the electrical system, so we tried to locate a hotel on a hill to bed down for the night. (The hill was to assist us in starting the car next morning.) No hills were available so we settled for a flat area, took a walk to the Shrine of the Eighth Imam; nearly got mobbed for being infidels near the Holy Place, and retired.

Stuart took responsibilities, including the management of the budget, with great seriousness. He was a masterful negotiator when it came to hotel room tariff. It was part of his religion that a clean bed was worth the equivalent of twenty-five cents a night and that no one but a cheat would ask for more.

Tired as I would be each evening after the day's drive, I could not help but be amused at the scene between him and the Iranian hotelkeepers as Stuart would shout "too much" over and over again in his Scottish brogue until he got an acceptable price.

At five am we assembled near the car and with a little pushing and luck, got it started. That day was an ordeal. The first fifty miles out of Meshed were well paved, and we breezed along beautifully. Then began-200-plus miles of the most God-awful road I have ever in my life encountered. It made the Tayabad-Meshed road look like a first class highway.

I drove twenty miles per hour over most of that stretch, and we were being shaken apart. Here, too, that nicely paved highway of the future was, for the most part in sight, but great barriers were erected to keep it virgin until the Shah deigned to open it.

In some sections we ran into "blow dust," a light powdery dust that had settled into and hid very deep ruts in the road that you could easily lose a wheel in. This vibrating caused the oil pan gasket and the differential gasket to spring leaks, and I began losing oil at an alarming rate. Fortunately oil is cheap in Iran and so we kept pouring it in every fifty miles. Nothing could be done about the differential however, and we all hoped the rear end would not burn up until we could find a repair shop.

It began to rain a bit just to keep things from being too easy, and we had no windshield wipers. We couldn't turn the engine off because of the battery. If we stopped but kept the engine idling, the oil would continue to leak out and the car would overheat. So we kept going at 20 miles per hour.

I decided to share my provisions with our hitchhikers, and they tried valiantly not to let on how hungry they really were. But I could not open those cans of food without sharing equally, and finally they let me twist their arms.

The Iranian road mileage signs are excruciatingly accurate, placed exactly five kilometers apart. I would drive an endless distance only to be reminded that we were only five kilometers closer to the point where paved road would again appear. Finally, after ten hours of virtually uninterrupted driving, we rediscovered asphalt.

Almost like a mirage, a town appeared, and along the road was an auto repair shop run by Ali, who spoke rapid-fire English he had learned while employed at "G.I. Joe's Construction Company" - the Gulf District U.S. Army Engineers. He was like manna from Heaven; and I regarded him as a personal sign from the Good Lord that He was watching over me. It is mute evidence to my state of mind that it took me two hours to discover that Ali spoke English but did not really understand what he spoke or what was said to him. It took another two hours to discover that he was an incredibly bad mechanic to boot.

Ali was excellent at taking things apart but had some difficulty getting them back together again, in part because he tended to mis-lay little pieces. Also, his first concern was not the oil leaking from each end of my conveyance but rather, you guessed it, the battery. So we went through it again. Pull out the generator, starter and cables (not the battery because the testing meter, that infallible aid to the auto diagnostician, showed the battery to be perfect and check them. Then reassemble and, of course, no juice. "Don't worry. One hour driving and everything will work." Thanks a load.

By this time the soft matter inside my skull, which had been shaken into loose jelly during the day's drive, began to reform itself and my fillings settled back into my teeth. I finally got Ali and a helper (who was a far better mechanic) to focus on the oil seals and it is to their credit that they worked the night through to have the car ready by eight am. Eventually it would be to my credit, as they hit me with a bill for $25.

As I walked from the hotel to the repair shop that morning I found a one rial coin in the street and regarded it as an omen that this was my lucky day. I have now concluded that the principle applies to all currencies except Iranian rials. After checking the repairs, paying Ali, and loading the car with baggage and passengers, we started out on what turned out to be the most unnerving day of the trip. In the first three hours of the day I had two accidents and three close misses.

The road was straight, flat, paved and relatively untraveled by Indian standards. As we barreled along at sixty miles an hour, one of two trucks traveling in the opposite direction decided to pass the other just as we were approaching. It took all I could do to avoid a head on collision. I pulled to the shoulder and braked and the truck just barely slid by. What a marvelous way to start the day.

Twenty minutes later, driving on an empty stretch of road, I noticed a man walking in the same direction I was traveling, along the shoulder in front of me. He was an elderly fellow dressed in the usual Iranian village attire-a worn double breasted pin striped suit which had been imported in bales from New York's second hand clothing dealers. These garments seem to be the vogue in rural Iran.

Over his shoulders he carried a twenty-foot bamboo pole. I tooted the horn to warn him of my approach. And that was a near fatal mistake. Without turning around, he strayed from the shoulder of the road into my traffic lane. I braked, held my hand on the horn and pulled way over to the shoulder trying to get around him. As I passed him there was a bump, and he went down on the ground. I stopped the car and ran over to him. He didn't move-just lay there on the· road, apparently unconscious. At this point a bus came along, its passengers witnessing the scene, and stopped.

I tried to recall precisely how this happened and thought of the possible consequences. It seemed to me that I could not possibly have hit the man. Then I noticed that his eyelids were twitching. He was lying with his face to the sun. The strong light made it impossible for him to fake unconsciousness. So I kicked him hard with my foot. No reaction.

Then I reached down, grabbed him with one hand by the collar and the other by his belt and picked him up in the air. His instinctive fear of falling made him react and we suddenly had a wide-awake peasant hanging in the air.

I put him down, shook him a few times and shouted some choice epithets that, though he could not understand English, should have gotten through to him. Then I shoved him to the side of the road and got back into the car.

I drove to the place where the bus was parked, located someone who spoke English and told him that the man had deliberately hit my car with his stick while I was passing him and then fell to the ground to make me believe I had struck him.

At this point, the man, seeing for the first time the large audience. ran at full speed to the crowd shouting that I had run him over, and then immediately lay down again in the road in precisely the same position in which I had first found him. Fortunately the crowd saw the humor of it all, gave him a few cat calls and told me to go along.

It was only ten am but I needed a drink, badly. The vision of arguing that one in an Iranian court was enough to make me long to reach the Turkish border with all deliberate speed.

The next incident did not occur for at least forty minutes. As I was driving along the **Caspian**, a fully laden donkey ran onto the road from behind a hill in front of the car, his master nowhere in sight. I managed to evade him. This incident, while sufficiently unnerving taken by itself, is hardly worth mentioning in this day's chronicle. But I include it only in the interest of complete reporting.

Hardly fifteen minutes had passed when another set of trucks driving in the opposite direction decided to play games, and I was again eyeball to eyeball with an on-coming truck. This time the shoulder was narrow and so I could only stop the car. Fortunately the truck's brakes held, and we sat there staring at each other. Ordinarily I would have gotten out and punched the driver in the nose. That day however I was simply too drained to do so. Finally the trucker smiled and waved happily, signifying, I suppose, that Allah watches over idiots like him, and drove on.

So we drove on, carrying with us a full realization of the driving skill of our Iranian friends. We wanted to lose as little time as possible in reaching the Turkish border. But all of this was just a buildup for what was to come. The picadors had done their work, and now the Gods of that one rial piece were about to deliver the coup de grace. It came in the form of a bespeckled middle-aged accountant type driving his family around the town of **Babol**.

Driving through town and trying to read the Iranian road signs, I happened to cut into his lane of traffic. He regarded this as a personal affront, honked his horn as the injured party and maneuvered around me to regain his rightful place in the world. You know the type. I was hardly in a mood to argue, and returned to him his honor. Knowing full well that I would have to pass him again on the open highway, I stayed fairly close to him. As he turned a corner a taxi parked by the side started to make a U-turn in front of him. You can well imagine his reaction. Naturally he refused to give up his right of way, indignantly tooted his horn and kept on going. I braked, fearing the worst, but happily the taxi stopped in time and my little friend continued on. I relaxed and followed along. He continued on until he got just past the taxi. Then he slammed on the brakes and stopped in the middle of the highway. I slammed on the brakes and stopped in the middle of his trunk.

The crash of metal against metal was followed by the clatter of cast zinc pieces as my, until then, undamaged grill dropped on the pavement. I got out and, in the most civil tone I could muster, asked him why he chose that moment and that place to park his car. He explained that he had stopped to reprimand the taxi driver and thereupon proceeded to do so, completely ignoring me or the damage to our respective cars.

Their argument soon degenerated into what, by Iranian standards is a fight - the two began slapping each other in the face. I let that go on awhile and busied myself by picking up the broken pieces of grill, surveying the damage and trying not to think of the possible consequences this episode might have on the next three weeks or more of my life.

Finally, I broke up the fight and asked the driver what he wanted to do. He pointed out that Iranian law places the responsibility for such collisions on the rear car and said we had to call the police. I allowed that there would be time consuming delays and that he might never collect a dime and asked him how much he wanted to settle on the spot. I paid the 50 tomans ($ 6.50) he asked and drove off wondering whether he might change his mind later, report the incident to the police and get me sent back at the border.

It is simply not possible to describe how I felt at this point. I felt a marked man; I felt remorse at my situation and at the idiocy of undertaking this trip; I felt anger at the world in general and at the sovereign state of Iran in particular and regret that I had once spent my energies over a four-year period to give aid and assistance to this group of madmen. But most of all I felt lonely, demoralized and lacking in self-confidence. It was to the credit of my hitchhikers that they appreciated the state I was in and came to my rescue. Had I been by myself, I think I might just have given up.

We proceeded without further incident through the new pass in the Elburz mountains through **Tehran**, on another superhighway to **Karaj** and decided to do a bit of night driving to get us as far as **Gazvin**. That would mean that with an early start we could make it to the Turkish border by nightfall of the following day.

Night driving in Iran is quite an experience. For reasons that to this day are not clear to me, approaching cars or trucks turn their bright lights completely off and, after two seconds, turn them full on again. One's first sensation to this treatment is to fear that his eyes have gone up in flames.

I began to suspect that my headlights were badly focused and the oncoming traffic was trying to call my attention to it, but the pattern persisted even when I turned all but my parking lights off.

We were relieved to reach Gazvin and bedded down early. The hotel had a hot bath and so we all, in turn, tried to revive our numbed senses in preparation for the next day.

It was raining heavily at 4:30 am when the watchman woke us. What a marvelous day to sleep late, I thought. But the consequences on the schedule of a further delay were too great and so we packed up and waited in a state of readiness for the rain to stop. Luck was with us and, after a cloudburst, it began to clear. So we pushed the car to get it started, cruised through the town of Gazvin until we found the road and began our journey at 5:30 am, just as dawn was breaking.

The road to **Tabriz** is excellent, winding its way across sparsely populated rolling, but arid hills. It looked as if the land should be quite fertile, but nary a blade of grass was to be seen-only reddish brown rolling hills. On we rolled at sixty miles an hour without another car in sight.

On this road we experienced the first indication of erratic car trouble that was to plague us for three days before we finally located the difficulty. While driving along, the car suddenly began to cough, lost power and finally stopped. However, the motor continued to idle.

I looked under the hood but could see nothing wrong. After a minute I got back into the car and we drove off. The car gave no sign of any problem and we continued on to Tabriz without further incident. My senses were very much alert to any sign of malfunction; my mind was puzzling over this erratic behavior.

In Tabriz we located the American Consul, Tom Greene, a very helpful fellow. It was Friday and there was no question of getting to Ankara by Sunday as my schedule required, so I sent messages to Delhi and Ankara giving a revised arrival time. Tom also gave me the latest information on the roads and provided me with his own driver to help us find a reliable auto repair shop, to see if we could locate the problem. They checked what I thought it might be but found nothing. Finally we stood in danger of not getting across the border by dark (Tom Greene warned me not to drive on the roads in Eastern Turkey after nightfall) and so we drove on northwest towards the junction of Iran, Russia and Turkey.

The overcast of the morning had now turned into a clear blue autumn sky and the bright sun cast a warm golden hue on the hills, broken by stark shadows growing longer with the passing of the afternoon, a reminder to make haste lest we get to the border after it closes. The borders of these countries follow severe mountain ranges virtually unbroken except for a few river valleys, the largest being the one followed by the excellent road from Tabriz through **Marand** (where the cutoff to Dzulfa and the U.S.S.R. is to be found), **Khoy** and **Maku** to the Turkish border.

I thought we would have to do some tricky mountain driving, but to my surprise the valley was quite wide and we saw no snow-caps on either side. Suddenly, and I do mean suddenly because I have no recollection of when it first appeared, towering over us, was Mount Ararat. Seventeen thousand feet of grandeur, very similar in shape to Mount Fuji and also wearing a glistening cape of snow and ice. it so dominates this ancient caravan route between the Persian Gulf and the Black Sea that it is small wonder it acquired a place in the Bible as the highest point on earth.

The road drew us closer and closer to the mountain, and we thought about the different civilizations that had somehow been touched by that promontory, when the car began to act up again; the same erratic behavior-coughing, loss of power and stalling. Our attention was quickly redirected to our dilemma and to Tom Greene's warning that the entire border area into eastern Turkey was no place to be on the road after dark, particularly with women in the car.

Oddly enough the car, once stalled, was not difficult to start again. I would let it sit for a few minutes and it would again operate normally for another ten minutes or so. Then the trouble would reappear. We were approaching Maku and just eight miles beyond was the border. Do we try to locate a mechanic on a Saturday night in Maku or do we try our luck into Turkey? I put it to the passengers and the consensus was to proceed through the border and on to **Dogubayazit**, the first Turkish town about twenty miles beyond the border. There was a strong desire to leave Iran. So up the mountain pass we drove-chug, chug, sputter, stall; chug, chug, sputter, stall, and finally rolled into the border station.

The formalities took about an hour and we drove onto Turkish soil just as the last rays of sun were disappearing ahead of us. Because of the car's sickly behavior and the lateness of the hour. I took along an extra two French hippies (both boys, I think) and we proceeded to Dogubayazit without any mishap, located "the" hotel and enjoyed some excellent shish-kebab and rice. There was no mechanic to be found and so we decided we would take a chance and proceed in the morning to Erzurum.

It had become very cold in the evening, the wind blowing through the valley, and I was concerned about the engine water freezing. The car was a bit more difficult to start in the morning, but at five thirty am, the sun behind us casting a long shadow of the car before us, we found ourselves on the road to **Erzurum**.

My passengers and I (we left the French hippies in Dogubayazit) proceeded along an excellent road for about two hours before-you guessed it-chug, chug, sputter, stall. I tried to puzzle over this strange behavior. The carburetor was newly fitted just prior to departure from Delhi, so that wasn't it. Could it be that the coil was overheating? Could it be the condenser? I looked under the hood. No, the coil was not inordinately hot. I tapped this and that, then got the crew to push, and the car started up again,

If I tell you that there was no further trouble until ten miles outside of Erzurum, would you believe me? We were just congratulating ourselves on the outskirts of Erzurum when precisely the same automotive behavior pattern began. I began to think the car had a complex. You know there are brilliant people in this world who simply cannot finish any task. Well, here was a car that broke down regularly just before getting to its destination. So we limped along, chug, chug, sputter, stall, and the last ten miles into Erzurum took us one hour to complete.

It was Sunday morning and I needed an English speaking mechanic in Erzerum. So we located one! Sharp-eyed Tony spotted a courtyard in which were situated about ten small repair shops. This sort of cooperative-style grouping is quite common in Eastern Turkey. You don't find auto repair garages managed by a single entrepreneur who does integrated repair work. Instead, a collection of small shops, each specializing in a different line (electrical, body and paint, carburetor, radiators, etc.) would set up in a common area. Of course they were all closed, but word spread that a foreigner was in town and, in short order, a mechanic appeared, dressed in his Sunday best. And he spoke a smattering of English.

He tried to start the car and found no juice. So he tested the battery. "Good battery," he said, and as my heart sank, he pulled out the starter motor, the voltage regulator and the generator. My protestations were of no avail and. one by one, he satisfied himself that all were working properly. Then when he got to the generator, the armature virtually disintegrated in his hand. Ha! Success! He had found the trouble!

It took two hours to put in a new generator. Most of the time was spent adapting the brackets to take the new generator, as 1938 Buick parts are in short supply in Eastern Turkey. In the meantime we bought some good Turkish bread. We broke open some cans of sardines and relaxed.

I couldn't figure out how a worn out generator could cause the kind of problem we had been experiencing, but it was quite clear that the generator needed repairing. So we applied the philosophy of the Middle East - wait to see what happens next.

I had always been led to believe that foreigners, particularly Americans, were not very popular in Eastern Turkey. If this is so, I saw no sign of it. In fact the helpfulness of the people on a Sunday morning, the friendly chit-chat of the mechanic and his eventual price (which turned out to be quite fair) all attest to quite the opposite.

I paid the mechanic, thanked him profusely for working on his day off (in his Sunday clothes) and we drove off. Ten miles on the other side of Erzurum - you guessed it - chug, chug, sputter, stall. It was three pm already and sundown was at five, so there was nothing to do but proceed to Erzincan.

And now what would you say if I told you that along the tortuous mountain roads to Erzincan we had no trouble at all until, that's right, five miles out of **Erzincan**. We couldn't see the city lights yet, but the road sign was clear. This time we stalled and try as we might, couldn't start up again.

It was pitch dark. The road was deserted and I had some very frightened passengers in the car. We tried everything. I added gas into the carburetor, and the engine momentarily came alive, but died again just as I put the hood down and climbed into the driver's seat. After a few minutes a small pickup truck drove by and stopped.

Three men got out and walked to the car. I fingered my hunting knife and the girls ducked down.

Ever since my two - year assignment in Turkey (1960-62) I have been singularly impressed with the capability of Turks to hold liquor. Well, these three fellows were feeling no pain. One waved a half empty bottle of raki at me and suggested we pour the contents into the carburetor. Another suggested they push the Buick the remaining five miles. Eventually we decided to lock up the car where she sat at the side of the road, and ride with them into town. The Turks offered to have the women ride in the cab, but we insisted on staying together. We piled into the rear of the pick-up ready to bail out if things up front got out of hand. Somehow, in just ten short minutes, we were dropped at a fairly decent hotel where my passengers bedded down for the night.

During the next twenty-four hours I was to require, and receive, a great deal of help. The first problem was to get the car into town. The second was to locate a mechanic. As luck would have it a local tractor operator was sitting in the lounge of the hotel (it was a local hang-out) and I contracted with him to tow the car into town.

Cold as it was, I must confess to a certain exhilaration at riding out of town on the mudguard of the tractor to find the car. It had not been disturbed in the interim two hours, and we hitched it to the tractor. In another twenty minutes the car was parked in front of the hotel. I drank three Coca Colas and retired, grateful that we didn't get stuck farther out of town and have to spend the night in the fields.

As I look back on these events, now that I know the happy ending, I tend to forget how mentally fatigued and downright disturbed I was at this point in the trip. In retrospect it is simply a series of problems and solutions. At the time however, I was not at all sure the car would actually make the remainder of the trip to Ankara. I had visions of abandoning it in some small town, and then not being permitted by Turkish customs to leave the country.

It was Monday, the day I was to begin my meetings in Ankara and I still had five hundred miles to go in a car that would not start. Early in the morning I walked over to the town's auto repair area where about thirty small repair shops were located. Luck was again with me, and I recognized a large trailer truck that had crossed the Turkish border at the same time as I. Fortunately the truck driver (a Turk) also recognized me and, with a very limited common vocabulary of mixed Turkish and English, I told him my tale of woe.

His action is mute testimony to the friendliness of the Turks and to their willingness to come to the aid of a person in distress. Cemal parked his truck and locked it. He then came with me, helped me move the car from the hotel across town to a repair area. and worked with me and other mechanics until the car was running again. For this work he accepted no remuneration.

I suspected the fuel pump and the carburetor as being the culprits of the piece, therefore located a mechanic who specialized in these components. When he discovered that the battery was dead and there was no juice, he refused to work on the car until that problem was attended to. So we found an electrician.

Yes indeed - same story. Battery tested out okay, so we check the ...

After again pulling out these components and checking them we persuaded them to get a substitute battery. No six volt batteries were available so we used a 12 volt, but sparingly. At this time the carburetor repairman did his bit. He opened the top of the carburetor, looked into the chamber just before the needle valve and with a suitable flourish, fished out a small piece of dirt that somehow had eluded the filters. The entire operation took the carburetor repairman fifteen minutes and the erratic trouble that nearly caused me to spill my marbles was repaired.

It was one pm and we were again ready to roll. I thanked Cemal profusely and we parted. My faith in humanity was restored, though my nerves took a bit longer to quiet down.

That afternoon we drove to **Sivas**.

We planned to start out again at the crack of dawn to complete the last 250 miles of the trip and arrive in Ankara before noon on Tuesday slightly less than forty-eight hours behind schedule.

We left Sivas early in the morning and encountered our first snow of the trip. Fortunately the snowflakes melted on contact and so we pushed on. It took about one hour of driving to get through the storm. From then on the weather remained dry even though the steel grey sky threatened all the way. We no longer had to drive over any major mountain ranges but rather proceeded over rolling barren countryside. The scenery can best be described as bleak.

The road became progressively better, the closer we got to Ankara, and so my confidence grew with each passing mile. Only one mishap remained to mar the last phase of the trip.

I noticed that the motor temperature was climbing to unusual heights. A look-see under the hood disclosed a leak of significant size in the radiator. We decided to try to make it to Ankara and to add water as often as required. We had a two gallon water jug with us, and so we proceeded. By the time we reached the outskirts of **Ankara** we were adding water every ten miles.

BUT WE HAD MADE IT!

We had covered about 4,500 miles since our departure from Delhi eleven days earlier. The car, with all it had endured, seemed little the worse for wear. (After all, we didn't even have a flat tire.) But I was totally exhausted.

So there you have it. My charges thanked me and left two days later for Istanbul by bus. I arranged to have the car stored in bond until we pick it up again next spring.

It was an experience of a lifetime. I have no intention of repeating it but am glad it is now a part of me. And most of all I take pride in that ancient vehicle that, after thirty-two years, was better able to withstand the punishment of the trip than I was.

Your loving husband,

Lu Rudel,   - September 1969

- Driving the Buick from Ankara to Paris – 1970

As a postscript to the above story, here is a letter written in the summer of 1970 to Frank Thomas, a colleague who remained in India after we departed.

Dear Frank:

Tomorrow we leave Paris for Washington. The Buick is now safely ensconced, or at least in the custody of, the Compagnie

Generals Transatlantique for a (hopefully) safe voyage to Baltimore. So the odyssey of the l0,000 mile drive from New Delhi to the U.S. (7,000 miles actually, not counting the Atlantic Ocean), seems to have reached a happy ending.

In view of your (and others') interest in this our trip, I thought I would record in this letter what may be termed as phase II of the Rudel's odyssey, supplementing my letter to Joan which was reprinted in NEWSCIRCLE magazine last March and in one fell stroke transformed me into a leading literary figure of the New Delhi scene.

You may recall that with some difficulty I had placed the Buick into the custody of Turkish Customs last October. We had greater difficulty in getting it back from them. It seems as permitted to leave a car at Customs for only four months. On the first day of the fifth month it becomes transformed into the Turkish equivalent of a pumpkin. I was informed that it would no longer be possible to release the car for export. It was also not possible to release the car to be retained in Turkey. The problem was not one of language; my very good friend, Emin Boysan, a very senior Turkish Government official went with me and he was as perplexed as I. Numerous suggestions were made, one of which was to load the car on a railway wagon and ship it out of the country. But we worked our way up the hierarchical ladder and finally the Director of Customs himself, amused by the quaint conflict of Turkish regulations, ordered the car's release.

That took care of the legal formalities and it was accomplished in barely 24 hours. The next problem was physically moving the car out of the Customs storage area. You will recall that the battery was dead even last October. It seemed futile to try to rejuvenate the car in the storage area and drive it out on its own steam. So we located a repair shop near the Customs area and began negotiating with a taxi driver who happened by, for him to tow the car to the repair shop. Amongst some 15 spectators who gathered out of nowhere, I concluded the negotiations. Then the taxi driver smiled and asked me to help him get his car started. You see he had no battery either.

Here the spectators came in very handy. Not only did they get the taxi started but they all piled into the taxi and, in a festive mood, accompanied us to the Customs area. There they busied themselves advising each other how to link up the two cars with a tawdry piece of rope that the taxi driver furnished for the purpose of towing this enormous Buick. After three attempts towing it - the rope broke regularly - the crowd simply pushed my car out into the open. This time the taxi driver was directing them. Once the car was out of the Customs area, someone came up with an old set of snow chains and rigged these into a makeshift tow rope. Again we helped get the car started and proceded in caravan fashion to the repair shop; first the taxi, then the Buick, then the cheering crowd.

Fortunately, I paid my bills promptly. Immediately after I paid the taxi driver a handful of lira, a loud explosion ensued from the taxi engine and steam gushed forth out of a burst water hose. It seems that pulling the Buick had over-heated his engine. That put a strain on the cooling system and caused his hose to burst. Such are the risks of private enterprise. But social justice prevailed and I gave the taxi driver another fistful of lira.

It's a tribute to Turkish ingenuity that they were able to get the car started in another 24 hours. Mechanics and apprentice mechanics swarmed over the Buick fixing this and tightening that until the car was operable. The body work was done in less than two hours and I must say it was quite a good job. All traces of my Iranian encounters were removed. The grill was repaired. I had arranged to get the windshield wiper motor repaired in the

U.S. and this was installed. Unhappily, however, only the windshield wiper on the driver's side was operable and so in the rain Joan was veiled behind beads of water on the windshield, which caused great anguish and strained family relations as I relied on her for navigational aid. Exactly six days after our arrival in Ankara we were again ready to go.

Ankara has changed almost beyond recognition in the eight years that we have been away. I can remember driving from Ulus to Chankaya in my Jaguar in seven minutes. The same distance with vastly improved roads now takes 45 minutes to cover. To a traveler from India, Ankara looks as western and developed as any European city. There are many signs of prosperity and, in the tradition of the 1970's this is accompanied by manifestations of student protest. We had our fill of doner kabob (which I consider good and sufficient reason for us to assure Turkey's continued alliance with NATO), and revisited the old familiar sites of Joan and my courtship (our first date consisted of a visit to Ataturk's Mausoleum).

During the first leg of the odyssey my mind was totally occupied with the problems of keeping an aging car running in remote areas where help was scarce. We were now moving into areas where help is more plentiful but the problems of attending to five passengers compensated. On the morning we left Ankara for our 375 mile trip to Izmir, five year old David had a 104.8° temperature with a strep throat. Happily the Air Force Hospital supplied antibiotics and David recovered splendidly. In **Izmir** we stayed at the Air Force Billets, the Kordon Hotel, directly on the waterfront. Excellently run and immaculately maintained facilities, which I recommend to any travelers through Izmir. They require that you be traveling on official orders. The food and service are unbelievably good, and the prices are equally unbelievably cheap.

We drove the car onto the SS TRUVA on Friday afternoon and after an uneventful 36 hours during which our children's Tibetan nurse, named Yangchen (her first time at sea) developed seasickness, we landed in **Brindisi**. The TRUVA is really a car ferry and it was as easy to load and unload the car and our belongings as it would be to drive onto the Staten Island Ferry. The weather in Southern Italy was unbelievably beautiful but there was a cold wind coming from the Adriatic that prevented Joan and me from joining the children in romping in the water. The kids seemed oblivious to the cold and enjoyed themselves immensely. We drove north along the Adriatic, stopping two nights in a village north of **Bari** (Trani), then proceeding further along the Coast.

I must say that the problems of pollution are not endemic only to the U.S. The beaches were littered with broken beer bottles and we had great difficulty in keeping the kids from getting cut up. The car made a hit wherever we went and my faith in its reliability grew.

Just north of **Pescara** we decided to detour to the town from whence John Funari's family hails. That particular area of Italy with its rolling hills amidst snow caps, is one of the most beautiful parts of Europe. Europe had a severe winter and so there was plenty of snow and plenty of water in the streams and rivers. The landscape was unbelievably green.

The village of **Norcia** is in one of the most remote areas of central Italy. Naturally that is the place where our Buick decided to give us a bit of trouble. The 70 km of road from Ascoli to Norcia begins with a 40 km hill. About 35 km along the way the car began to sputter, gasp and eventually died. For its demise it chose a particularly narrow and steep section of the road. So here we sat. We decided the only thing to do was push the car to what we laughingly called the side of the road and walk to Norcia. We locked up everything and then decided we ought to take along our passports -- YES, the passports.

It was only then that I remembered having turned over all our passports to the hotelkeeper in a small town outside of Pescara where we had spent the previous night. That completed my demoralization.

At this point a small Fiat appeared on the horizon and the kindly gentleman driving it stopped to explain that there were no mechanics on the road towards Norcia and that we would be best off turning around and rolling back a few kilometers. Since we had to go back to regain our passports, his advice seemed sound. Only one small problem remained. How to turn around a twenty foot car on what seemed to be a ten foot wide road. We did manage to turn around and then we rolled and rolled and rolled back towards **Ascoli** until we reached a town with a telephone with which to summon a mechanic.

The remainder of the trip to **Paris** was uneventful. I then left the family there, drove the car to **Le Havre**, put it on a ship for Baltimore and rejoined my family in Paris for the flight home.

Cheers,

Lu Rudel,   - May 1970

- FAMILY CAMPING TRIP TO THE CANADIAN ROCKIES –1981

A seven-week family camping trip across the country and into western Canada, taken in the summer of 1981, was a wonderful family bonding experience. I had retired from the Foreign Service a year earlier and was engaged to do some work for the Department of the Interior on their management of the US Trust Territories (Palau) while, at the same time, pressing ahead to get the Pennsylvania resort over its threshold. Joan's employer had recognized her talents in the fledgling computer technology business and she was earning serious money, sufficient to send our three children to college. The trip was welcome time off.

Our group comprised the five principal family members (the three children, Joan and I), accompanied by Joan's mother and father, who had never before done any camping, plus a Scottish friend of Ruthann who she had met while working on an Israeli kibbutz the previous summer. We drove to Wisconsin to pick up Joan's parents, then headed west across Minnesota to the Badlands of South Dakota, through the National Parks in Wyoming and Montana and into the Canadian Rockies up to Banff and Lake Louise. We had rented an eight-seater van for the trip and Joan managed the packing and loading for the entire voyage.

After picking up Joan's parents, Emma and Romy Fogltanz, we hightailed it to Rapid City South Dakota and into the Badlands. It was there that we first pitched our tents, and, within a few minutes, enjoyed our trip's first thunderstorm. The winds took down all but one of the tents (the one that housed Joan's parents); the rest of us congregated in the van. That introduction to our camping trip chastened us all.

I saw the children mature during those seven weeks. The interaction of the children with their only set of grandparents was a joy to see. Each child asserted him or herself in a different way. David, always the first to rise, daily built a fire and made coffee. He relished that responsibility. Joanna began to feel and act the equal of her older siblings. Ruthann, who early had shown signs of serving as the family's social conscience, enjoyed her friend's company, absorbed the natural beauty of the western United States and noted the fragility of the environment. She focused her decidedly "rebel" feelings on environmental protection. Joan's organizational abilities came to the forefront as we daily camped and decamped all the way into Canada. And Grandma Emma, with her Bohemian heritage and in-built penchant for cleanliness, was often seen spending time "sweeping out the tents."

Overall perhaps, the photos on the website (www.rudel.net) can tell a better story of the trip than I can. But several events have remained in my memory and are worthy of note. Ruthann and her friend had planned to go on a three-day hike through Grand Teton National Park. I drove them to their starting point and we made arrangements for me to pick them up three days later at another point. They had their tent, sleeping bags and other provisions in two backpacks. I waived these two seventeen-year olds off, trying to hide my trepidation about the dangers of their hike.

Three days later, as I waited at the designated pick-up point, I heard that some hikers had had an encounter with a bear. Needles to say, I was worried. Soon, Ruthann and her friend made their appearance. I was so happy to see them safely back that I did not notice they had only one backpack between them. On the ride back to our camp the story came out. Indeed, the bear encounter occurred with our very own young campers.

Two hours after being dropped off three days earlier, as they rested for a moment on a log along the path, they encountered a bear. Various guidebooks give advice about what to do in this situation. Some recommend that the person should roll over and play dead. Others say to stand and back away. Ruthann said she was puzzled as to what to do since she did not know which guidebook the bear had read. They slowly rose from the log and walked away in the direction opposite to where the bear stood, leaving their two packs sitting on the ground. The bear did not follow.

They warned other hikers coming along the path not to proceed and waited a half hour. They then carefully approached the point on the path where they had last seen the bear. Their packs were visible, but so was the bear. After some more time elapsed, they again attempted to return to the site. This time the bear was not to be seen. One pack, the one that contained their tent and sleeping equipment, was unmolested. The other, the one that contained their provisions, was torn to shreds with their food either scattered or gone. But through word of mouth (this was before the advent of cell phones) the bear story spread through park's "grapevine." Other hikers that encountered them in the deep woods gladly shared their provisions with our two teenage campers in return for a retelling of the story, and they both ate very well for the entire three-day hike.

Following this incident, we proceeded on our planned route through Yellowstone National Park, then north into Montana. While visiting Glacier National Park, David did a bit of rock climbing. Later, while camping in the park, David complained of severe pain in his abdomen. We feared a ruptured appendix and called for an ambulance. It turned out that the nearest hospital was located on the other side of the border, in Canada. The ambulance, being on an emergency call, took David (and me) to that facility, notwithstanding our lack of documents. What a wonderful relationship we enjoy with our neighbor to the north. Fortunately, David had simply strained his belly muscles while rock climbing. It was a false alarm.

By this time though, we could see that the trip was becoming too much for Emma and Romy. So before crossing the Canadian border, we took them to the Helena airport, said farewell and put them on a flight back to Green Bay. We then continued our trip to Banff, Lake Louise and Jasper.

The return trip east and back to the U.S. was fast and uneventful. All of us have long cherished the photos of the trip, as well as our collective memories.

- AUSTRALIA AND NEW ZEALAND - 1994

This seven-week voyage to the southern hemisphere took place shortly after I returned from phase two of my World Bank assignment in Riga. It had been cold and wet in Riga. It was cold and wet in Washington. Joan and I wanted a warm place to defrost our bones and hibernate for the remainder of the winter.

My participation in the UN's international conference circuit had made me curious about New Zealand and Australia. Their representatives, especially the Kiwis, as we tended to call the New Zealand delegates, had been interesting people. They maintained a certain independence from their British colleagues and had a practical and constructive approach that appealed to me. They seemed to have a built-in "baloney detector" which was usually turned on when listening to the speeches of their fellow delegates.

But besides this, I treasured my recording of the world famous New Zealand Maori soprano, Kiri te Kanawa, whose golden voice melts my heart as she sings Strauss' *Four Last Songs*. Plus, David would occasionally sing "And they Sang Waltzing Matilda", the melancholy ballad describing the tragedy of the 1915 Battle of Gallipoli, in which the British generals cavalierly deployed Australian and New Zealand troops to attack and scale the cliffs of the Dardanelles while the Turks, firing from above, decimated their ranks.

We were dealing here with a very large area to explore. Australia constitutes an entire continent. New Zealand is comprised of two big islands, (North Island and South Island) plus a myriad of smaller ones. That is a lot to cover in seven weeks. Our plan was to start in New Zealand to explore North and then South Island over a period of three weeks. We would then fly to Melbourne, Australia, at a distance of 1,300 miles. We selected four key areas of Australia to visit. These were Melbourne and surrounding areas (particularly the southwest coast towards Adelaide), the island of Tasmania, the area around Sydney, and finally the Great Barrier Reef and the area along its nearby shore.

We landed in Auckland, North Island, dressed in our Washington winter clothes, to find ourselves in a tropical setting. The temperature was in the eighties and it was South Pacific weather. We had decided to use youth hostels instead of hotels because the former had developed a reputation for cleanliness, favorable location and economy. Our reservations at the Auckland youth hostel turned out to be quite acceptable.

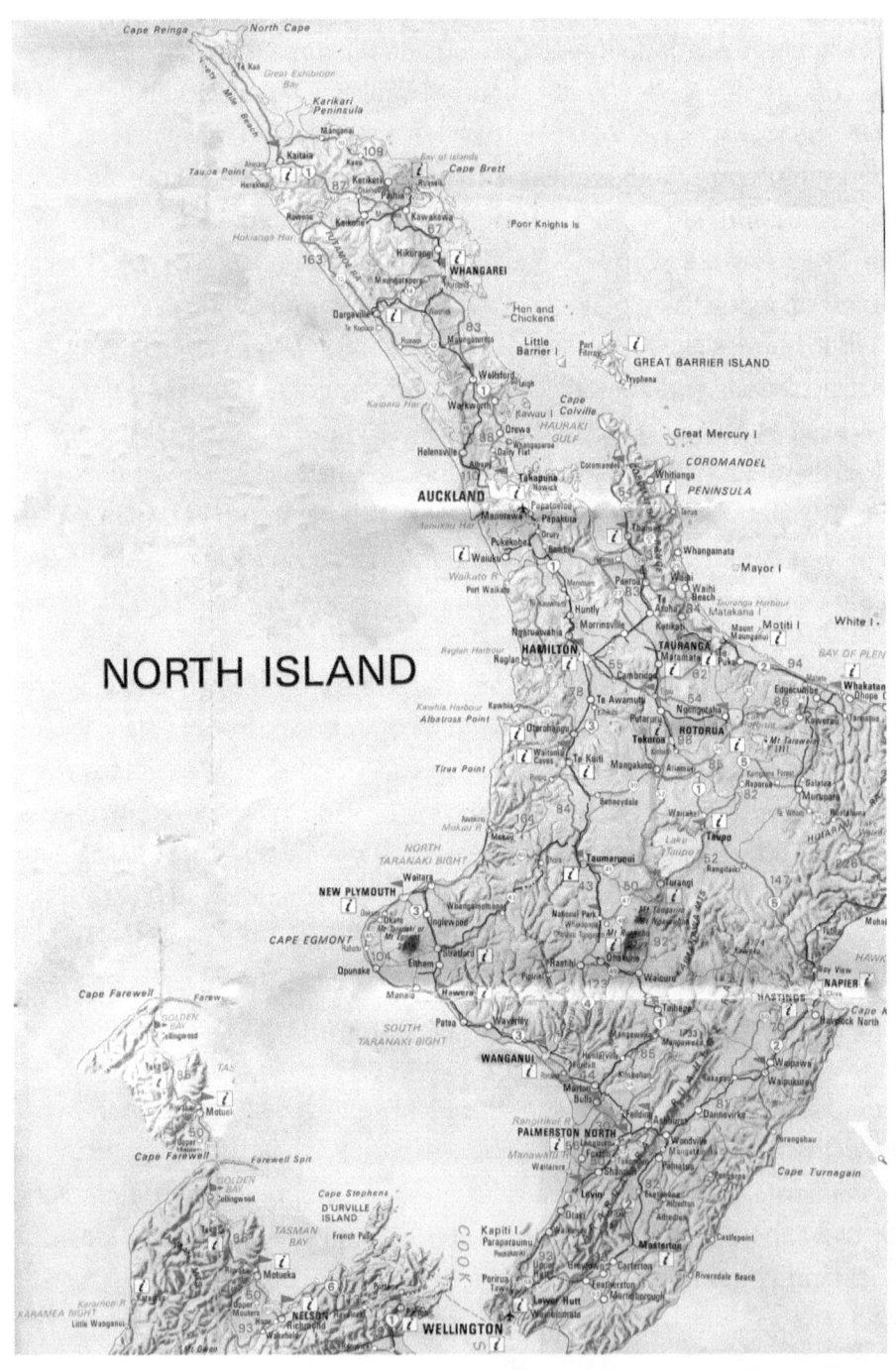

Auckland is a port city. It had been the capital of the colony until 1865 after which Wellington became the capital. The city's harbor is well protected and there are many islands in the bay. There are some large rock outcroppings around which a small cruise boat can meander, providing the tourist with great photo opportunities. We enjoyed a three-hour cruise that took us through a hole in a massive rock. We were even able to swim at a stop on one of the islands.

After enjoying a tour of the city, a Mauri dance recital and concert featuring traditional music, plus a visit to the museum that featured the Maori culture, we rented a car and drove north past Whangarei to **Cape Brett**, doubled back and explored the **Coromandel Peninsula** and saw the thousand year old Kauri trees. It looks like a landscaped garden surrounded by the blue sea. We then proceeded south, past beautiful sand beaches to **Tauranga**, and then **Rotorua**, with its Polynesian hot baths and thermal pools. The roads were excellent.

Joan's letter to Jack and Joanna describes the next leg of our journey:

"We continued south around **Lake Taupo** to Tongariro National Park and decided to spend a leisurely night at the Chateau Hotel. We ordered drinks and watched the clouds circle and then move away from **Mt. Ngauruhoe**. It is 2300 meters high. Next morning we took a lift to the summit to see its ski area. We were then high above the tree line and saw nothing but volcanic rock in the distance. It looks like a moonscape. But then, we descend on a three-mile circular hike to **Taranaki Falls**. We walked past meadows of mountain heather and great vistas, then reached the falls where we ate our lunch. The pool beneath the falls is deep ink blue. We returned to the car through dense forest following the cascading stream.

"On to **Wanganui**, situated on the island's west coast at the Wanganui River that has its headwaters on **Mt. Tongariro**. It is an attractive city of 23,000 and we decide to rent a room at the Youth hostel. Its manager, a woman that loves to care for each and every backpacker that passes through. On line in front of us is this young male British packer with golden ringlets. He tells her "Madam, I need a bed" and she hovers over him, suggesting restaurants, supermarkets and is marking up a city map for him. She suggests a place called "The Quay", which is pronounced "key" around here. She rushes off to show him his bunk so he can "put down his heavy pack, poor dear." Soon, she returns to take care of us.

"After we settled in, we decided to find out what the Quay was all about. It is a nice, upscale bar on the river, fairly crowded with very young folks. We walked in and took seats at the bar as all the tables were occupied. This is obviously a serious drinking bar. When Lu announces to the female bartender that we plan to have dinner, she looked a little perplexed, even though a food menu is in evidence. I suspect it has been a long time since anyone has come here "for dinner". She is a gracious and efficient bartender and soon provides us with beer and food. Loud live music soon begins. The place becomes packed and we watch in disbelief at the quantity of alcohol being consumed. All the "kids" are very friendly to us although they show surprise at finding senior citizens at their watering hole.

"Next morning we depart for **Wellington** through sheep grazing hills and rich farmland. We have only one hour to see Wellington if we are to catch the ferry to South Island because we had bad information about the location of the rental car return. The city is built on a series of large hills and we kept finding ourselves on the wrong side of the hill to get to the downtown area. We do manage to take a quick tour through the antique car museum."

—⊙❀⊙—

We debarked the ferry on South Island in the town of **Picton** and rented another vehicle. The shoreline there is simply magnificent. We walked and motored along toward **Blenheim**. I had heard about an airport there, where it would be possible to charter a small plane to fly around the area. And indeed we found the airfield on the outskirts of the town. It was a large grass field, about a square mile in dimension, with no clearly defined runway. At the time of our visit, it was the only airport I knew of that permitted aircraft to land and depart in any direction, even though the prevailing winds were from the west. Pilots could choose to land or take off into the wind, should the wind direction shift. Joan chose to stay on the ground and scouted out a good place for us to lunch after my joy ride. The tides are quite high in **Cook Strait**, approximately twenty-five feet, and so from the air, one can see the waters rushing through the rock formations along the coast. Small boats can be seen moored along the shore. The mountains along the coast are good protection from storms that normally arrive from the west. After I landed, Joan took me to a nearby winery that served an excellent lunch. We sat in the open patio, warmed by the sun, and savored this remarkable moment.

We then drove along the coast, stopping occasionally at sandy beaches and the many rock outcroppings that hosted seal colonies. The seals are very sure of themselves in the water, and will let you approach them, indeed they will play with you while swimming around. But, on land, they know their own limitations of movement and will not allow a human to get too close. We kept a respectful distance from them as they lay on the rocks and basked in the sunshine. Our next stop was **Kaikura**, on South Island's east coast where we had scheduled a whale watch boat ride, but the sea became too rough and the voyage was cancelled.

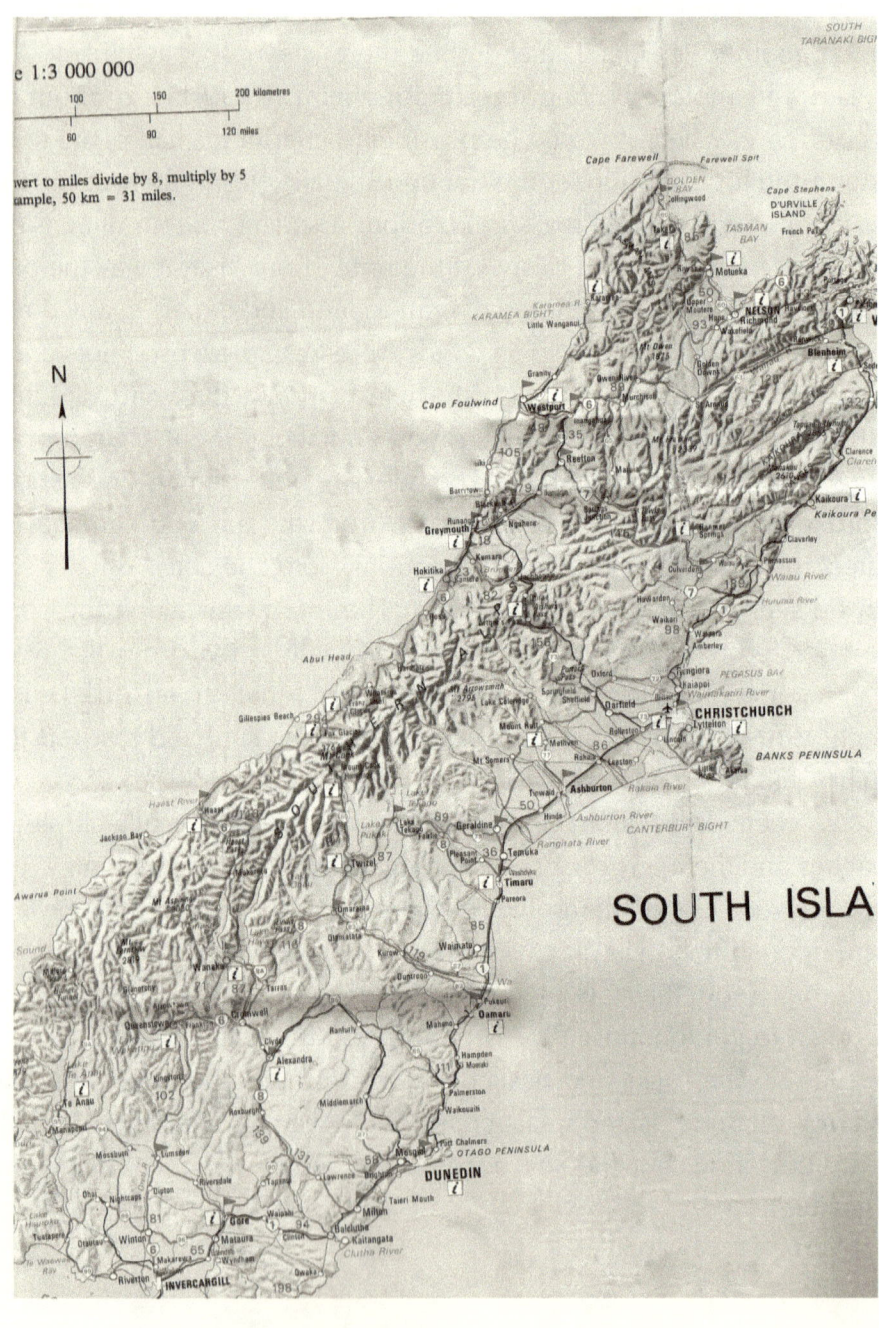

At the foot of **Fox Glacier** we walked on the residual alluvial rocks, The foot of the glacier has retreated more than a kilometer inland since 1750, providing strong evidence of global warming. Then we engaged a helicopter and pilot for a ride to the top of Franz Joseph Glacier, landing on its shoulder, just below the crest. On the return flight, the chopper tracked the glacier to allow us to see the deep crevices in the ice. The top of the glacier is a collection of huge ice boulders as it descends down the mountain at glacial speed.

We continued our drive along the island's west coast, with the ocean on one side and mountains on the other, crossing the **Haast Pass** as we drove inland and along the shore of **Lake Wanaka** to Queenstown, our most southerly destination on the island.

Queenstown offers a number of fun activities for the tourist. If one is into parasailing, there is an organized launch point on a nearby mountain. There are instructors who will strap a rider to them and will jump off, in tandem with a parasail, to give the rider a feel for the sport, without having to learn it. There are jet boats on the Shotover River to give the tourist a ride into the mountain gorges. The jet boat can operate even in a bare six inches of water. There is an airport where one can charter a small plane, with pilot, to tour the area and also to fly into Milford Sound on the west coast just on the other side of the Southern Alps mountain range from Queensland. We did the last two, but only observed the parasailing, even though Joan looked longingly at the parasail instructors and thought long and hard about trying it.

Our flight to **Milford Sound** was quite dramatic. The distance from Queensland to Milford Sound is just fifty miles as the crow flies. But airplanes sometimes do not fly like crows, particularly when there are high mountain peaks in between. Pilots tend to follow valleys and gorges. But some gorges can become dead ends. When one finds himself flying in a gorge that narrows and has no pass at its end, there may not be enough room to turn around. It is well to take along someone that is familiar with the terrain, to select those valleys and gorges that are known to let you through to the other side. For us, it was a spectacular, twenty-minute flight to Milford Sound, something hikers do in four days. There were no clouds as we crossed at an altitude of six thousand feet with mountain peaks towering above us. We flew past a two thousand-foot waterfall, then cleared the ridge and began a rapid descent to land on the one-way runway, hoping the wind at our tail was not too strong. As we shut down and opened the aircraft door, we were attacked by squadrons of mosquitoes. We bundled up as best we could and ran to the harbor to arrange for a boat ride on the Sound. Once at the water's edge, the mosquitoes disappeared, allowing us a leisurely cruise to sightsee. The pilot waited for us patiently, locked in his aircraft to fend off the mosquitoes. After the cruise, we returned to the airport where he guided me in following the special take off procedures: "A short field departure to four hundred feet, bear right to the canyon wall, then turn to the left and slow circling flight, climbing to six thousand feet before attempting to cross the ridges."

Departing Queenstown, we headed north, first along a prairie, something like one finds in Montana but containing many sheep ranches. We stopped in the town of **Twizel** and were invited to attend a sheep show, in which the differences among different breeds were explained and a live demonstration was given of how sheep are shorn.

Before driving the last leg to Christchurch, we made two detours. The first was to the foot of Mount Cook to visit that magnificent twelve thousand-foot mass as it dominates the entire scene. On the way, we strolled along the shore of **Lake Tepako**. It was another day of perfect weather and we took our cappuccino and role as we sauntered about. The second detour was to explore the Banks Peninsula out to the town of **Arakoa**. Foley's hostel, where we stayed, has a well-tended flower garden. A dirt road led us to Pigeon Bay and **Port Levy**, which is a very serene place.

In **Christchurch,** over two days we visited the newly built Town Hall, the library, the museum with its exposition on Antarctica, the art gallery and the botanical gardens. We attended an organ recital at the cathedral. A meal of fish and chips at the Oxford Tavern on the Avon River provided satisfying nourishment and also reminded us of the cultural ties the Kiwis continue to maintain with Great Britain. After dark, we searched the heavens to look at the Southern Cross.

We decide we enjoyed South Island more than North Island. Having spent a wonderful twenty-two days in New Zealand, we headed for the airport and returned the rental car. It was time to depart for Australia.

The flight to Melbourne took three hours. We checked in to the Queensberry Hill Youth Hostel and were given a very attractive room with a private bath. It was the ninth of March and we were to depart Australia on the fifth of April. First on the list of things to do was to strategize how we would use the remaining three and a half weeks of our voyage to explore this entire continent. We decided to forego Alice Springs, the Northern Territory, Canberra and Perth. Instead, we would concentrate on four regions: the coastline between Melbourne and Adelaide, the island of Tasmania, Sydney and the Great Barrier Reef. We made the necessary bookings to meet our schedule and Joan began to review her guidebooks, focusing on these four destinations.

The city of **Melbourne** has many things going for it. We started our tour with a city bus ride to the university area, or the "Uni Area" as the Aussies like to call it. There are many fine restaurants on Lygon Street and we enjoyed some delicious lamb chops with potatoes.

We rented a car and headed west. We had been urged, by an Aussie that we had befriended, to visit the **Grampian Mountains**. These are located in a national park inland, about eighty miles north of the coast. That was our first overnight stop. Joan managed to rent a small camper in the park for the night and I made believe it was fine with me. It was well worth the stop. The topography is beautiful. The rock outcrops are startling but not useable by those of us who suffer from vertigo. The trees and the waterfalls are beautiful.

After our visit to the Grampians, we headed south to the coastal road then east along the coast, called the Great Australian Bight (the name does not derive from the field of dentistry). Highway B100 hugs the coast along a cliff about hundred and fifty feet above the water. There are many rest areas where it is easy to pull off the highway to gaze upon the rock sculptures that have been naturally created by the crashing waves. At the **Loch Ard Gorge** we saw sandstone pillars named The Twelve Apostles. In several places there were towers, bridges and tunnels carved out of the rocky extensions into the ocean. What a wonderful display of natural beauty! We slowly proceeded along the highway to the coastal town of **Torquay**, and finally returned to Melbourne, ready to take the ferry to Tasmania.

The island of **Tasmania** is where the British sent their worst convicts. The scenery is truly wild and natural. Some areas are totally uninhabited by humans. It was an overnight run for the large ferry to reach **Devonport**. There were 315 cars and 1,300 passengers on board. Upon disembarking in Tasmania, we immediately drove west along the coastal road to see the dunes. They are three to four miles deep and abut directly onto forestland. The dunes move about three to four feet per year inland, encroaching on the forest. We witnessed a spectacular sunset on these dunes and then headed south to Cradle Mountain Park.

We continued to **Rosebery** and then **Strahan**, where we boarded a small ship to cruise the Gordon River in Franklin-Gordon Wild Rivers National Park. A five-hour cruise took us into a rainforest that is otherwise impenetrable. Two thousand-year old trees whose wood is heavier than water, such as the leatherwood and a variety of Eucalyptus, grow there. Waterfalls adorned with large ferns, undisturbed by humans, can be seen. After the cruise, we headed west to **Bronte Park** and took a cabin for the night at Peddler Lake Lodge.

The next morning we noted that the temperature had dropped. It was not so bad in the cabin's bedroom, but going out to the sitting room and the bathroom, we could see our breath. Never mind. We went for a short walk before driving on through **Hamilton** and then to **Strathgordon**. The road, still in the national park, was built by the power authority as access to a dam site developed for hydroelectric generation. There was lots of clamor from the "greenees" in opposition against the hydro project but the dam and reservoir were completed anyway. We took a walk to **Russell Falls**, a lovely, tiered waterfall. Each scene seemed to be better than the last one. On our fifth day on Tasmania, a Saturday morning, we left the Gordon National Park by the same road we entered but stopped at **Bushy**

Park because we had heard there was a hop festival. We joined the celebration because we knew how important hops are to the making of beer. There were vendors offering Turkish doner kebab, wallabies (kangaroo) sandwiches, Indian curry and samosas, lamb with goat cheese. There was wine tasting, folk dance and tours of the kilns. It was a lot of fun as we mingled with the Tasmanians.

In the afternoon, we arrived in **Hobart,** Tasmania's capital city. We had really explored many sections of the island and were scheduled to depart by the coming Tuesday's ferry. For the meantime, Joan arranged accommodations for us at the youth hostel. The city of Hobart has a few things to offer. We visited the botanical gardens, the beach, and the casino where we lost some cash, and then decided to drive to the airport.

There, I inquired of the chief flight instructor, Jonathan, whether we could arrange a flight to an interesting destination. He asked me if I would like to fly to **Cox Bight Beach**. When I asked him how long the runway was, he informed me there wasn't one. We could land on the sand beach. I jumped at the chance to do this crazy thing and we arranged to meet at the airport the next morning. Joan agreed to join us in the 172 aircraft.

The flight to Cox Bight Beach took about forty minutes. We passed waterfalls, a tin mine, rainforests, Mount Federation and Bathurst Bay before finally approaching Cox Bight Beach. I followed Jonathan's instruction to land neither too close to the water's edge nor in the dry, loose sand. The beach had a slight curve to it so landing the plane was a new experience for me. Once we had set the plane down safely, we cut the engine and walked onto the beach. Jonathan pointed south at the ocean and told us that the next landfall in that direction was Antarctica. After about half an hour of gazing around us in a 360-degree arc and asking ourselves if we really understood where on the planet we were just then, it was time to leave. We taxied the aircraft back to the point of touchdown, turned around, added flaps and began our soft field departure roll. We rotated quickly to get the wheels out of the sand, then gained speed at straight and level flight before climbing in a gentle left turn as the aircraft headed out to sea. The return flight was uneventful.

In Hobart, we had already checked out of the hostel. The car was loaded and we headed north to spend the night in **Launceston** before boarding the ferry back to Melbourne. The ferry was hauling an entire circus, including performers, animals and keepers back to the mainland. No cabin for two was available and so Joan wound up in a women's six-passenger dorm and I in a similar facility for men. If you, dear reader, have never found yourself sharing a cabin with a group of circus hands, your imagination may not fully extend to the shenanigans that these folks like to pull off. Let's just say I had a sleepless night and leave it at that.

Overall, it had been an exciting, yet relaxing week for us in Tasmania. We had two days left in Melbourne before leaving for Cairns and the Great Barrier Reef. The first afternoon, we went to a matinee concert at the symphony hall. We entered from street level and found ourselves at second balcony level. It appears that the hall was built underground. It has very fine acoustics. We heard them give an excellent performance of Saint-Saëns' *Cello Concerto*, after which we headed for Chinatown and a delicious dinner.

We also decided to visit **Phillip Island** to learn about the penguin colony living on its beaches. The great mystery about these penguins is their navigational ability. They leave their hutches, swim out to sea in search of food, traveling as far as one hundred miles offshore, then find their way back to their hutches, all of them arriving at about the same time just after sunset. As it grew dark, we waited expectantly for their arrival and were not disappointed.

The following day, we departed for **Cairns**, a flight of seventeen hundred miles, looking forward to the next phase of our voyage, the **Great Barrier Reef**. Joan had booked us into the Cairns youth hostel but this one turned out to be a lot more primitive than those we had stayed in previously. She managed to get us a private room with a sink, but the showers were at the end of the corridor. The room reminded me of descriptions I had read of the Lubyanka jail in Moscow. As it was for only one night, I agreed to stay but not very graciously.

Joan had scheduled us to join a group of eighteen divers traveling to the reef on a small boat. The boat was to stay out for three days and two nights. It had just one cabin and the young folks allowed us old people to claim it for ourselves. We were the only snorkelers; all the others had very fancy diving equipment. But what an experience! We were perhaps forty miles offshore at **Tongue Reef**, with no other boats about. The weather was good except for one afternoon when the sea became rough. We spent a lot of time in the water and Joan was in her element. She explored the colorful reef and swam among the tropical fish, not all of which were to my liking. I saw barracuda and shark many times. She observed huge clams, with diameters of at least three feet, which were so plump they could not close. When I tired of being in the water with her, the skipper would swim along to keep her safe. Indeed, she did get into trouble once when the sea became rough; she took in some water and began to choke. It was a happy thing that he was there to help her. It was there, on that boat, that I realized how diametrically opposite Joan's and my hobbies are. I love being in the air; she loves being in the deep.

Upon our return to Cairns, we said farewell to our diving buddies and took a train ride to **Kuranda**. The route was first used in the 1880s when the gold fields were in operation. It is now only a tourist attraction. The train penetrates the steep, mountainous area slightly inland from the coast and one can see beautiful scenery and more waterfalls as it moves through the mountain passes.

Before flying to Sydney, the last stop of our journey, we arranged to join a safari tour traveling north along the coast toward **Cape Tribulation**. During the ride, we stopped at a water hole in Daintree Rain Forest where most of the group stripped to their bathing suits and took a swim. I was not so inclined, having read about salt-water crocodiles in the area, but Joan was undaunted and took the swim.

After landing in **Sydney**, we still had three days before our flight home. We had enough time to see a ballet version of Massenet's *Manon* at the

Sydney Opera House. We visited the botanical gardens and took a walk along the waterfront to admire all of the sailboats moored there.

On our long flight back to the U.S., we took stock of our overall impressions of Australia and New Zealand. We recalled that the typical "Do not…" signs seen in Australia, on roads and in public places, cautioning people not to do certain things, either for safety or just to assure civil behavior, were not as much in evidence in New Zealand. It is as though the Kiwis just seem to do the right thing without being told. We also noted that the remnants of the Maori culture suggests that theirs was richer and more sophisticated compared with that of the Australian aboriginals. Today, the Australians seem rougher around the edges, but tend to be wealthier than the New Zealanders who are more agrarian and laid back in their lifestyles.

It was a voyage we will long treasure.

- Galapagos & Machu Picchu, Peru - 2001

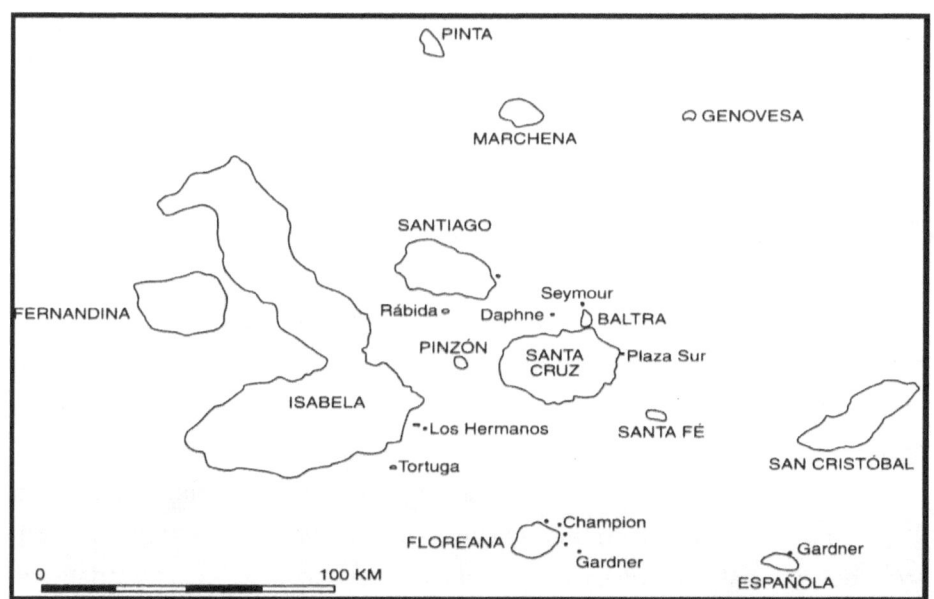

A delightful two-week break from the East Coast's winter weather took us to the Galapagos Islands, off the coast of Ecuador in the southern Pacific Ocean, where Charles Darwin's work during his voyage on the HMS Beagle led to the theory of evolution. The tour began, however, with a visit to Peru to see the amazing stone works and ruins of the ancient Indian civilization at Cusco and Machu Picchu. That civilization had thrived there for one hundred years before the Conquistadores landed from Spain and virtually wiped them out. For a time, I had mistakenly thought that the Inca civilization had dominated Peru for many centuries before the landing of Pizarro and his conquistadores in 1532. It seems, however, that the Incas conquered the area around 1400. Prior to that, there is evidence of many other Indian societies controlling that region, dating back to the eighth millennium BC.

The ruins of Machu Picchu are said to date back to 1450. The city was built during the reign of the Inca emperor Pachacuti but was abandoned by the time of the Spanish Conquest. Although known locally, it was not known to the Spanish during the colonial period and remained unknown to the outside world before being brought to international attention in 1911 by the American historian Hiram Bingham.

An uneventful flight brought us to **Lima** where we met our other tour group members and Meliton, our guide. He took us to the city cathedral, the statue of the virgin of Magdalena, the San Francisco Church, the Museo Nacional de Arqueología, Antropología e Historia del Perú and other tourist sites. We were made aware of the effect of the Spanish conquest, the destruction of the Inca civilization, and the imposition of Catholicism by killing. I had spent four weeks in Lima in 1974 (see Volume I) and so some of this was not new to me.

We flew to **Cusco** the next morning. We hade no difficulties with the high altitude and were taken around town. We saw beautiful Spanish architecture that had been placed directly on top of Inca foundations.

There was the Sun Temple (now Santo Domingo Monastery), Plaza Armas, and impressive Inca walls built with giant boulders that had been shaped to fit perfectly together and on top of each other without connecting mortar. The photos on the website tell a good story but here are our notes from the tour:

Sacsayhuaman: In the hills near the Jesus statue, most likely an Inca temple, also used as a fortress. It has zigzag walls, concentric rings of foundations.

Qenko: A sacred site with a monolith called 'seated puma'.

Puca Pucara: Probably was a hunting lodge on one of Inca's private estates.

Tambomachay: The Inca baths, possible center of water worship.

Next morning, we traveled for three to four hours by train to **Machu Picchu** downhill along the Urubamba River Valley. We arrived at the Machu Picchu Pueblo Hotel, beautifully set in botanical gardens, in Aguas Calientes at the foot of the mountain where the ancient city is located. It was warm and humid. A minibus took us up the mountain to Machu Picchu. After a few hours of wandering, Joan and I returned to the hotel at the base of the mountain for the night. The following morning, we went back up for another tour. We hiked to the Gate of the Sun and sat there; the perfect spot to meditate. In the late afternoon, we returned by train to our hotel in Cusco.

A side trip to **Pisac**, a village thirty-two kilometers from Cusco, had been arranged for the following day. The village boasts a citadel with huge terraces that have spectacular panoramic views. It was market day in the town and we purchased trinkets for the grand-children. We returned to Cusco and enjoyed lunch at the home of a Cusco family, all arranged by Meliton, our tour guide. It was the best meal we had had on the trip to date.

On Sunday, February 11, we flew to **Guayaquil**, Ecuador. We then boarded a charter flight to San Cristobal Airport on **Baltra Island** in the **Galapagos**, a distance of a thousand miles. A van drove us to Lobo Beach where we spent the afternoon. The ninety-two-year old, two-mast schooner, *Mondriaan,* was waiting there for our eighteen-member tour group. The *Mondriaan* would be our home for the next week as we sailed around the Galapagos Islands. The ship traveled by night. We spent our days exploring the islands and interacting with animals that have no fear of humans.

Here are our notes from that fabulous week:

Feb. 12, Monday, Espanola (Hood) Island, Gardner Bay-

AM We see swallowtail gulls (nocturnal), marine iguana, sally light foot crabs, Galapagos and Hood Island mockingbirds. We swim, snorkel and see some manta rays.

PM Ponta Suarez: It is flat and dry. A two-mile hike takes us to see some sea lions, marine iguanas, masked boobies, and hawks fighting. There is a blowhole but no albatross in this season.

Feb. 13 Tuesday, Floreana Island-

AM Their "Post Office" and mailbox is a whaler's barrel. Punta Cormoran, steep small volcano cone, nice beach. We snorkel near the rocks.

Flamingo Lagoon: We see only four or five at a great distance. We proceed to Turtle Beach. There are many flamingos in the water. It is egg-laying time. There are ghost crabs.

Devils Crown: The island is the cone of a volcano. There is excellent snorkeling from the zodiac boat. We see sharks, starfish (red/orange and yellow/green), very clear water, and then a cave. We did not swim into it.

PM We ride a truck to the Highlands. It is cool and green. We see a vermillion flycatcher. There is a cave that was the home to the Witmer family when they came from Germany in the 1930s. Ingeborg (daughter) and Erica (granddaughter) now manage a Pension and shop on Floreana at Puerto Velasco Ibarra.

Feb. 14, Wednesday, Isabela Island-

We ride the Zodiac to the harbor. We see the flamingo lagoon (but there is just one flamingo), and the new Darwin Center for raising baby tortoises. We hear about the illness that wiped out many tortoises. Then, a bus ride and a 1.5 kilometers. walk up to the Sierra Negra crater, green, ferns, hawks and egrets. We eat our boxed lunch. Late afternoon we are invited to use the beach of a small hotel, then walk into the village for ice cream.

Feb. 15, Thursday, Santa Cruz Island-

We visit the town of Puerto Ayora. It is the largest of island towns in Galapagos and has a busy harbor)

Charles Darwin Research Center: These islands formerly had fifteen species of tortoises; now only eleven are left. There is a tortoise incubator, heated with a hair dryer. One cannot change the position of eggs until after the first six weeks of incubation as they have liquid interiors. They are the size of a tennis ball. A tortoise will lay only one or two eggs. Temperature affects sex of the tortoise: 28 degrees Celsius is normal; 29 degrees produces more females, 27 degrees more males. We meet Lonesome George, the last of his species. He has not mated successfully, weighs four hundred pounds, is more than a hundred years old. A tortoise can live to 150-160 years.

We note the mangroves and the *Opuntia* (prickly pear) cactus.

The bus takes us to the lava tunnels and the twin craters on the road to Baltra.

Feb. 16, Friday-

AM Bartolomé Island: It is a dream landscape, the best snorkeling, a copper-colored beach. We climb Pinnacle Rock and walk the Summit Trail (372 steps). We swim/snorkel at the beach on one side. On the other side is the shark/turtle beach. We visit the beach and see a turtle drop an egg at water's edge but she does not recover the egg. Some tourists start to walk toward the egg. Whitman, our guide, chases them away, then carefully picks it up and buries the egg in the sand. The total human population of Bartolomé & Santiago islands comes to thirty.

PM Santiago Island, Sullivan Bay: The lava fields were created 150 years ago. They are of a solid black ropey design and there are 110 square kilometers of them. Lu sees two golden manta rays with a three-four feet span. Joan sees the tail of a white tipped shark, sleeping with its head buried in a hole in a rock.

Feb. 17, Saturday, Baltra Island-

AM We stop at Baltra Island to get fuel, the take a 20 minute zodiak ride to North Seymour Island. We hike to see frigates, lots of red puffed males (lazy birds, no oil on feathers), swallowtail gulls, sea lions and pups and lots of Iguanas digging nests and laying eggs.

We snorkel in two places against rocks, jumping off the zodiak. Lu & Whitman join in. Whitman says it was some of the best snorkeling he has ever done. It is deep water and there are many playful sea lions. We see a 6 foot manta ray, 2 snakes, several huge schools of fish, and, as usual, a variety of parrot, angel, trumpet, cornet, jack and bulls-eye puffer.

PM at Plaza Island: We see marine iguanas, blue footed boobies. Some swallow tails (with red feet & bill) were mating.

Feb. 18, Sunday-

We are to fly out of Baltra. We wait at the airport from 9:30 am to 1:00 p.m when the aircraft finally arrives. In Guayaquil, a tour of the city was arranged. We see the riverfront, cemetery and have dinner at the hotel.

Feb. 19, Monday-

We fly from Guayaquil, to Miami, then to Dulles airport and home.

- NORTHERN EUROPE – FINLAND, RUSSIA, NORWAY, DENMARK, GERMANY, CZECH REPUBLIC, AUSTRIA - 2004

Here is a letter we sent to our family at the end of this trip:

LU AND JOAN'S TRAVELS ALONG THE BEAUTIFUL WATERWAYS OF EUROPE - September 2004

From the Neva in St. Petersburg, the Gulf of Finland, the Sognefjord in Norway, the Elbe in Germany, the Vltava and Lužnice in [the] Czech Republic, the Danube in Austria, across the Baltic and North Seas, the month of September let us travel through some of the most majestic mountains, valleys and coastlines of the world, and see historic structures and monuments built in the glory days of past civilizations. The opulent palaces, art collections and churches of the tsars and princes of Russia; of the Hapsburg and Hohenzollern Kaisers, of the kings of Norway and Denmark, restored to their earlier splendor. All public buildings now, they are accessible to the masses and illuminated to form a regal nightscape, giving our experience a fairy-tale quality.

There were also some more horrific reminders of the brutality of man against man in our more recent history. The area of Hitler's bunker where he and his senior staff killed themselves at the end of World War II; the Berlin Wall which incarcerated an entire city for thirty years; the memorial for the nine hundred days of siege by the Germans [of] St. Petersburg in 1941 to 1943 during which two million of its citizens died; the domination of the Czech Republic by the Russians for more than forty years; various *denkmals* or monuments to the horrors and destructive forces of war, air raids, the Holocaust– sadly one could go on.

We had great luck and good weather, great food and mostly great accommodations (*mit Fruhschtuk*). Lu and Joan find they can still "wing it" when they travel. Public ground transportation, both local and intercity, is reasonably priced with discounted fares for seniors, fast, superbly organized and easy to use. The more northern people are very slim. The further south we go, the fatter they get. Everyone smokes all the time and everywhere (the Norwegians are just beginning to restrict smoking). All the beds were comfortable with the whitest sheets and fluffy down comforters and none were more than eight inches thick. So why in the U.S. do we have mattresses fifteen inches thick?

Helsinki – Wonderful harbor and market. Visit the Rock Church, hewn out of a rock outcrop in the middle of town. We stumble into [a] great new fish restaurant. Tram ride tour of city. Solve our financial crisis when we convince Nordea Bank to cash our Bank Austria checks.

St. Petersburg – Peter built the city in 1720s but Catherine built the cultural window to the west in 1780's through art acquisitions and by absorbing western thinking (Voltaire). Beautifully restored buildings along Neva River. The Hermitage with acres of magnificently restored parquet floors, gold gilt rooms and fine art (none of it Russian); Yusupov Palace where Rasputin's murder took place; Lenin's sale of Rembrandts to Mellon who then built our National Gallery; Ballet, city walks and visit to Pushkin Town (Summer

Palace). A Russian lunch at typical restaurant with vodka bottles on the table. The system makes a Russian guide indispensable for tourists. Hotel is [a] converted factory. Russian guide thinks living conditions today are worse than under the Communist regime.

Norway – The purity of the air and water, a very environmentally conscious nation, sparsely populated with a citizenry that is considerate, helpful and polite to each other. It is a very expensive place to visit (Beer at eight dollars per glass). Tour Oslo on trams and visit Vigeland Sculpture Garden. The picturesque towns along the Sognefjord, (Flam, Lærdal, Sogndal) accessible either by ferry boat, train or road (with very long tunnels – a great way for them to spend their oil revenues), have wonderful accommodations and offer delicious food. Tourist season is over. One morning we take [a] bus to Fjærland, hike about three kilometers to Mundal, take ferry to Balestrand. People spend leisure time outdoors, hiking, biking, mountain climbing, skiing. Our bus to Geilo picked up fifty hikers and returned them up the mountain to their parked vehicles. Great weather. Overnight cabin ferry from Oslo to Copenhagen.

Denmark – All kinds of herring preparations, lachs and other seafood is served on the wharf. We visit Tivoli Gardens and the Herzegovina Restaurant. A very permissive environment. We get tickets to see Mozart's *Titus* at the opera house and the Queen is in attendance. Elsinore Castle is located in a charming town. We take in the Louisiana Art Museum with Jim Dine's bath towel display. Then the Thorvaldsen Sculpture Museum. We enjoy great weather.

Berlin – The City Circle Tour, all day on and off. The Russians had the best part of the city beginning with the Brandenburg Gate and the Reichstag. Lots of rebuilding but things looked garish to us, although the general consensus is the architecture is quite exciting and fresh. Berlin Philharmonic concert at Kulturforum; Berggruen Art Museum near Charlottenburg Palace with many

Matisses, eighty Picassos, forty Klees, and Giacomettis. A bombed out church remains as a *denkmal*. Kranzler Café Haus. The Jewish Museum (Liebeskind) features German-Jewish history from the eleventh century. Doner Kebab at many street corners. Great weather. Boring train ride through what was East Germany to Dresden.

Dresden – Again a City Circle Tour with on and off all day. The Elbe flows through the city. The big item of public consciousness is the air attack of February 1945, three months before the Russians overran the city. New concept for us- "The German as Victim", presented like it was an unprovoked natural disaster. The irony of the Nazi Gauleiter's villa still standing – it had been totally undisturbed by the allied bombing. The major structures (Opera House, Palace, Churches) have been rebuilt at great expense. The city center is beautiful; the outlying areas are ordinary and boxy. Walk along the high road paralleling the Elbe. Many coffee houses. Great food and great weather. The train trip from Dresden to Prague along the Elbe is magnificent.

Czech Republic – The Prague bus station is a zoo. A different class of people travel by bus vs. train. The bus follows the Lužnice river south past Tabor (where, in the 1400s the Hussites experimented with collectives (kibbutzim)). Cĕské Budĕjovice is a large town with a magnificent city center and great beer. We arrive after dark but a taxi pulls up and we get the last room at a neat pension (selected from Joan's guide book "bible") in the center of the old town. (Luck!) Next day we bus to the beautiful but hilly Cĕský Krumlov. It seems solely inhabited by tourists. We attend a concert of encores for piano, violin and horn trio. No reason to stay here. We depart by bus to Kaplice and train to Linz. There we catch the train that takes us along Danube to Durnstein.

Dürnstein – We arrive after dark. A German and his "daughter" also alight and he points us to the Tourist Information Office. It is closed but they have a list of pensions with direct phone connections. We pick one, press the connect button and the pension manager answers. We cut a deal and walk there. It is grape harvest time. There is ample *Sturm* (recently pressed grape juice, slightly fermented) for Heuriger celebrations. We do a bike ride along one side of the Danube to Krems and return on the other side. Then we hike through the vineyards. We enjoy more good weather, good wine and good food (schnitzel, blood sausage, kraut, *spätzle*, strudel, *Wachauer Laberl*). We take the train to Vienna and I leave my brand new Tilley hat on the train. I am hatless in Vienna.

Vienna – We arrive at Pension Nossek and our shipped luggage awaits us. We attend High Mass at St. Stephen's. A visit to the cemetery to visit Lu's father's grave and also the Jewish Museum. We buy box seats for Donizetti's *La Favorite* at the Staatsoper. A hike in the Wienerwald from Simmering to Kobenzl to Grinzing. More good weather, good food and drink! We are invited to have *jause* at [the] Landtmann restaurant near the Volkstheater with Mary Steinhauser. "Alles its Gemutlich" in Lu's hometown.

See you soon! Love, Joan and Lu

After returning to our home in Bethesda, I was tormented by the loss of my Tilley hat. I had received in the mail from the company that produces the hat, a guarantee to replace the hat if it should be lost or destroyed. So, I send the company the following message:

October 29, 2004

Alex Tilley
Tilley Endurables Corporation

West Seneca, New York 14224

Dear Mr. Tilley:

I just received your "Straight Shooter's Statement of Loss"
You must be a wonderful Boss!
Your letter came just in time,
I lost the hat last month while it was still in its prime.
On the train along the Danube going to Vienna.
Boy, was I in a dilemma.

The hat was properly marked with name and number.
But the Viennese just like to waltz and slumber.
And will not make an international call to one who they think is "dumber".
I enclose your certificate, but without my visa number.
Because I fear identity theft! But please have one of your people call
My phone number; it will ring down the hall.
And I will provide the number while standing tall
Fully dressed, but still hatless you will recall.

Then you will have all the necessary data,
To process the charge which I will pay later.
And I shall be ever so grateful
To have a Tilley hat again in my estate-ful.

Yours with much appreciation and gratitude.
And that's not just another platitude.

Sincerely,
Ludwig Rudel

- ALASKA - 2007

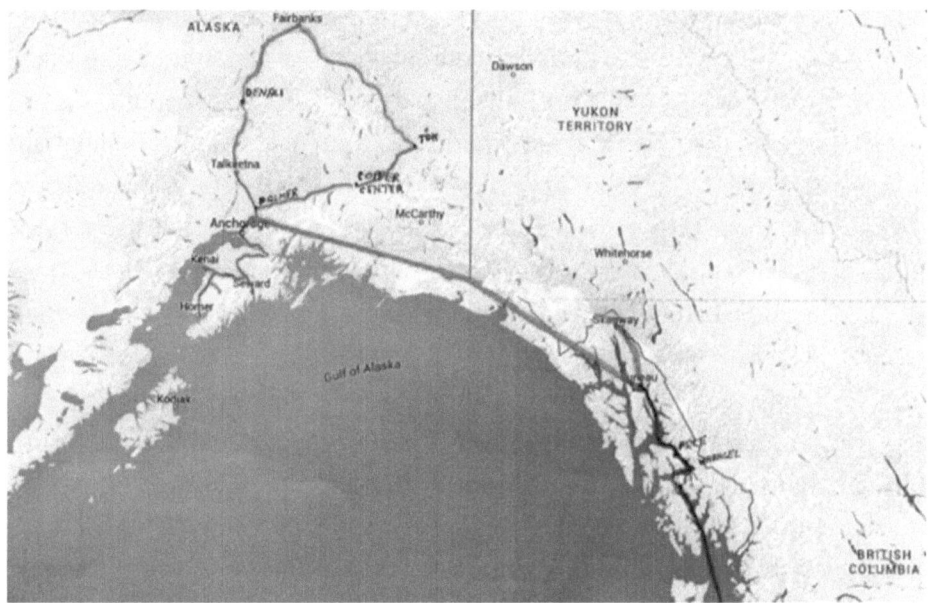

Robert Service is one of my favorite poets. His writings about the people who make their home in the Yukon and the wilds of the northwest fascinate me. One of our close friends from our days in India, Bob Satin, had moved to Alaska just after the turn of the millennium following a painful divorce. Shortly after his arrival there, we were surprised to learn that he had been elected mayor of the town of Seward. Bob seemed to have responded well to "the call of the wild." Apparently, longevity and deep roots are not a requirement for public office in Alaska.

During the summer of 2007, Joan and I decided to explore this outlier state to learn what distinguishes it from "the lower forty-eight." Road travel is highly restricted due to Alaska's topography and the scarcity of roads; thus, flights by small aircraft and water passage with scheduled ferries are the norm for public transport there. In fact, a large ferry plies the waters with scheduled voyages from Bellingham, Washington, along the coast of

Canada, then through the inside passage between Alaska's coastal islands. It terminates at Juneau. One can hop on and off the ferry at any of its many stops along the way. Since both Joan and I have an aversion to cruise ships, that was the mode of transport we chose to make our trip.

Our overall plan was to fly to Seattle and then take a bus to Bellingham where we would catch the ferry to Alaska. The five-week trip would be divided into three phases. The first would be the ferry ride to Juneau, stopping at Ketchikan, Wrangell, Petersburg, and Matanuska. Some of those stops lasted for just an hour while the boat loaded. At others, we spent a couple of days. At Juneau we would arrange a day trip to Skagway by rail and then fly directly to Anchorage.

For the second phase we envisioned making a large loop by car, north through Palmer to Talkeetna, Mount McKinley (Denali) and continuing north to arrive in Fairbanks on June 21, the summer solstice. We had heard that the entire city of Fairbanks holds a twenty-four hour non-stop celebration on that day. We would then continue the loop by driving east and then south via North Pole, Deltana, Tok, Copper Center and Valdez to return to Anchorage. Finally, our third phase would also be made by car and would take us on a southerly loop from Anchorage to Seward and Homer, Halibut Bay, then back to Anchorage where we would catch our return flight back to Washington D.C.

In Seattle, on Wednesday, May 30, we caught the Greyhound Bus to Bellingham, checked into a hotel for two nights and boarded the ferry on June 1 for a 6 pm departure. The voyage to our first stop, Wrangell, took two nights. During the ride, we found our cabin to be quite comfortable. The rear deck was taken over by the back-packers who pitched their tents. The weather was ideal and we sailed up the Canadian coast, past Vancouver and Rupert until we again entered U.S. waters. The ferry's first stop was Matanuska. There was a new growth of fresh green on the trees and snow-capped mountains in the distance. During a short walk near the harbor, we noticed how the cruise lines had taken over the tourist trade of the town by setting up fancy shops. The locals had little choice but to work for them. We then re-boarded for the remaining leg of the journey to Wrangell, where we got off. It was Sunday afternoon and we checked into Bruce Harding's Sourdough Lodge. They served a family style dinner to their guests and each of our plates of food could feed a family of four. From conversations around the table we learnt that a large part of the land upriver from the town had been declared a federal wilderness area. New federal regulations restricting logging had hurt the town's economy.

Next morning, on a walk around the town, we saw rusted out and abandoned debris everywhere and realized that waste disposal was a big problem there. We then took a five-hour ride on a jet boat to view the Stikine River. Despite it being early June, there was still ice on the river and snow on the shore. After dinner we took a cab to the boat terminal and waited for the ferry, due to dock at midnight, for our onward journey to Petersburg. The cab driver in Wrangell, a woman, provided us with a view of the life style prevailing on these islands. It is very accepting of human foibles. She told us that at midnight she usually takes home the drunks. After midnight, she takes home the bartenders.

We slept for the brief four-hour voyage on the ferry. Getting off at 3 am, we found that the B&B next to the ferry dock, where we were booked, was still dark. So we dumped our luggage on the porch, walked into town, saw a light in the harbormaster's shack and knocked on his door. George, the harbormaster, was on duty and invited us in for a cup of coffee. We enjoyed a pleasant chat and then moved on to have breakfast and check into our B&B. The B&B had crab pots in the water and provided their residents with free Dungeness crabs, nicely steamed and ready for eating. Petersburg is a large town surrounded by pristine forests and there were things we wanted to see. Thus, we decided to stay there until Friday.

One of the most memorable experiences for us in Petersburg was a boat ride upriver to the Le Conte glacier. It was rainy and a bit foggy but we saw beautiful scenery. There were aqua and cobalt colored icebergs, the size of houses, floating down the river next to our boat. Seals were stretched out on the icebergs, having just given birth, and the bald eagles flew about, eating the placenta. We also hired a seaplane and pilot to fly us over the glacier. What a view!

Next, we rented a car and drove down Mitkof highway to visit the Tonga National Park. At a picnic area, we ate our salmon and cheese and did some walking on the paths and specially built walkways across the wetlands. We saw the cannery. It employs three to four hundred Mexican workers and provides them with food and housing in addition to a salary. College kids also work there but they set up their tents near the airport.

On Saturday morning we checked out of the B&B, walked next door to the ferry terminal and board at 5:45 am for Juneau. It took us thirteen hours to get there. En route we watched whales and their pups swimming just yards from the ferry. We were to remain in Juneau for six days before flying to Anchorage on Friday, but intended to make a side trip to Skagway as well. Juneau is most memorable for our visit to the Mendenhall glacier, the Tracey Arms glacier and also the north and south Sawyer glacier. We saw waterfalls, granite walls and the usual array of seals with pups, eagles and whales.

The three-hour trip to Skagway by high-speed catamaran was spectacular. It began with sunny weather and ended in rain. This town played an important part in the 1898 gold rush. We viewed a video prepared by the Park Service that described life during that historic period. The town was the closest point to the gold fields approachable by boat, but a very steep climb was required from Skagway to White Pass, at the Alaskan border with Canada. In fact, it is reported that 3,500 horses died in those days due to overloading for the climb. As for us, we rode by rail to White Pass at the Canadian border in a fine rain. The area is truly picturesque.

On Friday, June 15, we departed by air to Anchorage, immediately picked up our rental car and drove to Homer to spend the night. Our daughter and son-in-law, the Devines, had close friends, Paul and Cecily, living in Palmer and so we arranged to meet them for dinner. They were extremely helpful and gave us good advice about travelling in Alaska. Phase two of our journey was about to start.

Our first stop was Talkeetna, the launch pad for the Denali (previously called Mt. McKinley) mountain climbers. We stayed at a climber's hostel and watched how they would pack and prepare for the ordeal. In a conversation with one climber who had descended the day before we arrived, I asked him to describe his climb and was surprised when he told me it took him twenty-five days to go up and down. First, he got a small aircraft to fly him and all his equipment to the base camp at seven thousand feet. Then he started his climb but there was no way for him to carry all his stuff at once. So he went back and forth a lot, ferrying equipment, about three thousand feet at a time, to his next stop. Up and back he went like a porter, hauling his provisions, oxygen, tents, sleeping gear, warm clothes, etc. The higher he went, the fewer provisions he had to ferry but he had to acclimate his body to the thinning air. Sometimes the weather did not cooperate and he had to wait for the storm to lift. Finally, maybe three thousand feet below the summit, he waited for good weather to make the last climb to the peak and then down again the same way. I make a mental note never, ever, to try doing this for fun.

Nonetheless, I arranged to make a flight in a small aircraft called a Beaver, to a relatively flat snow field near the base camp, and enjoyed the landing and subsequent take off. There were lots of glaciers to see, as well as many mountain peaks to navigate around and between.

After this, we drove north, to the left of Denali, and found our reserved cabin near the entrance to Denali Park. We quickly learnt that driving there could be dangerous at dusk, when the moose wander the roads. Their long legs make their heavy bodies windshield level. If you hit them broadside, the body will wind up in your lap. Decapitations have occurred. But being a good place for walking, we spent five days there, including a day trip into the park itself to walk on Mount McKinley.

The next day, we bought tickets for a tour bus to drive us into the park, to the resort at the foot of the big mountain. The drive into the park was great; we saw bear, moose and fox. We enjoyed some refreshments and a walk among the wild flowers that everywhere were plentiful.

On the ride back, a storm suddenly develops and it begins pouring rain and hail to the point that mudslides close the road, both in front and behind the bus. The driver exclaimed he had never seen such a storm in all his years traversing this route, which, of course, does not give us much comfort. He radios for help and we were assured some equipment was on its way to open the road. Even so, we decided to get off and brave the rain because we could still see mudslides and boulders rolling down the steep side of the road and falling in close proximity to the bus. If the bus got pushed over the cliff, we did not want to be in it. Eventually, a large front-end loader appeared to clear a path, and the bus proceeded to drive out of the park. Everyone was safe.

On the way to Fairbanks and our rendezvous with the summer solstice celebration, we drove into Nenana, at the junction of the Chena and Tanana rivers, and stopped for lunch at a restaurant with a parking lot full of motorbikes. Our waitress turned out to be from Switzerland, working her way around the world. There were human interest stories everywhere; Alaska draws odd persons to it. In Fairbanks the solstice celebrations were under way. The sidewalks were full of people dancing and singing, several music bands and lots of buskers. We joined in the fun. We also visited the university museum and walked along the promenade of the Chena River, which runs through town. There was no nightfall on this day as we were only a few miles south of the Arctic Circle.

On Friday, we headed west to the North Pole and then south to Delta Junction, where we left the Chena and drove onward to Tok. Our tour now took us southwest to Copper Center, with its beautiful roaring stream, and then to Valdez, the scene of the big Exxon oil spill, where we saw big oil pipelines. The salmon had just started running and we saw fishermen, fifty feet apart along both banks of the river, hauling out the fish. The scenery from Copper Center to Valdez, as we cut through the mountains, pass Keystone Canyon and cross Thompson Pass, is extraordinarily beautiful. We bedded down at a beautiful cabin, ten miles outside Valdez, high over Robe Lake. While we did not actually enter Valdez, we were told that spill had been completely cleaned up.

On Sunday, we doubled back the way we came, on the road to Copper Center and then rolled on to Anchorage, to meet our friend, Bob Satin. He welcomed us as "outlaws" and told us the difference between in-laws and outlaws was that outlaws were "wanted." We were treated to deliciously prepared Alaskan king crab, after which we toured the city, including the aviation museum. It was a chance to learn about Bob's new life. He is a geologist by training and had become a volunteer guide at some of the national park sites where there are many glaciers. His term as mayor of Seward was now over but he still remained involved in local affairs. Bob had remarried and his new wife is a key person at the Anchorage station of National Public Radio.

After a couple of days in Anchorage, we were ready for phase three of our travels. The last loop would not involve as many driven miles as the previous one. The road system is so sparse that we had to retrace some portions of our route to see what we wanted to see. We drove first to Seward with Bob and Susan who gave us a tour of the town. On Saturday, June 30, Joan and I drove further south on the peninsula to Homer.

The drive to Homer took us past Kenai. We drove along the Kenai River and again saw fishermen on both banks, hooking salmon as fast as they could pull them out of the water. This time they were standing much closer to each other; about ten feet apart. One fisherman told us he "… lost one to a bear this morning."

Homer has a very helpful visitors' center which assisted us in finding accommodations and then arranged for a boat, the *Danny J*, to take us across Halibut Cove to a small town with a wonderful restaurant the next morning. In addition to a delicious lunch, the boat trip afforded us some spectacular scenery on the way. On the way back, we stopped at Gull Island where we saw cormorants, puffins and, of course, lots of gulls.

In Homer, we struck up a conversation with a pony-tailed motor-biker who told us that the town was "… a quaint drinking village with a small fishing problem." It was all good-natured banter. I no longer remember his personal story, which he was not at all reluctant to share with Joan and me. But I do recall the story confirming our impression that Alaska is not a sought after destination in and of itself; rather, it is a place where people go if they want to get away—escape-- from their former lives.

The tour of Alaska was truly memorable. All in all, after five weeks of touring, we concluded that "Seward's Folly"-- the purchase of Alaska from Russia in 1867 for two cents per acre-- was truly worth it.

- WINTER TRAVELS WITH THE FAMILY

For modern families who have chosen to live their lives in geographically dispersed locations, coming together for major holidays is perhaps the best way to reconnect. During the early period of our family's growth, when our wallets were leaner, we chose our home in Bethesda or the farmhouse in Pennsylvania as the meeting place. That was where we welcomed the twenty-first century on December 31, 1999. We would also routinely gather for a week or so in the summer at our farm in Pennsylvania. But, as we aged, it became more interesting to find a location in the tropics for our biennial family gatherings. Since the turn of the century, we've holidayed in Edisto, South Carolina (2003-04), Conch Key, Florida (2005-06), Belize and Guatemala (2007-08), Costa Rica (2009-10), and Vieques, Puerto Rico (2011-12). Often, Joan and I would remain at these destinations for several weeks following the children's departure to enjoy the warm climate. [10]

Here are two reports of these winter travels that we sent to our family and friends.

Costa Rica – Winter 2009-2010

Hello Friends and Family:

It is January 17, 2010, and we are exactly midpoint in our ten-week Costa Rica sojourn. We hope each of our friends and family are safe, warm and receiving mental and physical sustenance. As we are! The one thing we miss here is the stimulating company of our good friends and family. Please be assured that we think of you often, as we explore this beautiful country.

What follows is detail of the experiences of our travels. Regrettably, it brings to mind the invidious "Christmas Letter". If you are busily engaged, do not read further. Some of you know Costa Rica better than we. On the off chance this holds interest for you (just possibly you are at this moment suffering from the winter blahs) you might skim the rest of this message.

This country is one large lush tropical garden. Everything grows here. Joan is in her glory looking at the flora (and the fauna, i.e., the birds). All lands that have not been turned into parks are up for sale. There are literally hundreds of land developments that have been started (very few look like successes; most seem to be in trouble from the current economic decline) and an endless supply of parcels along every road have "For Sale" signs. Lu is not tempted.

Hotels are quite empty. We have not had to make advance reservations, which suits us just fine. We find many restaurants

---

10   That pattern shifted, in the summer of 2013, as the family gathered at David's cabin in the Sierras

closed. We travel with modest food supplies and usually seek out a facility with a refrigerator.

Plenty of "for sale" signs but few road signs. Try to find your way from one small town to the next … good luck. The main road, the Pan-American highway is the exception. This two-lane highway has a lot of trucks and when they want to pass, they pass. The smaller roads (most of them dirt) remain unmarked. So one consults one's map? There are roads on maps where no roads exist. Or there may be roads but no bridges. Road conditions are not always as shown. It is advisable to be off the roads and settled in your B&B by dark. We rented a fou-by-four drive small vehicle. It had less than five thousand kilometers on it and we got every kind of insurance they offered. When we return it in another five weeks it will have taken a lot of hard wear from us. May it still be serviceable at the end of our trip.

The mountains - Our first venture after leaving the luxury of the Hilton near the airport was to drive to Rincón de la Vieja where Joan landed us in a B&B that looked like a stage coach stop (or a DAK bungalow) with mosquito netting. Two Dutch couples and two German couples. The hike in Rincón was spectacular from waterfalls to boiling geothermal pools. Then off to Lake Arenal (about 2,500 feet elevation) with lots of howler monkeys and beautiful scenery, a visit to the Observatory Lodge (set up years ago by [the] Smithsonian to monitor the volcano) and our "awakening" about CR roads. We are grateful to our four-wheel drive wagon to keep us safe. The scenery, the panoramas, the natural beauty is always greater than one can describe. The volcano at Arenal was rumbling and periodically blew out huge boulders which we watched tumbling down the side of the volcano.

The "Playas"- We arrived in Nosara (on the Pacific coast of the Nicoya peninsula) on December 19 and got into our casita, stocked it and scouted out the landscape. It is a surfer's paradise. The long rolling waves and the gradual sandy beaches are legendary among the surfing community. On the flight to the airport at the city of Liberia, there were surfers who were hurrying to get here because they monitored the weather systems and a set of storms were on their way to cause big waves! The family arrived a week later on Christmas Day.

And then there were ten!

It now seems like a joyous blur of activity. Surf lessons – Caroline, nine, on her first surfing lesson was the first to get up on her board. David, Sandra and Ruthann followed with surf lessons. All the kids, including the six-year olds, loved the surf and are excellent swimmers. They would dive under/ dive over the huge waves and bobbed up every time. Far braver than we. So ... surf lessons, boogey boarding, canopy tour zip lines, yoga classes, conversations with laid back *Ticos* (locals), and, a fully air-conditioned *casa* with a clean cool pool where Lu can hide out while everyone else is trying new things. It is best to plan a long siesta (11 am to 3 pm) when the heat is simply too much. The sun rises at 5:30 am and sets at 5:30 pm. Mornings are really great. We get up at 6:00 and go to bed by 8:00...at least we older surfers do.

The kids and grandkids left January 5th. We packed up, cleared out of the villa and headed back to the mountains.

We drove into the mountains above Miramar and found a perfect little place to stay with cool temperatures called El Mirador (meaning lookout point). Just two cabins, great view, pool and beautiful garden. Built by a German couple and managed by their daughter, Ule, who has been most gracious to us. We have breakfast on our veranda each morning. Two lovely dogs - one a German shepherd keep watch.

On the 5th day, we decided to leave. It had been quite windy recently and the night of 10th the wind was so strong-- gusts over sixty miles per hour-- it blew the ceramic tiles off the front of our cabin and shredded much of the garden. The two dogs protected us all night by sitting on our veranda.

So, back to the beach, this time south of Jako, for another three days of ocean-front relaxing in a small cabana right on another lonely (and lovely) beach.

When we thought the winds had calmed down, we headed again into the mountains, past San Isidro and into the passes that lead to Costa Rica's highest peak, Chirripó (about four thousand meters). We explored the nearby river valleys (more like ravines) by car and on foot, ate rice and beans at small *restaurantes* and followed the one lane dirt trails as far as they would take us. Past the entrance to Chirripó National Park at the end of the trail we discovered the Cloudbridge Preserve. That is what the Garden of Eden must have looked like. Waterfalls, tranquility gardens, flowers in colors too varied to describe, trees, labyrinths, paths hewn out of rocks, and nary anyone within earshot or sight. Viktor, the *trabajando*, welcomed us with a big smile, unwilling to believe we could not speak Spanish.

These mountains appear to be like Kashmir without the background snowcaps, especially the racing river valleys. The rivers have glorious waterfalls and rapids and they are abundant with trout.

These are truly happy people, content in their ways. Everyone greets passers on the roads. We ordered wine at our hotel and, as the proprietor inserted the corkscrew, another customer known to him entered the restaurant. He stopped what he was doing and went through the elaborate ritual of cordially greeting the newcomer; then went back to opening the wine bottle...The fruits (papaya, pineapple, watermelon) are abundant as are some vegetables. We are served copious amounts every morning. All desserts and candy are sweet; even bitter chocolate.

The towns are limited in what one can get there. Shopping is done in San Jose.

So, another five weeks of this leisure life before we rejoin friends and family. We look forward to that. Be of good cheer, and, above all else, keep warm.

Lu and Joan

Puerto Rico – Winter 2011-2012

To Our Friends and Family. – January 21, 2012

Life for us in PR is great. After the family departed following our Christmas week party in Vieques, we have been bumming around, surveying and comparing the various beaches, surfs, vistas, foods and accommodations. Joan is very thorough in her research (we are toting around three guidebooks) and all I have to do is follow along. My challenge is to avoid mosquitoes and other biting bugs. There is also a small conflict going on between Joan and me. I like comfortable resorts. She likes small casitas where she has a kitchenette! My mother used to argue with my stepfather about the same thing. She wanted to go to a resort in the Catskills; he wanted to rent, what she called a *kochalein* (Yiddish for "cook for yourself"). She would complain that all year she cooks and cleans in our house. Then for vacation he wanted to take her to a country house where she could cook and clean there! So it goes! Except with a role reversal added! At the moment we are at a casita on the very edge of the beach, looking at the Atlantic Ocean and the wonderfully large swells rolling in. Soon the kite surfers will arrive and put on a show. Joan is cooking breakfast!

The time on Vieques with the kids was quite wonderful. The house worked out just fine-- seven bedrooms, two kitchens, two nice big porches overlooking the water. Nice beach, water a little rough for Lu and me, but the kids thought it was just great; they love the wild surf. We asked Declan, when he was swimming at the dangerous beach with Ruthann, "What shall we tell your parents if you drown?" Big smile, "Tell them I was having fun!" We also went to calmer beaches, of which there are many. Joan did all the breakfasts. Everyone else cooked the other meals. Good vibes and harmony.

Day after day, we rise to another seventy degree morning, the sun shining, the rolling waves crashing against the beach, the ocean expanse before us … and declare to each other, "...another typical shitty day in the tropics!" This small island, a part of a chain of islands running southeast from the tip of Florida, first Cuba, then Haiti and Dominican Republic and then PR, is in the "Atlantic time zone" an hour ahead of the East Coast.

Since 1898, when the U.S. fought and won a war with Spain, it has been a U.S. possession. But we really do not know how to manage colonial exploitation. Most PR residents know they enjoy the best of all worlds. They are U.S. citizens (as many in other countries eagerly seek to be) and elect all of their governing officers (no appointed officers by the U.S. Government), but pay no U.S. taxes. Any taxes collected here are used to meet the costs of their own government's programs. In addition, they receive U.S. funding for much infrastructure. We saw a number of signs announcing projects being funded by the U.S. "stimulus" program. They can serve in the volunteer U.S. military if they so desire but the Coast Guard, the Customs Service, the National Parks and their defense needs are provided by the U.S. at no cost to them. The standard of living seems to be quite high.

They are a really laid back people with a relaxed time horizon and a level of patience that we have not found in other societies. I can't imagine many cases of ulcers here. Their automobile driving reflects this. If a car stops on the wrong side of the road, blocks traffic to buy something from a roadside vendor, all traffic stops and patiently waits the completion of the transaction. A car horn is used only as a way to waive at or greet a friend. Everything is a party, including religious services. Playing a car radio loudly is considered a gift to those within earshot. Road signs and directions are not always accurate. Their highway numbering system is most confusing. To ask directions always elicits smiles and accommodations to help but often the directions will be in error.

Godly they may be, but cleanliness is another story. *Basura* (garbage or litter) is everywhere but no one seems to mind. Sound pollution is not considered a negative. Everyone speaks loudly and in an animated style. I would be interested to know how the EPA enforcement units operate here.

There is a sense that, at some time in the recent past, some took the trouble to make attractive improvements but these improvements were not maintained and have gone to seed.

Waiters serve you while talking on their cell phones. Cars drive down the street blaring music; they think they are adding something to others' well being by doing so.

January 18, 2012- We are now on the North Coast, West of Isabella at the Villas del Mar Hau. We are staying in a pastel colored casita right on the beach for a few days. They are most comfortable; with tiny kitchenette, two tiny bedrooms with tiny beds, big TV, lovely veranda, with a narrow boardwalk separating us from the beach and the ocean – close enough to occasionally feeling a spray from the waves. And, yes, there are waves, big swells, and they are getting bigger and the wind stronger with each day we are here. We had heavy rains last night. The casita has many windows "screened" with the jalousie closures so in the middle of the night we ran around turning knobs. The view from the veranda is spectacular – huge waves, white foam and sprays and the sound of pounding surf. Something like Vieques, but wilder.

Yesterday we took a ride down the coast to the Rincon area. Saw the surfers (perhaps a hundred of them) in two different areas. Where they go depends on the swells/waves and that depends on the winds. We looked at two places to stay south of Rincon, but there were not nearly as nice as what we have now. Rincon looks a little trashy, but it does have a good German restaurant – last night's dinner. We drove home in the dark which wasn't exactly fun.

After leaving Vieques and a night at the Fajardo Inn we shuttled to Enterprise Car Rental (strangely located in the parking garage of the Ritz-Carlton near the [international] airport). In our Mitsubishi Lancer we drove south on PR-52 and then into the hills on Ruta Panorámica to the town of Jayuya, located almost in the dead center of the big island. Lots of narrow roads with fifteen miles per hour curves – beautiful, lush, and occasionally tense. (Joan is driving and appears relaxed and Lu appears to have confidence in her driving abilities... a trip of appearances).

As we reach our parador it starts raining. The parador is the former home of a coffee plantation owner. Wood frame with many levels and add-ons. We are given the last room, lowest level, dark and damp, windows that don't really open, nice door to a little porch, no screens, ...need I say more. To add to all this unhappiness, Lu's one square foot pork chop at dinner cannot be cut, chewed or bent. We sleep sealed into this room. All the other rooms have wide open door[s] and windows. You know and I know that there must be mosquitoes happily living in our room from years past. Lu wakes up with lots of bites, very unhappy and I know we have to immediately leave. After a cup of coffee, we are able to delay our departure a couple of hours because it really is a beautiful location and a beautiful morning.

We head down to the Ponce on the south ...more fifteen miles per hour curves, but a beautiful ride. Ponce is the second largest city and we loved it. Stayed five days in Hotel Belgica, an old colonial hotel just off the main square for just under dollars hundred a night w/breakfast (and a refrigerator). We explored the city and celebrated with the city one of the more important holidays of the year – The Feast of Three Kings, twelve days after Christmas. [Almost] everything is closed which is not so great for tourists but there is much music (the sound truck was parked under our balcony at 6:00 am), lots of Christmas lights, and people in the central square – every child in the city receives a gift from the mayor and the Three Kings – parents and kids line up for blocks from early morning. The celebration went on for three days. On Monday we thought for sure we could go to the bank. No it was closed – celebrating the birthday of some esteemed Puerto Rican. We thought this might just go on until Lent when we can celebrate Carnival!!

We took a ride to Santa Isabel (a little village on the water east of Ponce) and had our first taste of *mofongo* – fried and mashed green plantains usually stuffed with meat or seafood. Lucky, it was a good restaurant. We had it with *pollo* and it was very good. We ordered some elsewhere – that one was very dry and tasteless.

Joan loved Ponce and the old colonial hotel, but it was time to head to the dry southwest coast. We found the place of Lu's dreams! A resort – the Copa Marina, located on the outskirts of Guánica, on the water with beautifully landscaped and maintained grounds, the room was just fine with a patio, chaise, chairs and table, several pools, tennis, etc. The occupancy rate was no more than five percent. As a result we never knew which of their restaurants would be open and when. Food (if you had the patience to wait for it) was quite okay. As the saying goes, "God sent Lu to Puerto Rico to develop patience." Lu was very happy. We may just go back. Joan enjoyed the short boat trip to Gilligan's Island (yes, that is its name) to swim and snorkel in the mangrove bay. It certainly dispelled her notion that mangroves grew only in swamps and housed a lot of snakes.

Out of Guánica and the resort we drove to Cabo Rojo – the southern-most tip of PR. Hot, dry and some beautiful beaches with no place to stay, and some non-sand beaches with lodging. We continued on to San Germain – a beautifully restored colonial city, but a little late in the day and much of it closed at 4:00 pm.

We leave Copa Marina Resort – Lu with tears in his eyes – and head back into the hills sort of in the direction of the Arecibo Observatory, more twists and turns, to our reservation at something called the TJ Ranch owned by Tony and Juanita. Had some difficulty finding it – deep in the hills of the Karst Country. (The guidebook describes the Karst Country as a region of crumbling limestone hills, some very high, smothered by dense jungle, deep gorges and pockmarked by cavernous sinkholes.) TJ Ranch has three casitas, an open air restaurant, their home and some other out buildings desperately in need of maintenance. They hail from New York/Boston and other vague locations. Juanita (Joan) with her sister purchased forty acres of this land when just out of college; Joan is now sixty. There are many parts to this story. Tony is an excellent cook. It was a very peaceful three days ...lots of reading and one day [at] the Observatory.

Most interesting. The Observatory is partially under the [administration] of the National Science Foundation. Originally started by our military. It is a single dish radio telescope receiving radio light waves (not audio), and is a thousand feet in diameter. They feature a good Visitor's Center. This site was chosen because the Karst country features natural sink holes (in which they could place the dish), and is sufficiently near the equator (it is at eighteen degrees latitude and can scan for twenty degrees on either side – for a forty degree field) which was a requirement. Use of this facility is available to all scientists worldwide (if they come with their own funding) and all research is published although we had difficulty finding recently published work on display.

We watch the weather report for both east and west coasts and are happy with our consistent eighty degree highs and seventy lows. We think of you often and say, "... wouldn't so-and-so love this!" The Puerto Ricans are a very happy and gentle people. Always willing to help and answer questions. Information is frequently just approximate. Most English-speaking Puerto Ricans we met grew up in Brooklyn or the Bronx.

In a few days we will go to the rain forest of El Yunque on the other side of the island and stay on the outskirts of San Juan the last three nights - we fly to Tampa and will be spending about two weeks in Florida. Plan to visit cousin Elaine at daughter Vicki's in Bradenton and cousin Helen & Roger on Marco Island. On the way home we plan to stop in Charleston (Frank Thomas and wife who are living there in a retirement community).

We hope to be home late February. Early March we go to New York for Juls' birthday and a wedding and maybe a few extra days.

Hope you are well. Winter has been kind to us thus far.

Love, L & J

7

CANADA

OUR FAMILY'S CAMPING TRIP into western Canada during the summer of 1981 had somewhat familiarized us and tantalized us with the charm and cordiality of our northern neighbors. I often thought about the attractions of life there. Shortly after the turn of the Millennium, Joan and I decided to travel to Nova Scotia. At that time it was quite easy to get there. A car ferry from Portland, Maine crossed the mouth of the Bay of Fundy to the southern tip of the Nova Scotia peninsula. One could return to the U.S. by circumnavigating Nova Scotia, crossing the isthmus, the land bridge connecting the Nova Scotia peninsula with the continent, west into New Brunswick, then drive south to Maine. Alternately, one could take another ferry directly to Bar Harbor, Maine. The further one travels north in Nova Scotia, past Halifax to Cape Breton, the more beautiful the scenery becomes, particularly along the shoreline. On a clear day, Prince Edward Island can be seen on the other side of the Northumberland Strait.

The history books claim that a man with the English sounding name of John Cabot had discovered this area, but eventually, one learns that his real name was Giovanni Caboto, an Italian, just like Christofo Colombo. The people living in these Maritime Provinces of Canada are of British and French Acadian stock and are very laid back. Even though the weather tends to be wet, and is an important subject of conversation among the locals, it seems the area has lent itself to pleasant mid-summer vacationing.

By 2001, we had fixed up our mountain retreat in Pennsylvania. How neat it would be to have another cottage by the sea!

It was another five years before we had enough cash to buy a property in the Maritimes. By then, we had gradually sold our remaining interest in Glendale. Yet, my motivation to search for a suitable property was two-fold. I had become convinced global warming could not or would not be halted by my fellow human beings. My second concern was that, some time in the future, there might be a worldwide food shortage. It would be good for our family to have close access to the seas. One can always go fishing.

In October 2006, I flew to Moncton, New Brunswick to explore the coastal areas of the Northumberland Strait along New Brunswick and Nova Scotia. I wanted access to the sea as well as some tillable land. I wanted property with an elevation of at least fifty feet above the present sea level. I focused on property in New Brunswick because the Northumberland Straits enjoy water temperatures much warmer than the Bay of Fundy; indeed warmer than any coastal area north of Philadelphia, due to its shallowness and the peculiar path of the Gulf current. I also saw that road access from Maine to New Brunswick was more convenient than to Nova Scotia. It did not require a ferry ride from the U.S. I was also interested in New Brunswick because it is a bilingual province from whence the Acadians came, most of who departed for Louisiana after the French and Indian War of 1754-1763 and became known in the U.S. as the "Cajuns".

I had researched property availabilities on the Canadian multi-list system through the Internet, and found specific referrals from Canadian realtors. I found the area to be a buyers' market with lots of property from which to choose. The Canadians have strict rules about a realtor not acting simultaneously as agent for both buyer and seller.

I also explored the Bay of Fundy coast but found that the tides produce wide areas of shore lands that, during low tides, expose muddy red clay. I saw no sand beaches; it was very unattractive. I then drove north of Moncton, along the coast to Richibucto (the Kent County seat) and Kouchibouguac National Park. That area is lovely but I thought it too iso- lated. The coastal land east of Moncton (Cap Pele and Cape Tormentine) is very low lying and densely populated with small properties and mod- est cabins at almost sea level elevations, directly along the water front- age. There was another area along that coastline with hundred year old farmhouses on larger parcels, but very little of that was being offered for sale. Shediac, and the areas to its north --Cocagne, Grande-Digue and Bouctouche-- seemed very interesting. The area is the center for tourism on the coast near Moncton. It is the lobster capital of the world. The entire area has a quality of "beachiness" like Rehoboth Beach, Delaware but is less sophisticated. Tourist season is from mid June to the end of August.

Just to complete my research, I crossed the isthmus separating New Brunswick from Nova Scotia and travelled eastward to explore Amherst, Pugwash, Tatamagouche, Pictou, New Glasgow, and Antigomish. These coastal lands are farmed and relatively flat. As one travels eastward the lands become hilly, not unlike central Pennsylvania. Antigonish is a univer- sity town. I arrived there on Halloween and saw a lot of students partying. Most restaurants were closed but I found one Chinese restaurant open. My fortune cookie said, "Your investment will have returns that exceed your wildest imagination." A good omen perhaps?

After all this searching, I concluded that the area north of Shediac (only a half hour from the Moncton airport) best suited my needs. The property I selected in the coastal village of Grande-Digue was a one level, two- bedroom cottage suitable for year-round living. It had an enclosed garage as well as 1,200 square feet of living space, located on a hard surface road with about eighty acres of land. From the picture window in front of the cabin there was a view of the waters of the Northumberland Strait. The water's edge was across the road and about 1,200 feet away. The house was thirty-five years old; the roof shingles were a year old. The septic tank and field had been renovated four years earlier. The house came with a well and could be expanded.

The farmland was a spaghetti-shaped parcel, about five hundred feet wide and about eight thousand feet long. The cottage was located at the front of the lot just off the road at about fifty feet above current sea level and the land then rose gently behind it to about ninety feet with a great view of the coastline. A local farmer had cut the land between the cottage and this high point twice annually for hay. Behind that field it continues to rise a bit more before it slopes down and eventually becomes a wetland at the back end of the property. It had a Tamarack tree that was just changing its needles and was a bright yellow-orange..

The realtor waited patiently for me to make the decision and then negotiated the purchase..

I became fascinated with the community in the small Acadian village of Grande-Digue and also with the potential of the farm. (Please see photos at www.rudel.net) I purchased the property and then shopped for just a few pieces of furniture, beds and appliances, mostly from the Goodwill Store. It has become my Shangri-La. At the time of purchase, I had no way to know what the remainder of the property looked like because the end of the hay field was bounded by an impenetrable barrier of fast and densely growing alders that gave it a fence-like effect We had acres upon acres of this dense brush. It took several years and a large amount of heavy equipment work and time to open up the property beyond the hay field. When we finally built access to the rear acreage, we found clusters of sugar maples, birches and also a few apple trees, eventually, leading into a bog. To discourage the re-growth of the cut alders, we planted pine trees in the portions of the field where we had removed them. It was a never-ending battle to keep the alders from taking over again.

Grande-Digue is a sleepy Acadian French-speaking community on the Northumberland Strait just six miles north of Shediac, a well known summer resort. Shediac has many restaurants, a nifty harbor and a beautiful public beach. Its beautiful coastline allows us to see Prince Edward Island on a clear day.

Grande Digue is only twenty miles from Moncton, an old established major city with a university. Moncton is the major city on the rail line and the Trans-Canada highway connecting Halifax with Quebec. A high speed, limited-access highway system connects Moncton with St. John and the U.S.-Canada border crossing at Calais, Maine, with a driving time of three hours. The Gaspe Peninsula at the mouth of the St. Laurence River, one of the most scenic coastal areas on the East Coast, is just north of this area.

Our numerous trips to Canada have left me with a number of observations about the country and its people. First, I sense there is, among most Canadians in my community, a greater respect for the educated and for the teaching profession than I have found in central Pennsylvania and many other places in the U.S. At the same time there is not the frenzy one finds in the U.S. to send every child that graduates high school on to college. The skilled working man or woman has more of a sense of self-worth, irrespective of the income derived from the work--for instance, fishing--than one finds in the U.S.

Additionally, the Canadian national character is not that different from that of the U.S. with respect to the questions of protection of individual freedoms, social fairness and equality, the rule of law and pride in their judicial system, as well as adherence to a political system for selection of representatives and rule by participatory government. However, there are signs of a greater willingness to accept non-Caucasian immigrants and to integrate them into society. Many Chinese or Koreans have melded into Canadian society and can be seen working at community markets.

On the other hand, Acadians in New Brunswick demand separate French-speaking schools. There are two hospitals in Moncton: one French, the other English-speaking. Some Acadians will not patronize shops that do not display prices and descriptions of merchandise in French. They are determined to preserve their French rooted culture. One of the most puzzling aspects of local attitudes is the seeming enmity of the Quebecois towards the Acadians. The Quebecois long for independence from Canada while the Acadians do not. I sense that at least some of the friction between these two groups stems from the fact that the Acadians were farmers while the Quebecois were traders who fancied themselves as far more sophisticated than the Acadian "peasants." Moreover, in the country in general, there is now perhaps a growing wariness toward immigrants that practice Islam.

A key difference from the U.S. though is that taxes are very high-- the sales tax in New Brunswick in thirteen percent-- but the government delivers many services very well, including welfare when required. The health system is totally run by the government and the public seems quite satisfied with it. Of course, it is a workable system for a country that borders on the U.S. When one becomes dissatisfied with a particular service, one can cross into the U.S. and buy the service one needs. There seems to be greater family and community cohesion. When a family member or community member is in need, others will extend help. This also extends to care for the aged.

THE 1988 MAZDA EARNS ITS WAY - 2011

This, essentially, is a story of my high adventure to save money in the travel business. Our trusty Mazda 323, purchased brand-new by Joan in 1988 for eight thousand dollars had served us well. After six years of service in Maryland, we moved this "econobox on wheels" to Pennsylvania where it was parked at the Barnhart airstrip so that, upon flying to Glendale, I had immediate access to transport to conduct business before returning to the airstrip to fly back home. It sat there, winter and summer, waiting for me to use it as a runabout, which I did about thirty times each year. In twenty-three years it amassed seventy thousand miles on the odometer and built itself a reputation for reliability. When we sold Glendale in 2009, the Mazda became surplus to our needs.

In the meantime, we had purchased the cabin in Grande-Digue, New Brunswick. But getting there proved to be quite expensive. A round trip ticket for a flight from the Washington D.C. to New Brunswick cost seven hundred dollars while a similar ticket to Bangor, Maine (which constituted three fourths of the thousand mile trip) cost 260 dollars. Even renting a car in New Brunswick cost about seventy dollars per day. At the time, I was traveling to New Brunswick three times each year so these costs were adding up.

The idea then came to me that if I kept a car in Bangor it would be a lot cheaper than flying to New Brunswick and renting a car. In April 2010, after fully servicing the trusty 1988 Mazda 323, I drove it all the way to Grande-Digue. To my surprise and pleasure, it cruised along beautifully in traffic on the highways and sipped fuel at thirty-five miles to the gallon. The Mazda was giving me everything I asked for. It ran back and forth to Bangor three times in 2010. After the final trip, I asked a friend, Phil Grimley, who had a cabin in Bar Harbor, about thirty-five miles from Bangor, to let me park the car in his open driveway for the winter. And there it stood until my first real adventure in it in 2011.

When my friends would ask if this was really saving me any money, I would laugh knowingly and assure them that it was. But, deep inside, I was not quite so sure. For one, I had auto registration and insurance to pay on the car. Then there was the summer storage cost of three hundred dollars. There was always some maintenance cost. I also chose to ignore the cost of taxis to and from the airport to the storage site. Plus there was no way to include the unreliability factor in the cost equation. Air Canada was much more comfortable and reliable than US Air. Also, a 1988 Mazda was still an old car. Still, I was confident that my system was creating substantial savings for me.

I provide this background so you, dear reader, can fully understand my excitement at achieving some real economies out of this carefully structured process. Thus, the stage was set, in the spring of 2011, to make my pilgrimage to Bar Harbor to pick up the Mazda. Joan took me to Reagan National where I caught the flight to LaGuardia for a connection to Bangor. My adventure was about to begin.

There were several items to note as I arrived at the LaGuardia departure gate. Many people were milling about. This was odd since the onward flight was a Dash-8, a propeller-driven small plane with about thirty seats. There were also murmurings that the three earlier flights to Bangor had either been canceled or left after bumping several passengers and that this was to be the last flight of the day. The young woman in charge of the gate was rushing about and offering five hundred dollar vouchers and overnight hotel accommodations to any volunteer who would agree to wait until the next day's flight. I found this out by asking around because that gate keeper was making these announcements by speaking into the P.A. microphone at a rate that would make little Emma's speech sound like a 78 rpm recording being played at 33 rpm.

Finally, some volunteers emerged, were herded together near the desk and the loading door opened to let us board. Once we were on board, the crew discovered that there were more seats than passengers and those that had been bumped were required to give up their vouchers and were allowed to board. The little Dash-8, scheduled for a 7 pm departure, would not get wheels up until 8:30 pm.

I found myself sitting in a very small seat next to a very large man who lived in Miramichi, just up the road from Grande-Digue. He, his wife and their two teenage sons were returning home from vacation. They too had made the discovery that international flights to Canada were far more expensive than U.S. domestic fares. Their were returning from a wonderful week in New York and their car was parked in Bangor. The man had been in the paper and wood products business as a plant manager and told me how Canadian production was "in the tank." It seems the old plants were being sold, dismantled and shipped to China and Russia. His kids would not be able to find employment in New Brunswick although they would like to live there. We also talked about the Canadian health care system that, he said, is very costly, although the costs are evenly distributed because it is all covered out of taxes. He seemed happy with the system they have, imperfect though it is.

We landed in Bangor at 10 pm and I took a cab ($10) to the Howard Johnson Hotel ($65). At 4:15 am my alarm woke me and the taxi ($11) took me to a bus that left at 5:15 am for Bar Harbor. I was very proud to have found a Downeast commuter bus since it only runs once a day and its fare was an amazingly low five dollars. I was on my way to pick up my Mazda.

Now, here is where the trip got really adventurous.

I took out my map of Mount Desert Island, on which Bar Harbor and Acadia National Park are located to ask the driver how close he'd come to Frenchman's Hill Road, on which my friend's cottage was located. The answer did not cheer me as it was three miles from the closest point on the bus route. Now I knew that I could walk two miles with my bad foot and had previously even pushed myself to do three miles. I was working on the edge of my limit here. Carrying the backpack and pulling a suitcase on a country road that was likely to be uphill, there was a new uncertainty in the equation. As I watched out of the bus' front window considering my plight, I noticed that the driver, from time to time, engaged the windshield wipers. So there was rain to contend with as well. Not a downpour, sort of a Seattle type dry rain. I guess I could have stayed on the bus to Bar Harbor and called a cab, but that would have impinged on my cost calculation and I feared that the data would show this whole exercise to have been in vain. Thus, I got off the bus at Knox Road and began the long pull. It was then 6:15 am.

The first a mile on Knox Road led to an intersection. The next mile on Gilbert Farm Road led to another intersection with Crooked Road and Frenchman's Hill Road, which was where the pavement ended. There was only one mile to go up the dirt hill of Frenchman's Hill Road to the

Grimleys' house and the Mazda. And this was, as they say, the last mile for me.

Would the Mazda start after sitting idle for six months? Did I leave it pointed downhill? Had it been hit by a tree? All these thoughts flooded my brain as the hill got steeper and steeper and my enthusiasm for this adventure diminished. At last, the Grimleys' driveway came into view in all of its inclined glory. I decided to leave the suitcase at the bottom, intending to pick it up once the old and faithful Mazda got rolling, and staggered up the driveway to the house.

There it was! No tree had fallen across its bow. It looked just as I had left it except one front tire was almost flat. I took out the key Phil Grimley said did not fit, opened the car door, plopped into the front seat, said a prayer, held my breath and then turned the ignition. Brroomm! It started right up. Victory was mine. It was 7:30 am. Not as long a trek as I expected it would have been.

Next I took a more careful look at the tire. The rim was not quite touching the ground. It was really as flat as it could go while still holding some air. I was too tired to jack up the car and put the donut on. Let's see; maybe I could baby it down the driveway, the dirt road and to an air source. Slowly, ever so slowly I got it moving. I noticed that it made a lot of noise as it moved. Apparently the disc brakes had frozen and it was grabbing. Oh well, a little oil would fix that. I went slowly down the driveway, picked up the suitcase, then continued at five miles an hour, avoiding the ruts. And so, at that rate, the Mazda pretty much drove itself three miles to a gas station. Four quarters were needed to get the air pump working (we'll add that to the equation later) and the tire came back up.

I had also scheduled an appointment with a mechanic to get the car inspected for Maine ($12.50 plus repairs of deficiencies) so I could put on the new Maine license plate ($64). With the tire back up, I tried a slightly higher speed, maybe all of twenty miles per hour, to drive to the inspection station. What was all that noise anyway?

The station owner looked at the car, then at me, then at the car again, shrugged his shoulder (aha! another Frenchman) and told the mechanic to get it inside. I took a seat in the waiting room. One hour later he called me in. The estimate to get it to a point where he would give it a pass was $1,568 and he would have to order many of the parts. It would take several days. It seemed that apart from the frozen brakes, the rotors and calipers needed to be replaced because of my driving to the inspection station. There was a break in the boot of the front left axle and a number of other problems. He asked whether I really wanted to put that much money into it? He said that if I got the car to a junkyard they might give me a hundred dollars for it.

I thanked him profusely but told him he could keep the car if he would drive me to a car rental agency. He did and I then rented a new Ford Fusion and drove to Canada where I licked my wounds and counted my savings. That is how my adventure, and the life of the Mazda, ended.

8

BY PRIVATE AIRCRAFT: OCCASIONALLY FLYING SOLO[11]

THE QUEST TO FLY

FLYING SOLO IN UNCONTROLLED air space, in command of a small aircraft, gives one the ultimate sense of independence and defiance. You are alone in the sky. You may choose to proceed in any of three hundred and sixty directions, climb or descend, speed up or slow down as the mood strikes. And all the while, you are defying Newton's laws of gravity.

During my flying career, I accumulated approximately two thousand hours as pilot in command. Pilots who survive their first three hundred hours usually make it into such high flight time. It's those initial hours during which the worst mistakes are made. As the saying goes: "There are bold pilots and there are old pilots. But there are no old, bold pilots." I am one of those old pilots and I remember well my first three hundred hours; there were several close calls.

My fascination with flying began as a high school teenager in Brooklyn. One of my neighborhood friends, Charlie Goldberg, came back from his summer vacation and said he had a flying lesson. This was after the end

---

11 Photos can be viewed on the Rudel web site as follows: Iran 1957; Ann Arbor 1964; India 1965 – 1970; Kitty Hawk 1984; Kenya 1985; Detroit, 1985; Milan 1986; Hawaii 1987; Egypt 1989; Florida 1990; Caribbean 1996; Argentina- Iguassu Falls 1997; New Zealand & Australia 2002; Alaska 2007; Los Angeles & Catalina Island 2012.

of World War II, and I had seen every war film that featured airplanes. My hero was my cousin, Sam Korn, who had served in the Pacific as a blister gunner on B-24s, had been on forty missions and lived to return at the end of the war. And so naturally, the thought that one of us kids could have found a way to defy gravity made me furiously envious. I asked Charlie to tell me about his flight. He was very skittish about the details and I wondered whether he might have made up the story. Floyd Bennett Field was in Brooklyn, not far from my home, so I took the streetcar there to watch the planes take off and land. But I did not get in the air.

My first airplane ride was as a passenger in a DC-3 at the age of 18. I had been hired by the international division of Radio Corporation of America (RCA) in New York as a clerk. One day, I was asked to take a document to Chicago. It was urgent that the document got there within hours. Someone would meet me at the airport to relieve me of my burden and I was to fly directly back to New York on the return flight. The travel section of the company made the flight reservation, gave me a round trip ticket and told me to take a taxi to the airport. As I was about to leave the office, one of the senior traders working there, a fellow named Robinson whom we all called "Robbie", came up to me, gave me fifty cents and told me to buy an insurance policy for the flight, making him the beneficiary in the event the plane crashed and I was killed. At that time such insurance policies were sold by automatic machines at the airport. One simply threw in the fifty cents, wrote one's name and the name of the beneficiary on the policy, and then dropped the policy in the mail. If the flight completed safely, the policy would be worthless. If the plane met with an accident, it was worth a thousand dollars. I asked Robbie why he was doing this. He gave me an evil looking smirk, looked me straight in the eye and said, "I feel lucky this morning!"

Later, during my college years, I enrolled in the ROTC at City College. But this was an infantry unit and there was no way I could transfer to a college with an air force unit. Still, after being called to active duty in 1953 and assigned to Japan, I managed to take joy rides with a helicopter rescue unit stationed in Sasebo. Finally, while at the University of Michigan in 1964, I went to the Ann Arbor airport and started serious training on the Cessna high wing aircraft. By the time I completed my course work for the MA, I had earned my license as a "private pilot, single engine, land."

I cannot explain in words my passion, almost an obsession, for flying. I have absolutely no interest in boating. On the ground, I suffer from vertigo when climbing mountains, particularly when the path runs along a hillside and one side has a drop-off. But in the air, I feel no fear doing steep banks, climbs, and turning descents. My sense of rebelliousness thrives when defying gravity.

In chapter five of Volume I, I describe my flying experience with the Indian "Pushpak" aircraft in New Delhi during my tour there. But during the early 1970s when we moved back to the States, opportunities to put in flight hours, given the time and financial constraints of a mid-career government employee, were rare. Occasionally, I would get to rent an aircraft at the Montgomery County airport and fly locally.

Dulles airport had just been built then but received very little commercial traffic, and so the air traffic controllers (ATC) loved our single engine "put-puts" because we provided them with a chance to practice. They would get very chatty and jokes would be passed back and forth during practice landings. Several pilots and controllers were golfers and there would be conversations about the golf courses surrounding the airport. One local golf course was declared unplayable by a couple of pilots because its members "...call fore, hit six and write five." Another time I heard an amusing exchange between an airliner on approach and the controller. The airliner was to land behind a small general aviation aircraft. The controller told the airliner to reduce speed to a hundred and eighty knots because it was gaining on the smaller craft. After a few moments the controller instructed the airliner to further reduce speed to a hundred and sixty knots because he was still closing in on the other plane. The airline pilot, feeling uncomfortable with these instructions, asked to the controller, "Dulles approach control, do you know what the stall speed of this airliner is?" Very quickly, the controller replied, "No, but ask your co-pilot. I'm sure he can get that information for you." But of course, Dulles ATC is very different now. A small aircraft is often regarded as an intrusion.

THE CESSNA 172

After retirement in 1980, I became more serious about flying and took additional training to qualify for flight under instrument meteorological conditions (IMC), meaning weather conditions that required a pilot to rely on instruments for navigation rather than on his or her visual abilities. Once certified as an "instrument pilot", I bought my own plane, a four-seater Cessna 172. We referred to it as if it were a member of our family and named it Charlie November for its call letters, 738CN. I flew Charlie November back and forth to Pennsylvania nearly every week during the early 1980s until I could recognize each and every cloud along the way. One of the locals near Glendale had built a 2100-foot airstrip on some old coal stripping just ten minutes away from our land development. He too owned an aircraft. He allowed me to keep a car on the field and to land if I promised not to crack up. This made it very convenient. I could fly from Washington D.C. in an hour and drive to Glendale in another ten minutes.

There were some memorable cross-country trips as well. At first, Joan flew with me. We flew to Wisconsin to see Joan's family and landed in Manitowoc, a distance of about eight hundred miles. We flew for about six hours, landing en route in Bowling Green, Ohio to refuel. The last segment of the flight required us to cross Lake Michigan. Prudence dictated that we gain an altitude of 12,500 feet before going over the lake to allow for glide time and distance in the event the engine quit. We landed safely in Manitowoc and were met by Joan's family

We also flew IMC to Florida once. I recall how impressed Joan was, after flying for almost four hours in the clouds, with our descent into

Savannah. We broke out of the clouds at an elevation of five hundred to find ourselves directly on the approach to the runway.

However, I did not realize, and Joan did not reveal, the anxiety she felt in a small aircraft until one fateful day in 1984. With Joan accompanying me on a flight to Glendale, I landed at another grass field, not the one I was used to, and a severe crosswind helped me mess up the landing. Thankfully, there were no injuries except for my bruised ego. The nose wheel had collapsed, the propeller had struck the ground, and the emergency locator beacon was blaring to the entire world that Lu Rudel had crashed his plane. The aircraft was "totaled" in insurance parlance, meaning it was damaged beyond repair. The damage was only monetary and the insurance covered most of it. But I had to satisfy the Federal Aviation Administration that I was qualified to take to the air because I had dinged my airplane. To comfort my hurting ego--surprise!-- I bought another airplane.

Yet, after that incident, Joan refused to accompany me on flights. It was not the crash alone that made her averse to flying with me. She is a water person. She is comfortable in water and loves to snorkel for hours at a time. She did so at many places including the Great Barrier Reef, off Australia. On the other hand, I find myself as uncomfortable in the water with her, as she does in the air with me. All I could think of as we snorkeled together off the moored diving boat in Australia, and watched the fish--some very large with sharp teeth--gliding past us, was that these waters were foreign territory. Joan took to that environment as the proverbial duck to water. I fluctuated between boredom and terror. I then understood what she must have been going through as she dutifully accompanied me in the air. As the song goes, "Birds gotta swim and fish gotta fly..." (Apologies to Jerome Kern!)

THE CESSNA 182

The aircraft I purchased to replace Charlie November was a larger, faster, more powerful model, the Cessna 182 Skylane. It was a truly beautiful, easy to handle aircraft. Its long-range tanks could take me many miles farther than the capacity of my own bladder. It had a more powerful engine that gave the plane more speed and faster lift. It is classified by the FAA as a high performance aircraft.

I continued to fly back and forth to Glendale but made other cross-country trips as well, normally without passengers. One such trip, in the summer of 1992, was to visit Detroit where Jul was scheduled to perform Verdi's *Falstaff*. That flight also gave me an opportunity to visit Hajime "Jimmy" Hayashi, the Japanese fellow with whom I had worked during my military service at Camp Gifu, Japan. I made other flights to Boston to visit Ruthann, to Cincinnati to visit my cousin Erika, and several times to Florida.

Another flight Joan and I took was to a camping site near Kitty Hawk, North Carolina. Imagine loading a tent, sleeping bags, and camping supplies into the luggage compartment of the aircraft and flying two hundred miles to the camping area. We also made flights in Hawaii, Iguassu Falls, Argentina, the Caribbean Islands (Barbados, St. Thomas), and Southern California. But one locale really stands out in my memory: Mount McKinley, also know as Denali, in Alaska.

Small aircraft are ubiquitous in Alaska. They are available for charter to fly tourists over glaciers, along the coast, into hunting lands, and to airlift hikers and all of their gear to the base camp when they are ready to make the trek to the summit. Joan and I spent the night at the hostel in Talkeetna, the starting point for climbers of Mount McKinley. We spoke with numerous climbers, some preparing for the ordeal, others having just returned either from successful or unsuccessful attempt. It was fascinating to learn of the logistics involved in climbing to the summit. The usual drill is to fly, with all your gear, to the base camp at an elevation of about seven thousand feet. Then, after a night or two of rest and acclimatization to the thin air, one begins ferrying supplies to the next stop, perhaps at nine thousand feet. The same drill is repeated to the third stop: on and on. Finally, the climber is in position to try for the summit.

The weather plays an important part in this planning and the climb may take as much as twenty-five days.

I flew in a Beaver aircraft from Talkeetna and landed near the Denali base camp; the plane landed in the snow on skis between rock outcrops and without the benefit of a windsock. I walked around for about an hour in this pristine setting with the other passengers, then boarded again to take off in the snow and returned to Talkeetna.

FLYING OVERSEAS

I also took advantage of every opportunity to fly small aircraft in whichever far off places our overseas travels took us. One of the highlights was our flight in Kenya in 1984. Flying over the East African Rift Valley brought back thoughts of Isak Dinesen's *Out of Africa*, not to mention Robert Redford and Meryl Streep in the film adaptation. One day we decided to fly around Mount Kilimanjaro and then land at the Maasai Amboseli Game Reserve (now known as the Amboseli National Park). As we made our approach and circled the field, the runway seemed deserted. But once on the ground, after we shut down the engine, we saw two Maasai warriors run out of the woods, spears in hand, and head for the aircraft. Joan and I were somewhat apprehensive, if I may be permitted a euphemism, until one of them asked in excellent English, "Want to take picture?"

Later in 1989, during my work in Egypt, I found time to do some flying at the Cairo Flying Club. The chief pilot owned a Dimona motor glider, made in Austria. It was built for aerobatic maneuvers and so we did loops over the pyramids. A photo of this flight may be seen on the cover of Volume I. He created an incentive for his students to use the glider capability of the aircraft by cutting the engine in mid-flight. He charged sixty dollars per hour when the engine was running and five dollars when the engine was off.

In 1986, I accompanied Jul on a charter flight to Milan, Italy. That trip came about because Jul had made an error in his conducting schedule. He was to perform at Carnegie Hall on a Sunday night but had also accepted a gig that would require him to begin rehearsals in Milan the following Monday at 4 pm. He had overlooked the six-hour time difference between New York and Milan and had barely twelve hours between the end of the Carnegie concert and the start of the Milan rehearsal. He asked me whether I could arrange a charter. I located a Lear jet in Salisbury, Maryland, and Jul invited me to accompany him on the trip. The afternoon of that flight I flew my Cessna to Salisbury, parked it and boarded the Lear. I few minutes later we were at LaGuardia airport, waiting for Jul to arrive after his concert. Once he boarded, the Lear took off for Milan, stopping three times, to refuel in Newfoundland, then Greenland, and then Shannon, Ireland. After an interesting two days in Milan and a performance of Strauss' *Frau Ohne Schatten* at La Scala, I made the return trip alone in the waiting charter aircraft, leaving Jul to complete his gig.

On our trip to Australia and New Zealand, Joan joined me, always with an instructor pilot onboard, to fly to glaciers, and other touristic places like Blenheim and Christ Church. Hikers take pride in completing the four-day trek over Milford Track through very rugged mountain passes. We did it in twenty minutes, landing at that mosquito-infested port on Milford Sound on a one-way runway that required a very tight pattern for both landing and departure through a single air corridor. On the island of Tasmania, we parked the Cessna on the beach at the southernmost point of land. The next point of landfall southwards would have been Antarctica.

Along the course of my travels, I found that a photo of my aircraft provided me with easier access through security into tightly controlled airports than my U.S. passport. In Islamabad and Dacca, I walked up to high iron gates on the back-side of these airports, banged on the gate and, when someone looked out of the peephole, flashed the photo of my airplane before them, saying, "This is my aircraft." Immediately they smiled and the gates would open. There is camaraderie among pilots the world over. For instance, I usually traveled with copies of hard-to-come-by flight magazines to give as gifts to flying clubs and I would often be offered a joy ride as a courtesy from the club's chief instructor.

After September 11, 2001 the air traffic control around Washington, D.C. became more burdensome for general aviation pilots. Many procedures were put in place that, in my view, did little to enhance security but gave the appearance to the mighty and powerful of greater safety. I began flying less. By 2004, I could no longer justify the expense of keeping the plane sitting on the tarmac. And then, the advice from a retired navy pilot I had met on one of our excursions to Central America finally convinced me to sell the 182. His claim to fame was an assignment to probe along the edge of Soviet air space near Alaska during the Cold War to see if his maneuvers would cause them to turn on their radar. When the Russians did, the AWACS (Airborne Warning and Control System) plane high above would pinpoint the Soviet radar site's location. It was a delicate flying operation to be sure. He was no longer flying because, as he told me, "If you are flying less than seventy-five hours per year, you get rusty and are a danger to yourself and others."

But this did not stop my flying. I settled for renting aircraft and flying with an instructor or check pilot to maintain my skills and avoid danger. But my well-behaved instructor knows how to remain invisible. He or she is there only in case I get into trouble and is only a minor infringement on my sense of independence. Most importantly, it is no infringement at all on my spirit of defiance of the force of gravity.

PART THREE

CONCLUDING THOUGHTS

9

OUT OF THE PAST - INTO THE FUTURE

"There are times when you want to spread an alarm, but nothing has happened. I knew! I knew then and there – I could have finished the whole story that afternoon. It wasn't as though there was a mystery to unravel. I could see every step coming, step after step, like a dark figure walking down a hall toward a certain door. I knew where he was heading, I knew where he was going to end. And I sat here many afternoons asking myself why, being an intelligent man, I was so powerless to stop it. …. And so, I waited here."

-- Alfieri, the lawyer, end of Act One of Arthur Miller's play, "A View From the Bridge"

WHAT A FORTUNATE LIFE I have lived during my brief moment in this universe. Of all the great periods in recorded history, I can think of none in which I would rather have lived. Over the past two hundred years, each new generation has been able to achieve a higher standard of living than its forebears. Joan and I, and now our children have been the beneficiaries of this trend.

At the same time, the challenges now facing the new generation seem overwhelming. I have never feared for the future of Western society during my lifetime as much as I do now. We seem to be sleepwalking into a time of severe troubles. The last eighteen months, since volume one was published, have been a fast moving period in global international relations. I take no comfort that some of my predictions have materialized. Here are ten of the most troubling events that have flared up during this short period. There is little evidence that the more powerful members of the international community have arrived at ways to manage any of them:

1 - Upheaval in the Ukraine, and the U.S. decision to intervene in that conflict, resulting in resurgence of hostility between Russia and the West.
2 - Sunni Muslim seizure of parts of Syria and Iraq to reestablish the Caliphate abolished by Ataturk in 1926.
3 - Iran's efforts to dominate the global Shite Muslim community and the heightening of tensions between them and the Sunni Muslim nations.
4 - The resurgence of the Taliban in Afghanistan.
5 - Increased migration flows from Africa and the Middle East across the Mediterranean into Europe.
6 - China's island expansions in the South China Sea to allow it to achieve dominance over that region.
7 - The inability of nations and international organizations to agree on a schedule of actions of sufficient scale to stop global warming, despite clear and obvious evidence of human impact on the climate, and its dire consequences.
8 - The rising friction among Western European nations in resolving the Greek financial crisis.
9 - The U.S. general elections of 2014 and the resulting dysfunction in our federal government's decision-making process.
10 - The weakening of the U.S. national security apparatus in collecting the needed information to safeguard the country against terrorist threats, and the outrageous behavior of the Fourth Estate in publishing secret data such as that stolen and released by Edward Snowden.

Perhaps the most puzzling phenomenon for me has to do with recent reports of the large-scale recruitment of young Muslims, the children of those migrant families that had recently settled in the West, to travel to ISIS-controlled Syria and Iraq and join the conflict. As a former refugee, who thinks my visa to enter the US in 1938 was the winning ticket of the big lottery, I am unable to comprehend this behavior. How does one explain these acts by children of families that have successfully navigated the perils of immigration into Western nations, to willingly give up claim to their new nationality so as to seek martyrdom for the caliphate? It brings to mind that phrase, used by J.D. Salinger in *Catcher in the Rye*, and attributed to the psychoanalyst Wilhelm Stekel: "The mark of the immature man is that he wants to die nobly for a cause, while the mark of the mature man is that he wants to live humbly for one."

As I gaze into the future and try to read the tea leaves of current events for clues as to how things may evolve for my adopted country, I puzzle over the expressed goals and the behavior of these self-proclaimed spokespersons for Islam, as they justify slavery, beheadings, crucifixions and the subservience of women for all whom they identify as apostates of the true words of Mohammed. The Nazis wanted to kill all Jews. These folks want to do the same to all non-believers, all Shias, even Sunnis that do not adhere to the ISIS extremist beliefs, a far more daunting task. How can one co-exist on our planet with such people?

Only a small minority of Muslims subscribe to the extremist views of ISIS or the Taliban. But, perhaps due to the transgressions of Western nations during the imperialist period, there is empathy for ISIS, or something like it so long as it is anti-western and embraces Shari'a law, among many of those who identify with Islam than is currently assumed. We do not hear widespread public condemnation of ISIS voiced by leaders of the Islamic communities. Nor are there signs of action by them to curtail ISIS financing and recruitment. The network of Wahabi funded madrasas continues to indoctrinate its youth with extremist dogma.

If Islamic extremism is to be defeated, that will only be achieved by actions taken from within the Islamic community itself. Still, the Western nations must mount a defense. The recorded history of the human species over the past seven thousand years suggests that there have always been bandits on the prowl for opportunities at self-aggrandizement, preying on weaker members of society. That is why every society allocates a portion of its resources and wealth to maintain a constabulary, a judiciary and a military force intended to "keep the peace". Several wise persons have pointed out that the price of liberty is eternal vigilance.

A review of history reveals that there is difficulty gaining the needed cohesion to meet new challenges, as a society matures and becomes more prosperous. Its members tend to become less willing to accept the needed inconveniences and sacrifices to address their society's security needs. Consider how, during the 1940s, the U.S. government organized the nation's productive capacities, through the War Production Board, to meet the needs of the war effort. The Chryslers and Fords fell in line to serve the national defense. How will today's multi-national corporations meet the call if ever a similar need should arise? How would the "me generation" respond to a military draft?

I think about the day-to-day life during the summer of 1914, in the weeks before the beginning of World War I and wonder whether anyone foresaw what was to come in the following months. As an octogenarian, I recognize the inability of my generation to now influence current world events. The ball has now passed to the next generation. I search for evidence that might point to a coalescing of human actions to resolve these problems, but see few signs of statesmanlike political leadership needed to evolve a consensus, either at the national or international levels. Indeed, there are strong indications that the ten problem areas listed above, daily become more critical, with less time remaining within which to resolve them amicably. The task of good governance, even in these United States, seems to have taken a backseat to the retention of power. It brings to mind the conditions that prevailed during the decline of the Roman Empire when the mantra for politicians, as well as their electors was *panem et circenses*. Give the people "bread and circuses."

The "circus" seems to include our free press, radio and TV commentary, and now, growing social media channels. Communications technology is evolving, with the organized mass media consolidating into mega-enterprises characterized by typical oligopolistic behavior (to serve its own interests over the interests of the nation) while social media channels provide opportunities to anyone owning a computer to engage in irresponsible disclosures, not subject to fact checking. The "privacy rights" of individuals are protected at the expense of national security: not so for the Government's privacy rights. My recent efforts to engage in the public discourse by offering thoughts on issues of national importance (See six "letters to the editor" reproduced in Annex One) have not been eagerly received.

One goes to the trouble of writing non-fiction out of a belief that he or she possesses some insight, some specific piece of knowledge that other persons will want to know or need to understand. I have written these two volumes to pass on to faculty and students of international affairs, and to my progeny, some of the insights gained along the course of my career that may have applicability to current or upcoming problems they, and the world around them, are facing. These thoughts are offered to stimulate their quest for learning in this important field.

Our current conflicts with Russia, China, Turkey, the Arab States brings to mind a phrase used by the historian David Levering Lewis, that western societies are embarked on a road of "… Reciprocally reassuring ignorance and an addiction to war as a substitute for the complexities of coexistence." My sense of history informs me that the "good guys" do not always triumph. If the "free world" does not quickly find ways to coalesce its efforts and resources to meet its burgeoning challenges, we should not expect our wonderful way of life to endure.

As I write this, I recall Alfieri's words: "And I sat here many afternoons asking myself why, being an intelligent man, I was so powerless to stop it. ... And so, I waited here." We must not sit and wait.

ANNEX 1 A

SIX LETTERS TO THE PRESS

IF ONE TAKES THE trouble to write a letter to the editor of a prominent newspaper, it can be assumed the issue weighs heavily on the mind; even more so, if he chooses to include it in his memoirs. My success in getting such letters published had been greater during my younger days. Some of those earlier letters were reproduced in Volume one. Here are the six more recent letters, all of them unpublished.

With respect to the first letter, on April 29, 2001, the New York Times Magazine published a story about an incident that took place in Vietnam thirty-five years earlier, involving retired Senator Bob Kerrey. Mr. Kerrey, a Medal of Honor winner who had lost a leg in the war, a former senator and the then, president of New School University in New York City, had led a group of Navy Seals into a village, Thanh Phong, to capture a Vietcong leader. The group killed 13 to 20 people, and then, Mr. Kerrey says, they discovered that all of them were unarmed civilians, mostly women and children. The story revealed nothing that had not been known thirty-two years earlier when an investigation into the incident took place and exonerated Kerrey. I was moved to write this letter:

April 30, 2001

Letter to the Editor
The New York Times - Magazine

Dear Sir or Madam,

Subject: Senator Bob Kerrey

I know nothing more about the Than Phong incident, and Bob Kerrey's role in it, than I could glean from your April 29th article. In the context of my own experiences as an Infantry Lieutenant during the Korean conflict, I offer the following reactions:

It is clear that the event would not have attracted such prominent play in your newspaper, 32 years after the event, had the person involved not been a prominent ex-senator. If the person involved had been just another John Doe, the Fourth Estate would not have engaged in this kind of sensationalist character attack. And then, you will again lament that competent people do not seek to enter "Public Life".

In his explorations to learn "the truth" about what really happened, the author compares and contrasts Kerrey's candid statements to him over a two-year period to show inconsistencies, as though the process reveals some diabolical cover-up. It does not. Rather, it reveals an honest attempt by Kerrey to dredge through his true recollections and lay them bare before the author, in the vain hope they would be understood. Regrettably, the author's reactions suggest that Kerrey's trust was sadly misplaced.

By quoting the paragraph from the Army Field Manual, the author reveals he is clueless when it comes to conduct, by all combatants, in combat situations. The first task of a combat leader is to stay alive, and to keep his men alive. Maybe he should check with Senator McCain to find out how the other side behaved.

If the author, and all others in the chain of decision makers who approved publication of this sensationalist, judgmental, voyeuristic and insensitive article are serious in their search "to understand", I commend this course of action: the next time your country finds itself at war and seeks the best people to put into harm's way, go and volunteer for the kind of mission Kerrey undertook. Only then, by observing your own behavior, will you be in position to understand "the truth."

Sincerely,

Ludwig Rudel

May 12, 2003

Letters to the Editor

The New York Times

Dear Sir or Madam,

Subject: Journalistic Arrogance – Jayson Blair

With respect to your disclosure of the misdeeds of Jayson Blair and your management's excuses for publishing his lies and misreporting, I offer these comments.

A large portion of the blame can be ascribed to the smugness and self-importance the reading and viewing public accurately perceives in the behavior of the "Fourth Estate" today. There seems to be ever present, the attitude that the truth has been given only to them to see clearly and that they have no one to whom they need answer. No humility at their own limitations of understanding is evident in their presentations. If you are a "member of the club" of journalists your word is accepted as gospel. And it is defended at all cost.

A couple of years ago I was moved to write a letter to your paper reacting to an article in the Sunday Magazine reporting on Senator Bob Kerry's action during the Viet Nam war while leading a patrol on a night mission. The article made profound moral judgments about his conduct. My objections dealt with these judgments, made by authors and editors who had never had personal combat experience of comparable dangers to themselves.

I sent a copy of my letter to Joe Lelyveld on the basis of a past personal relationship. He did me the kindness of responding individually to me, and sent the letter to the editor for possible inclusion among the published responses. It never saw print, even though (or perhaps because) it was the most critical of the reader responses to this article.

Journalists and their editors are in control of an instrument that has the capability to be used as a "weapon of mass destruction," Would Mr. Raines respond with the same excuses, had an errant military officer misused a comparable weapon placed in his custody?

Sincerely,

Ludwig Rudel

November 12, 2013

To the Book Review Editor

New York Times

Book review of *The Brothers*, by Kinzer

It has always been good sport among certain non-fiction writers to attack decisions taken in a completely different context of time. I want to tell them that some of the very decisions they are now attacking have kept them safe.

The author digs deeply into the secrets of America's foreign policy actions and breezily dismisses hostile provocations taken by the Soviets during the same time period without any critical examination. One wonders why both Kinzer and the reviewer give a free pass to the actions of the Moscow financed Comintern during the six or so years following the end of the Second World War in countries like Greece, Turkey, Iran, Czechoslovakia, Poland, the Baltic States, Bulgaria and Yugoslavia. If American foreign policy can be called "interventionist" what should one call Soviet policy in those days?

Kinzer seems to be a leader in a cabal of writers with an anti-American bent that enjoy smearing former government officials by taking events out of context. In the late 1940s and early 1950s the

Soviets were openly and covertly supporting the Tudeh Party, Iran's communist party. It is they who succeeded in pressing Mossadegh in 1951 to move against the Shah and the British oil interests just when the U.S. and the Brits were heavily engaged in rebuffing aggression in Korea. The Soviets, and Russia before that, had long coveted Iran's oil fields as well as its warm water port on the Persian Gulf. Soviet intentions were assessed as intending to make Iran another vassal Soviet State, just as they had done to the European Iron Curtain Countries, once the Brits pulled out.

Shah Pahlavi was as much an autocrat in that period as his father had been before the war and, for that matter, as is Iran's current "Supreme Ruler" - Khamenei. The Shah's action to dismiss his own Prime Minister does not rise to the definition of a coup. Our support of the Shah as he asserted his authority, has been vilified by those in Iran who would gladly do us harm. Why does your reviewer not treat these writings with greater objectivity?

Respectfully submitted,

Ludwig (Lu) Rudel

ps: I was the acting Iran Desk Officer at the International Cooperation Administration (predecessor of USAID) from 1956 to 1960.

Wednesday May 6, 2015
To the Editor
New York Times
Comment on Op-Ed column on European Migration, *Open Up! Europe* By Philippe Legrain

As one who immigrated to the USA from Austria in 1938, I am very sympathetic to those who are prepared to undertake the dangers and hardships of uprooting. But the writer's argument that

"Letting in millions more migrants makes good economic sense" hardly is convincing.

When I came to the USA, this planet had a total human population of less then 2.5 billion. Today's global population is 7.5 billion, a threefold increase in less than eighty years ... and very rapidly climbing.

Water is a wonderful resource but – how about a flood? A fire in the hearth may bring great benefits. So ... how about a forest-fire? There are limits to the absorptive capacities of nations in a given time period, particularly as technology makes labor less needed.

Many people in Africa, the Middle East and Asia sense that their own societies' future looks bleak and will not provide them with similar opportunities to those that prevail in Western nations. They desperately desire to relocate. Sadly, many do not admire the political and cultural values of their destination countries.

The idea of "open borders" as espoused by the writer is not the answer. Development aid to the poorer societies is the better way to go.

Respectfully submitted,
Ludwig Rudel

Letter to the Editor
To The New York Times,
March 28, 2015
Op-ed contribution offer:
A Lament for Hope and Change - Disenchantment with the Dems.

As an Independent who voted for Obama in both elections, I have been appalled at the ever increasing dysfunctionality of our political system during the past six years. There is no question that the Obama Administration's efforts to govern have been blocked by Congressional Republicans since the 2010 elections. Still, I have a sense of being let down by the Democrats as well. Opportunities for meaningful improvement in the performance by the federal government have been lost.

Speaker Boehner has used his position to block action on important bills, not even allowing them to come to the floor for debate if his Party caucus had not agreed to the measure. I wonder if he did not learn this trick from the previous speaker, as she pushed the authorizing legislation for Obamacare to a vote during the 2009 - 2010 Congress. There was no "reach across the isle" effort by the Democrats then either.

The Administration's approach to national problems showed little imagination. In cooperation with the Federal Reserve, it did brilliantly to reverse the economic slump the country faced in 2009, without cooperation from the Republicans. The unemployment rate was reduced slowly but steadily. Yet, efforts to deal with an overloaded labor market could have been enhanced if, for example, a "National Service" program had been introduced to delay the flow of new entrants, those graduating from high school and college, into the labor market. The Administration's efforts to mitigate the housing market crash and the massive foreclosure rate were equally unimaginative. Those few programs that were put in place were poorly administered. Suppose, for example, one of the housing agencies had been tasked to offer a deal to the banks, to buy their underwater mortgages at 75 or 80 cents on the dollar, but only if the mortgagee was still occupying the dwelling and was willing to refinance the reduced mortgage balance at the then prevailing low interest rates? Since the Treasury was able to borrow at these same low rates the cost to the government would have been minimal.

The major philosophical difference between Republicans and Democrats has to do with the intrusiveness and size of government. But there should be no conflict between parties with respect to the need for efficient and thoughtful implementation of existing government programs by its bureaucracy. There was lots of room for the Administration to improve the management of its departments even absent the cooperation of the Republicans. Instead, the bureaucracy was allowed to deteriorate. The debacle of the HHS website crash was, of course, the most visible evidence of high-level incompetence. But the White House security breakdowns made it clear that it did not provide adequate direction even of his own small staff. Nobody ever gets fired, it seems.

During the past five years phone solicitations by robocallers have invaded the tranquility of the average home even though phones have been placed on the "Do not call list". One might think that a country, whose intelligence community is criticized for creating a technological monster that eavesdrops and records billions of phone calls, should be able to put a stop to this nuisance. It is not the most important issue on the table. Still, the elimination of this nuisance would have been a very visible and politically enhancing demonstration of the administration serving its constituency notwithstanding Republican intransigence.

Perhaps the most distressing sign of bureaucratic deterioration has to do with the Civil Service recruitment system. Following the end of World War II, when government efficiency was shown to have contributed enormously to winning the war (i.e., the War Production Board) the Civil Service Commission offered an annual Federal Service Entrance Examination for college graduates. It was a wonderful recruitment tool, structured to select the best of the crop of college graduates, place them on a common list from which all federal agencies could recruit candidates for entry-level positions.

I was recruited through that system in 1955, following my Korean military service. That exam was discontinued in 1981 because the test had been criticized for unfairly penalizing those who came from poorer segments of the population and/or certain minority groups. Although the criticism may be technically accurate, no test can be made to equalize the chances for those who grow up in a deprived household, while still accomplishing the test's purpose. Now, thirty-four years later, this excellent program still has not been reconstituted.

The role of government and its regulatory tasks is bound to grow as multinational companies continue to merge and become oligopolies. It would have been helpful to build an effective bureaucracy during the last six years to perform these tasks. Democrats should not lay the entire blame for our government's dysfunction on the Republicans. There is enough guilt to go around!

Respectfully submitted,

Ludwig Rudel

June 7, 2015
Letter to the Editor:
New York Times
Subject: Journalistic Arrogance II – SEAL Team 6
Please help me understand how your front-page lead article about the actions of SEAL Team 6 is supposed to improve my well-being. Not one specific fact is contained in the first 25 column inches of the article. We then find this statement: "But the bulwark of secrecy around Team 6 makes it impossible to assess its record and the consequences of its actions…." Your writers left out two words from that sentence – "by journalists". The operations of Team

6 are constantly and systematically scrutinized by those who, unlike your journalists, are trained to do so.

Our country is engaged in a conflict with a sworn enemy that wears no uniforms by which to identify them and has no political infrastructure with whom to engage in discussion. Assuming the thrust of your article to be correct, why are you surprised that Team 6 has adapted its tactics to this situation?

I question whether you should be entitled to the safety and security provided by our military establishment, security that your so-called journalists seem to take for granted but are content to undermine in order to print sensationalist clap-trap.

Respectfully submitted,

Ludwig Rudel

ANNEX 1 B

OUR TRAVELS, FOREIGN AID AND THE CONCEPT OF NATIONAL CHARACTER

SHORTLY AFTER THE END of World War II, the U.S. undertook programs to provide economic assistance on a global scale, initially to rebuild Europe through the Marshall Plan, then under Truman's Point Four program. The U.S. was soon accused of imposing our system on other societies which had their own, very different, value systems and behavior patterns. The U.S. was said to be seeking to turn other countries into its own image with a "one size fits all" approach.

The International Cooperation Administration and then USAID took this criticism seriously. A battery of anthropologists and sociologists was hired to correct this bias. There was recognition that societies do not all follow some universal standard of behavior. What may work well in one country to serve its social objectives, may not work in another. It was argued that one should not be judgmental about the efficacy of one societal behavior system over another.

The bilateral U.S. aid programs were then reviewed to adapt them to local societal mores and conditions. But what if the recipient nation was rife with corruption? What if a caste system was present, denying upward mobility and causing poverty and malnutrition to one segment of the society? What if certain behavior practices are judged to be the very cause of the country's economic troubles and inability to grow? To what extent should a "change agent" insist on institutional change before releasing aid funds?

These murky questions are the topics of many discussions within the development aid community. They highlight the notion that managing such assistance tends to be more an art than a science. Most of us thought it was important to understand the aid recipient's culture in order to make a good assessment and plan for aid.

This approach took on the stigma of "political incorrectness", in that it might be seen as the first cousin to "racial profiling." It also ran headlong into a major controversy in academia, dating back to the middle of the twentieth century, concerning "national character."

The Psychology Dictionary says this about it:

"National Character is a group of characteristics or behavioral traits which are afforded to the entire or majority population of a whole nation. These characters primarily consist of stereotypes that are seldom accurate."

That definition is certainly consistent with a book, written by Peter Ustinov, *Diplomats*, published in 1960[12].In that photo collection, he clothes himself in diplomatic garb and is seen delivering humorous punch lines depicting the perspectives of different national representatives as they orate at the United Nations.

On a more serious side, a major work on national character is Ruth Benedict's book, *Patterns of Culture*, written in 1934. In it, she argues that, "A culture, like an individual, is a more or less consistent pattern of thought and action". Margaret Mead, in her foreword to the book, summarizes Benedict's conception as "human cultures being personality writ large". Benedict was one of the cultural anthropologists recruited by the US government after our entry into World War II. She played a major role in

---

12   Paperback,1960, publisher Bernard Geis, photos by William Read Woodfield.

grasping the place of the Emperor of Japan in popular Japanese culture and formulated the recommendation to President Roosevelt that the continuation of the Emperor's reign should be part of the surrender offer.

Well then, does a nation have a personality? What makes the Greeks act as they do? What makes the Turks act as they do? And what is to be said about the friction between these neighboring countries sharing a common border, that have quarreled for centuries? And what to say about the Haitians and the people of the Dominican Republic, who share one island in the Caribbean Sea but perform so differently with respect to their national goals?

Does it serve a useful purpose to analyze a country's national character to facilitate a successful and persuasive negotiation? Every citizen of that society will not behave in the same manner, but are there certain common traits, attitudes and beliefs that should be taken into account when designing an aid project, or negotiating with its functionaries and leaders? In the recent negotiations between the Greek government and the European Union concerning Greece's debt crisis, is it not likely that the European Union would have employed different tactics if the problem had been with France or Spain?

A 2015 study, titled *Cultures and Disasters: understanding cultural framings in disaster risk reduction*[13] examines how cultural factors influence planning and outcomes. The study emphasizes the role of the culture in decision-making and the importance of cultural factors in the success of interventions. So, it would seem that we do consider national character assessment in the conduct of foreign affairs, although, as a principle, we may not like to admit it.

---

13 Fred Krüger, Greg Bankoff, Terry Cannon, Benedikt Orlowski and E. Lisa F. Schipper. : New York: Routledge, 2015

ANNEX 2

THE FOGLTANZ - SCHLEIS FAMILY SINCE MIGRATION FROM BOHEMIA TO WISCONSIN AROUND 1850

IN THE 1850s FOLLOWING the European Settlement of 1848, a large migration took place from Bohemia to the "New World". It is believed that, with the political act to free the serfs and the actions by the nobility to mitigate this by imposing military draft of fourteen years on the youth of the freed serfs, life became dangerous and more difficult. The serf farming skills gave them hope that they could make a living in the U.S. mid-west more easily than carve out a place for themselves within the rigid social structure of their homeland.

All eight great-grandparents of Joan and her sister, Marlene are known to have migrated to Wisconsin from the villages of Mrakov and Kaut, near Domazlice, about 100 miles west of Pilzen, Bohemia, an area very close to the German Border. A personal visit to that area by Joan and Lu Rudel in 1979 did not readily identify possible living family connections, although more thorough research would certainly be in order. It is interesting to note that there seems little interest on the part of the older generation of Fogltanz and Schleis family members in learning about such connections. In all likelihood those who left Bohemia for the New World in the 1850s did not maintain an interest in contact with their past, perhaps because they had negative experiences to look back on, and this may explain the present day disinterest.

A study by a member of the Manitowoc County Historical Society contains the following passage: [14]

"Early Bohemian immigration to America, like many other ethnic groups, was closely tied to political and religious confrontations. During the 16th and 17th centuries, Protestantism and Catholicism struggled for supremacy in Europe. Bohemia was a focal point of this controversy. People were persecuted for their religious beliefs and many escaped to other European nations. Later, they would be among those people traveling to America.

"Bohemian movement into Manitowoc County, Wisconsin, began in the late 1840's as evidenced by the 1850 census report. By the 1860 census, over 1700 Bohemians were living in Manitowoc County. Most of these immigrants came from Domazlice, Mrakov, Pilsen, Straz, Tabor, (Kaut), and Prague, Czechoslovakia.

"Wisconsin was admitted to the Union in 1848. One major factor in the movement of immigrants to Wisconsin was the Immigration Commissioner (established in 1852) the state maintained in New York City with quarters near the waterfront. His job was to persuade people to settle in Wisconsin. Advertisements for Wisconsin were extensively circulated in Europe.

'Come! In Wisconsin all men are free and equal before the law .... Religious freedom is absolute and there is not the slightest connection between church and state .... In Wisconsin no religious qualification is necessary for office or to constitute a voter; all that is required is for the man to be 21 years old and to have lived in the state one year.'"

Although only a few miles of railroad was built in the Midwest in the mid-1800's, Wisconsin had the advantage of ports on Lake Michigan. Ships

---

14   "Early Bohemian Immigration", Dan Juchniewich, Manitowoc County Historical Society, 1979)

docked in Chicago after coming up the Mississippi. The Erie Canal opened travel from the East Coast to the Great Lakes. Travel was by boat and foot.

Many early settlers were farmers and the Wisconsin land appealed to them. Winters were colder than in Central Europe but many crops that could be grown in Wisconsin were familiar to the settlers. There was no competition from slave labor and taxes were low. Citizenship could be obtained in one year. Although most Bohemian immigrants were farmers, there were also skilled tradesmen and merchants. Sawmills, gristmills, tanneries, breweries, stores, hotels, dance halls, and taverns were established. The Catholic church was one of the first community buildings to be built with donations of land, money and labor. The first church in Manitowoc County was built in 1858 (Nativity of Blessed Virgin Mary). Prior to that, the Pivonka family (Joan's paternal grandmother's mother's family) had a dance hall in the Francis Creek-Michicot area and it was used as a church for prayer and singing of hymns. Priests would appear a couple of times a year. Horses and oxen were scarce and schools are not mentioned in Wisconsin's early history. The Schauer's Brass Band was formed in 1856, playing for weddings, church festivals and dances (Frank Schleis Sr. was a member). The Bohemian immigrants were "fun" loving, fond of music and beer. Even during prohibition Joan's relatives made beer.

The Wisconsin Telephone Company installed the first phone in the area in 1887. Mail was brought in weekly by boat and then horseback. There were no banking facilities until 1917.

New immigrants would stay with and work for established immigrants until such time as they had enough money and found land to settle. This area was heavily forested and much effort was required to clear the land for agriculture. They first built log shanties for protection against the inclement weather and wolves.

EARLY HISTORY OF THE FAMILY

One of the difficulties in tracing our past was that these immigrants rejected their past. Life was not good in the "old country" and they rarely talked about it. In 1979 we attempted to track the roots of the first eight family immigrants by traveling to Prague, Pilsen, Domazlice, Mrakov and Kaut, Czechoslovakia. We found a cemetery on the hill above Mrakov, full of Vogeltanz' recent graves. Below those graves we were told there was another layer of graves. We could not find the grave markers from the late 1700's and 1800's. It is clear that freeing of the serfs in 1848 by Austria-Hungry, plus new social pressures placed on them (i.e. conscription) and personal accounts of misery and hunger, caused the emigration from Bohemia.

While we have no idea how to identify our family tree prior to 1850, the following is the U.S. family tree. We know this about Joan's eight great-grandparents:

Schleis:

> **maternal** - John Schleis (1845 -1918) came from Domazlice
> married Kathryn Krummel
> children: Mary, Katie, Matthew, Barbara (Joan's grandmother)

> **paternal** - Wencel Schleis (1850 - 1920)
> married Catherine (1853 -1928)
> children: Barbara, John I., Frank, Kathryn, Mary I, Emma, Theresa, Helen, Wencel J. (Joan's grandfather)

Fogltanz (original spelling was Vogeltanz)

> **maternal** - Frantisek Kozlovsky (1832 - ?)
> married Anna Pivonka (1832 - 1923)
> children: Anton, Katherine, Anna, Mary, Frank Jr., Joseph, Adolph, Emma J. (Joan's grandmother)

paternal - Tomas Fogltanz (1839 - 1927)
married Marketa Sladkey (1849 - 1928)
children: Joseph, Wencel, Mary, Anna, John (Joan's grandfather)

Koslovsky, Frantisek (Frank):

Parents were John and Anna (Horene) Koslovsky, who were engaged in farming in Bohemia and had three children, Joseph, Philip and Frantisek (Frank). Anna died in Bohemia when Frank was eight. At the age of 12 Frank learned the tailors trade and worked as a tailor for six years in Bohemia. At age 18 Frank sailed from Bremen, Germany, landed in New York after a nine-week journey and continued to Chicago. He traveled to Port Washington, Wisconsin, via wagon and then on foot to Manitowoc, a distance of 65 miles. He cleared land for over a year and then bought 80 acres in Cooperstown, working for over a year clearing that land.

On January 19, 1856, Frank married Anna Pivonka, walking 14 miles with two witnesses to the justice of peace in Manitowoc along a "good snow path". The couple lived in a shanty for four years until Frank was able to build a "proper dwelling". Frank made and sold shingles which provided him income until the land could support him. Six years later he sold the land and bought 120 acres in New Denmark Township, Brown County. This again was totally new land with no roads, only Indian trails over which Frank carried supplies from DePere and Green Bay. Once again he cleared the land and made it productive. He had no horses or oxen with which to plow and all the ground was prepared by hand with a hoe.

Frank was a Democrat, a township supervisor clerk of the school board, a devoted member of the Catholic church and donated land for the building of the church. In 1862 he was drafted into the Army, sent to Madison, Fond du Lac and then home. Drafted a second time, he was sent to Green Bay.

Frank and Anna (Pivonka) Kozlovsky had eight children: Anton, Katherine, Anna, Mary, Frank, Joseph, Adolph and Emma (Joan's grandmother).

Fogltanz, Tomas (1839 – 1927):
He was literate. He regularly received the Czech newspaper LASATEI. He loved to smoke his long pipe but by age 80 it made him dizzy and his wife, Marketa, took it away from him. Joan's dad, Romy, often took care of Tomas in his old age. When Marketa was away from home, Tomas would find the pipe, smoke it, get dizzy, fall down, and Romy age 12 would have to get this big man back into his chair or at least prop him up against the wall.

Grandparents:
    maternal - Wencel J. Schleis (1880 - 1937)
    married Barbara Schleis (1883 - 1942)
    children: Anton, James, Edward, Catherine, William, Melvin, Emma
    L. (Joan's mother). All children lived in Denmark and environs.

    paternal - John Fogltanz (1871 - 1939)
    married Emma J. Kozlovksy (1880 - 1962)
    children: Wencel, Edward, Mary, Charles, Roman (Joan's father)

Schleis, Wencel J. (1882 – 1937):
Wencel had a farm in Stanglesville, then a tavern in Denmark. He owned land in Lark, made lumber and built a house in Manitowoc. When Emma (Joan's mother) was twelve, he sold the tavern and moved to a small farm across from the *20th Century Bar and Bowling Alley* on County road R, two miles southeast of Denmark. Wencel was a member of the Pilsen Brass Band, played the clarinet (polka and waltz) at village and church picnics, and had a uniform. He is described by Emma as a strict disciplinarian, "not always very nice". He died of a stroke at home.

Schleis, Barbara (1883 - 1942) :

An easy-going, good hearted person, Barbara cared for Anton's children when his wife, Leena, died at childbirth. Barbara died of lymphoma.

Fogltanz, John: (1872 – 1939) (Joan's grandfather)

A big man, a farmer, who wore bib overalls except for church when he dressed impeccably in a three piece suit and highly-polished shoes. He wore glasses and a good-sized moustache. Joan has warm memories of joining him in his kitchen every afternoon, sitting on his lap and sharing his bottle of beer - one shot glass of beer for Joan. His sons always smiled when talking about their father. He supported and participated with them in many of their "crazy" projects. When he was in the barn milking cows, he frequently gave his sons a little extra money - mother was not to know.

John fell off a load of grain and died of a broken neck. Friends and family gathered at the farm for the "wake" - his open coffin, with candles burning, was placed in the living room of his home. Joan remembers attending the wake, at the age of five, in a pink ruffled taffeta dress.

Kozlovsky, Emma (1878 - 1962): (Joan's grandmother)

A neat-looking woman, with long hair beautifully styled in a bun, wearing long dresses always covered with a home-sewed apron. She was quite strict, but loving and kept a neat home. She loved her garden and its large berry patch. Joan frequently had breakfast with her, eating cream of wheat, "kashi", sprinkled with graham cracker crumbs. She made wonderful kolatches (prune and poppy-seed), and deep-fried pastries sprinkled with powered sugar called "listi". After her husband died she lived by herself in a second house located on Joan's parents' farm, spending much of her time in her rocking chair, looking out the front screen door. Joan now uses that rocking chair. Emma would walk to Joan's parent's home every evening for a visit. Her mother tongue was Czech. She was able to write letters to Joan in phonetic English. In 1958 Joan's parents sold the farm and built a house in the village of Denmark. Emma moved into their home. She died there of cancer in 1962 while Joan was living in Turkey.

Aunts and Uncles:

Anton Schleis (1902 - 1966) nicknamed Hap.

married Leena Hengel.

children: Claude, James, Bonnie, Helen.

Leena died in childbirth while delivering Helen. Anton worked at the Denmark Brewery and Lake to Lake Dairy. Claude and Jimmy were truck drivers, Bonnie and her husband Ken Prybelski (a plant manager) live in Indiana. Helen, the youngest child was raised by Katie and Herman Geigel, married Roger Shavlik, a businessman, and lives in Green Bay.

Edward Schleis (1907 - 1967)

married Lillian Pelishek.

children: Gerald, Edward Jr., Patricia, Victoria, and Thomas.

Eddie was drafted during World War II, saw action in Belgium and France including the Battle of the Bulge. He owned and operated the *20th Century Bar and Bowling Alley*.

James Schleis (1904 - 1951)

married Mildred Jorgenson.

children: Nancy, Ronald.

Jimmy, together with Eddie, owned and operated the *20th Century Bar and Bowling Alley* just outside Denmark. Nancy married Gordon Larsen and resides in Green Bay. Ronald, experiencing several marriages and occupations, is now settled.

Catherine 'Katie' (Schleis) (1908 - 1978)
married Herman Geigel;
They "adopted" and raised Anton's youngest daughter, Helen, when Helen's mother died in childbirth. Herman and Katie operated the Denmark Hotel.

Emma L. (Schleis (1914 – 2011)
married Roman Fogltanz.
children: Joan, Marlene

Melvin Schleis (1921 - 2014)
married Doris Knutson.
children: Wendy, Deborah
Melvin, nicknamed Ozzie, was drafted during World War II, stayed in the U.S. due to bad knees. Both Melvin and Doris were funeral directors, owned and operated Knutson's Funeral Home. Both daughters are interior designers, currently living in New York.

Wencel Fogltanz (1899 - 1990)
married Marcella Siebolt.
children: Elaine, Donald.
A large man, Wencel worked on boats that operated on Lake Michigan and as a boilermaker at the Manitowoc Shipyards. The memory is of Wencel carrying his "lunch box" with "speck" sandwiches. He died in a nursing home in Manitowoc. Marcella, a schoolteacher prior to marriage, was a marathon volunteer with her church and Girl Scouts. Marcella died in St. Mary's Nursing Home in Manitowoc. Elaine married Claude Goetz, an accountant. They have 13 children. Her brother, Don was a draftsman for a yacht builder. He and his wife Sue have three children.

Edward Fogltanz (1905 - 1982)

married Mary Kvitek.

children: Jean.

Ed and Mary bought a farm a mile and a half from Ed's "homestead". For many years Ed had a polka band, playing at weddings, church and village picnics. Jean married and divorced Don Pelishek. They had two sons. She is now married to Dick Hipke, lives in Manitowoc and works as a supper club manager. Jean dances the polka and waltz a minimum of six hours each week. She requires no medications and leads a healthy and happy life.

Charles Fogltanz (1912 - 1964)

married Sybil Schleis.

children: Roger.

Charlie and Sybil bought a farm in the same 640 acre square mile as the Fogltanz homestead. He enjoyed farming and playing in Ed's polka band, but his adult life was sad: his wife was mentally ill and their son, Roger died at age 16 in a tractor accident. Charlie died of alcoholism in California.

Mary Fogltanz (died as an infant)

Roman (Romy) Fogltanz (1908 - 1999)

married Emma Schleis (1914-2011).

children: Joan, Marlene

Romy and Emma's Farm

The 160 acre farm, in Manitowoc County, three miles southwest of Denmark, offers memories of good times and hard work. The Manitowoc County Historical Society document referenced earlier, mentions Yakish's mill and dam, a half mile from the farm, and the tavern at Kozlovksy Corners, a half mile from the farm. This homestead farm (previously farmed by Joan's grandparents, John and Emma Fogltanz), boasted of two homes, one occupied by Romy and his family, the other in which his parents lived. The farm also had, a cow barn with haymow, a horse barn with haymow and chicken coop, a granary and woodshed, two machine sheds and a workshop. The land was hilly, with a river and forest. Approximately 20 Holstein dairy cows, some pigs, a team of horses, always a dog, - with crops, mainly of oats, some corn, occasional barley - provided their livelihood. Milk was stored in cans and driven to the cheese factory after the morning milking. They owned an Essex car which Romy converted into a truck. It was the vehicle in which Joan learned to drive at age seven.

The Fogltanz home was considered very nice and modern for a farm-house. After all, her mother was a "city girl". There were French doors between the living and dining rooms, and a sun porch. Electricity came in 1928, an indoor bathroom was installed by Romy in 1930 using a pump jack with a gas engine to pump the water from the basement cistern, which held rainwater, to a tank in the attic. The bathroom had mauve colored fixtures with a built-in tub. Hot water for the kitchen was supplied by pipes passing through the fire pot of the wood range and stored in the stove's water tank. During World War II Romy dug a basement under the second half of the house and installed a wood/coal furnace, and a water pressure system. Prior to that, heat was supplied by the wood cooking range and a wood stove in the dining room. During the winter the furniture in the living room and dining room where switched and the living room was closed off to conserve heat. The house had one bedroom on the ground floor and an unfinished attic. Joan slept in a crib in her parents' bedroom until she was nine and her sister, Marlene, was born.

The family worked in the fields during the summer: cutting, raking, gathering hay, shocking grain (stacking 6 bunches of tied grain in an upright position for drying purposes). Joan's mother could drive the team of horses or the tractor as well as she could bake a cake. Joan describes her early life on the farm as follows:

"In the fields I picked stones, the worst job on earth. I learned to drive a team of horses pulling a wagon and broke wagon poles by making too tight a turn. I rode o the back of pigs, almost killing them in the summer heat. During warm weather the cows had to be gathered from "the back 40 acres" twice a day with the dog's assistance. Our dog, Buddy, was with us 14 years, great with cows but he did not have a playful gene in his body.

"Threshing was a festive time for me. The four boys (my dad-Romy, Wencel, Ed and Charlie) worked together. They jointly owned a threshing machine. Neighbors would join in the work and were repaid for their labors by having their grain harvested by the "four boys" and their threshing machine, their tractors and the team of perhaps twenty workers. My aunts came to prepare food and there was always a keg of beer. With the heat of August and the heavy labor and sweating, there was never a danger of anyone getting tipsy. Wencel would take his vacation from the shipyards, and come out from the city with Marcella to help with the harvest. He would be there at 5:00 am, greasing, oiling and maintaining the machinery: the thresher, feed cutter, conveyer and several tractors which supplied the power to the machines.

"With the right education Dad could have been a great inventor/ engineer. In 1943 he built a barn cleaner for removing manure from the cow barn. The idea came from a picture in a catalog. No one in the area had such a device and Dad had never seen one. He located scrap iron and hired a blacksmith. It had a six foot sweep, a roller chain with a transmission and moved the manure into the manure spreader waiting right outside the barn door. This barn cleaner served him for 15 years at which time he sold the farm."

The One-Room School

The Twin River School, a one-room school house for grades one through eight, was a mile and a half from our farm down a gravel road. It had no electricity or running water. One teacher taught all grades with a student population between ten and fifteen. Romy's brother, Ed, lived across the road and every Monday morning started the wood and coal furnace. Every evening after classes the teacher would bank the fire to keep it going during the night and add new fuel to the coals in the morning. Students maintained the school during the school year. Parent volunteers did the big cleaning/ maintenance at the beginning of each school year. Student "duties" included carrying in water from the outdoor pump for hand washing and drinking. Students also swept the outhouses and classroom floor with "compound" every evening. They also shoveled snow. The superintendent visited the school during the year to be sure that ashes were removed from the furnace and the outhouses were in good repair. It was a different view of education!

Mrs. Herold was Joan's first teacher, followed by Miss Fenlon from 1944-1948. Miss Fenlon was 19 when she started teaching, after just two years at the Manitowoc County Normal School. There was a library of about fifty books including an old set of encyclopedias, and one dictionary. When the teacher requested additional reference books, the school board of which Joan's Uncle Ed was a member, asked if the students had read all the books currently in the library and decided not to buy additional books until that was done.

The school closed in 1958 with the consolidation of school districts. It was then used as a clubhouse by a motorcycle club. The Twin River School disappeared during a tornado on July 5, 1994.

The Village of Denmark

The Fogltanz farm was three miles southwest of Denmark. The town had a population of approximately 1000 and it was there that Joan went to high school. It was in this village that the family bought most of its provisions, farm supplies, and had grain ground into animal feed. Denmark has a heavy emphasis on agriculture, a couple of rural-oriented industries that offer the bulk of the community's jobs and a conservative nature. Its population now is middle age and older with a lot of retired farmers.

The first settler was a German named John Bartelme, but he was quickly followed by Danes and others of Scandinavian descent. In 1848 it changed its name from Copenhagen to Denmark.

In 1904 the Chicago and Northwestern Railroad built its tracks through the village. Scandinavian affection for cooperative ventures led to the formation of the Denmark Co-op. After prohibition ended, the Denmark Brewery was built. It introduced "20 Century Pale" (a light beer) and "Old Town Lager" (a dark beer). The brewery went bankrupt in 1945. The building was then purchased by Atlas Cold Storage for storing cheese and later bought by the Brown County Publishing Company. Lake-to-Lake Dairy, established in 1949) is the most recognizable building in Denmark. It embodies the community's dairy heritage. Its predecessor dairy had been established shortly after the advent of the railroad and was known as the 'Denmark Condensed Milk Company". Lake-to-Lake now ships one million pounds of milk daily to the Chicago area in bulk milk trucks. In addition to processing and shipping milk it makes. In 1979 it had 1300 farmer members and fifty employees.

Dufecks Manufacturing has been making cheese boxes since the early 1900's. Popple wood is boiled and readied for veneer, made into boxes and dried. Many of its 25 employees are semi-retired and workweeks are split among the employees. Some employees are part-time farmers.

There are two new bank buildings: Denmark State Bank and M & I Bank (formerly Valley Bank, formerly Badger State Bank), but attracting new industry is a problem. While some residents would welcome it, many would rather pay higher taxes then have new industry move in.

Denmark has a nonfunctional Industrial Development Corporation. The new Interstate 43 highway brings Denmark closer to Manitowoc and Green Bay and makes Denmark attractive to people who work in the two cities and prefer small-town living. Denmark has good housing for its elderly and an active senior citizen center. It has a large school complex with a relatively new elementary, middle and senior high school. The school population totals 1500. Joan's high school class of 1952 had 35 graduates.

Establishments Joan remembers from her childhood, but have now disappeared, include Kriwanek's Grocery, Lodl Meat Market, Shoemaker Hansen, Denmark Co-op Grocery, Denmark Hotel (owned by Joan's uncle and aunt, Herman and Katie Geigel).

A story that is told and retold is the Denmark bank robbery of 1949. It was a day like any other day, then Denmark made the big time. The bank burglar alarm, which was connected to the Denmark Hotel lobby, went off and Herman Geigel who was tending bar, shut it off and was irritated with the alarm, which frequently went off without reason. He looked out the window and saw three men loading sacks of money into the trunk of their car. Herman grabbed his rifle, aimed and click...the ammunition was locked in the safe. George DeBroux, bank president, fired a couple of wild shots as the thieves sped away with more than $38,000. Three area men were convicted and all but $5000 was recovered.

www.ingramcontent.com/pod-product-compliance
Lightning Source LLC
Chambersburg PA
CBHW030417290526
45786CB00001B/13